Translation Studies in Africa

Continuum Studies in Translation
Series Editor: Jeremy Munday, Centre for Translation Studies,
University of Leeds

Published in association with the International Association for Translation
and Intercultural Studies (IATIS), Continuum Studies in Translation aims
to present a series of books focused around central issues in translation
and interpreting. Using case studies drawn from a wide range of different
countries and languages, each book presents a comprehensive examination
of current areas of research within translation studies written by academics
at the forefront of the field. The thought-provoking books in this series are
aimed at advanced students and researchers of translation studies.

Translation as Intervention
Edited by Jeremy Munday

Translator and Interpreter Training:
Issues, Methods and Debates
Edited by John Kearns

Translation Studies in Africa:
Edited by Judith Inggs and Libby Meintjes

Translation Studies in Africa

Edited by Judith Inggs and Libby Meintjes

continuum

Continuum International Publishing Group

The Tower Building   80 Maiden Lane, Suite 704
11 York Road   New York
London SE1 7NX   NY 10038

© Judith Inggs, Libby Meintjes and Contributors 2009

British Library Cataloguing-in-Publication Data
A catalogue record for this book is available from the British Library.

ISBN: 978-1-8470-6177-5 (hardback)
        978-1-8471-4589-5 (paperback)

Library of Congress Cataloging-in-Publication Data
The Publisher has applied for CIP data.

Typeset by Newgen Imaging Systems Pvt Ltd, Chennai, India
Printed and bound in Great Britain by The MPG Books Group

Contents

Notes on Contributors

Paul Bandia is a Professor in the Department of French at Concordia University in Montreal, Canada. His research interests are interdisciplinary, bringing together concepts and knowledge from a variety of fields including postcolonial studies, sociolinguistics, cultural studies and history. He has published widely in the fields of translation studies and postcolonial francophone literatures and cultures. He is the author of *Translation as Reparation: Writing and Translation in Postcolonial Africa* (St. Jerome, 2008) and is the co-editor of *Charting the Future of Translation History: Discourses and Methodology* (University of Ottawa Press, 2006).

Anne-Marie Beukes is an Associate Professor in Linguistics and Head of the Department of Linguistics and Literary Theory at the University of Johannesburg, South Africa. She has some 30 years' teaching and research experience in language policy and planning and language facilitation (translation) in both the academic and professional spheres. She is the author of some 40 scholarly articles and chapters in books, and has presented more than 40 conference papers. She is also the chairperson of the South African Translators' Institute (SATI) and represented South Africa on the Council of the International Federation of Translators (FIT) for nine years (1996–2005). From 2003 to 2005 she was also the Vice-President of FIT. As an experienced language planner she headed the South African government's Language Planning section in the Department of Arts and Culture from 1993 to 2003 where she was closely involved in policy development and implementation in the first decade of democracy, serving on the Pan South African Language Board (PanSALB) from 1996 to 1997.

Johan Blaauw is Head of Language Practice in the Language Directorate of the Institutional Head Office of the North-West University (NWU), South Africa. He is a simultaneous interpreter, translator and editor, accredited by the South African Translators' Institute. He has been a language practitioner for 30 years and his current position includes work in all three of these fields. He is also responsible for the initial and in-service training of the interpreters in the educational interpreting service team at his institution (which provides some 500 hours of interpreting weekly in a wide range of academic fields), as well as for quality monitoring. Because an interpreting service of this magnitude in a controlled environment offers extensive research opportunities, he has almost by default become a researcher in the field of spoken-language educational interpreting. This has in recent years resulted in a number of individual and co-authored articles on interpreting in various research publications.

Leon de Kock is Professor of English and Head of the School of Literature and Language Studies at the University of the Witwatersrand in Johannesburg, South Africa. He has published widely in several fields, including postcolonial studies, literary historiography, South African literary criticism, whiteness studies, translation studies and mind-body ecologies. He is the author of *Civilising Barbarians* (Wits University Press, 1996), a monograph on missionary colonialism in nineteenth-century South Africa, editor of several collections of South African writing and criticism, translator of Afrikaans author Marlene van Niekerk's paradigm-breaking Afrikaans novel, *Triomf* (1999) as well as other works of literary translation, and author of two volumes of poetry, in addition to many essays in the South African press.

Ileana Dimitriu is an Associate Professor of English and Translation Studies at the University of KwaZulu-Natal in Durban, South Africa. Her main research areas are postcolonial translation studies and comparative literature in South African 'post-ideological' contexts. Her more recent publications include the monograph, *Art of Conscience: Re-reading Nadine Gordimer after Apartheid* (Hestia, 2000). In 2002, she was the editor of a special issue of the South African journal, *Current Writing* 14(2) entitled 'Translation, Diversity and Power'. In the last few years, she has also produced a number of chapters in books published by Lit (2006), Rodopi (2004), Peter Lang (2001), Maastricht University Press (2001), and articles in specialist journals.

Judith Inggs is an Associate Professor in Translation and Interpreting Studies at the University of the Witwatersrand in Johannesburg, South Africa, where she has been training translators for the last 20 years. She is an accredited member of the South African Translators' Institute and has extensive experience as a practising translator and editor. She has published a number of articles on both translation and children's literature, including the translation of English children's fantasy into Russian, the translation of Russian poetry, the translation and adaptation of South African folktales, and studies on aspects of South African youth fiction. Current research interests include representations of sexuality in South African youth fiction, the translation of South African youth fiction into French and German, and a cognitive linguistic approach to the translation of poetry.

Haidee Kruger is a Lecturer in Language Practice and English Literature at the Vaal Triangle Campus of North-West University in Vanderbijlpark, South Africa, where she teaches editing, translation and twentieth-century poetry and fiction. She has also worked as an editor, translator and materials developer, mostly in the field of educational publishing in southern Africa. She holds an MA in English Literature (on the Beat poetry of Allen Ginsberg) and is currently reading for a PhD in Translation Studies at the University of the Witwatersrand, focusing on the translation of children's literature in the South African educational context. Her research interests are diverse, and include contemporary literature, literary translation, the role of language practitioners in promoting multilingualism in South Africa, and translator and editor training. She is also a writer and poet.

Libby Meintjes is Senior Lecturer and Head of Translation Studies in the School of Literature and Language Studies at the University of the Witwatersrand in Johannesburg, South Africa. She has been involved in training translators for over 25 years and is also a practising professional translator. She has published in the field of translation and ideology and the semiotics of translation. Her current research interests are in the area of translation in fiction, and in self-translation, with specific reference to South African literature.

Marné Pienaar is Professor of Linguistics in the Department of Afrikaans at the University of Johannesburg, South Africa. Her research interests include cognitive semantics and interpreting studies. She has published substantially on various aspects of simultaneous interpreting in South Africa. Recently published articles include 'Simultaneous interpreting as an aid in parallel medium tertiary education' (*Spil Plus* 2006), 'Four languages, one classroom: "Reasonably practicable"? (*SALAS*, 2007), and 'Educational interpreting and the role of the interpreter: visible agents of cultural sensitivity' (Maastricht, 2007)

Tajudeen Y. Surakat is a Senior Lecturer in English Linguistics at the Ahmadu Bello University, Zaria - Nigeria. He is currently the coordinator of the English Language Linguistics Programme in the Department of English and Literary Studies. He was previously Head of the Department of Languages, Literature and Linguistics at the Islamic University in Uganda where he served as a technical expert sponsored by the Nigerian Government. His research interests include Applied Linguistics (Translation Studies & TESOL) and Developmental Psycholinguistics.

He has published a number of articles in reputable international journals including two in LACUS (Vol. 30, 2003; Vol. 32, 2003). He has attended more than 30 academic and professional conferences in Nigeria, Uganda, Kenya, the UK, USA, Canada, and Germany.

Marlene Verhoef is Director of the Language Directorate of the North-West University, one of the so-called merged South African universities. She is responsible for the overall language management of this multi-campus institution. This venture is particularly challenging when taking into consideration that the NWU actively pursues the establishment of a functionally multilingual working environment. Her current research interests are focused on the continuous investigation of the viability of establishing a workable multilingual university environment in a developing country such as South Africa, with particular reference to using simultaneous interpreting for the facilitation of teaching and learning.

Frances Vosloo is a doctoral student in Translation Studies in the Department of Afrikaans and Dutch at the University of Stellenbosch, South Africa. Her research interests include the sociology of translation with specific reference to translators as social agents in the South African context, and the multi-disciplinary nature of translation studies. The title of her dissertation is 'Antjie Krog as vertaler: 'n Sisteemondersoek'. She has previously published on Antjie Krog as translator in *Stilet* (XIX (2), 2007) and in *Current Writing* (19(2), 2007).

Charmaine Young studied education and languages at the University of Pretoria during the 1990s. She then studied at the Université du Tampon in Réunion, and subsequently taught French and English at secondary school while completing an Honours degree in Linguistics (Translation Studies) in 2000. In 2007 she received an MA for her dissertation 'Transfer in film and narrative: the "griot" translated'. Her particular research interest is in the way in which aspects of culture are transferred in literature and film, especially in the African postcolonial context. Recent developments in African film and the study of its translation or 'subtitling' have increased her interest in the transfer of culture within film and she regards this field as a focal point for future studies.

Acknowledgements

The editors would like to express their gratitude to all those who contributed to the preparation of this volume, most particularly Jeremy Munday and John Kearns, who were always willing to give advice and support, and those colleagues both in South Africa and abroad who provided invaluable feedback in reviewing the contributions. Thanks also to Gurdeep Mattu and Colleen Coalter at Continuum for their patience and assistance.

Introduction

This volume examines a range of considerations on translation and interpreting in Africa. Four different perspectives emerge in the collection: the role of translation in disseminating African worldviews; the personal and the self-conscious in the praxis of translation; the cultural and its relocation in translated literature, and perspectives on translational and interpreting issues in education and training. Some of the chapters in this volume developed out of papers delivered at the Second International Congress of the International Association of Translation and Intercultural Studies, held at the University of the Western Cape, Cape Town, South Africa, 11–14 July 2006. Others were especially invited for this collection.

The first contribution by Paul Bandia provides a contextual frame from which to examine translation processes on the continent. Bandia examines the importance of translation in shaping African history and culture, extending the notion of translation beyond the mere transfer from one language to another to include contemporary understandings of transnational and transcultural encounters in the global context. The chapter traces translation activity on the continent and the representation of Africanness from pre-colonial to post-colonial times. In his discussion of literature in West and East Africa, Bandia considers how the notion of colonial subjects as 'translated beings' and African oral tradition have informed African writing and expression. Writing orality, he says, 'paradoxically imposes a state of bilingualism' marking African writing as different and making it possible to subvert and challenge dominant literary hegemonies. The translation and representation of Africanness through the writing of orality becomes a movement from a 'relatively homogeneous oral culture to a more heterogeneous or hybrid global culture'. He concludes that the relationship of African writers to language is one of translation, and the assertion of identity through linguistic difference challenges rather than submits to the 'unsavoury legacies of colonialism' while constituting an important aspect of the creative hybridity of African writing.

Leon de Kock's contribution engages with this same creative hybridity on two levels. First he considers the theoretical implications of the literary translation project in Africa, and South Africa more specifically, and then relates this to his own experience as a working translator. He uses his translation of Marlene van Niekerk's award-winning Afrikaans novel *Triomf* (1994) as a case study to corroborate the first part of his discussion. He argues convincingly that the nature of South African literature as a site of both convergence and divergence complicates the task of literary translation. This task becomes a dangerous balancing act which is compounded by the translator's attempt to approximate 'a higher ideal of expression' (Walter Benjamin's elusive 'pure language') and is made more difficult by the 'experiential and conceptual recasting of *modes of being* across languages'. This task is further complicated by the irreducible nature of individual literary expression and the complexity of the South African literary context which is one of relentless heterogeneity and hybridity, characterized by tension, and which De Kock describes as 'a rich textual seam', marking it as enduringly different and forcing the translation project towards the very brink of untranslatability.

The contribution by Frances Vosloo approaches the South African literary translator from the perspective of Antje Krog's *A Change of Tongue* (2003). In this work, Krog, a well-known South African poet, writer and translator, presents her reader with her discourse on translation through five intertexts, all of which relate directly or indirectly to the concept of translation. These intertexts serve as possible spaces of interpretation and allusion in which the reader is able to engage with Krog as writer and more specifically as translator. Vosloo argues that multiple readings of these intertextual references provide a way of accessing Krog's own theoretical assumptions on, and conceptualization of, translation, and this means that she has to consider the issue of whether the intertext does indeed serve the function and purpose an explicit intertext is generally believed to serve. Through a rich reading of one of these intertexts, Vosloo concludes that the intertexts function not only to signpost Krog's discourse on translation and her own ideas on change and the transformation/merging of the individual, but to provide a frame for 'translating'/mediating Krog's own voice.

Following on this theme of writers and their relation to translation, the contribution by Libby Meintjes examines the responses of a number of South African writers to the translation project and the translation partnership. In contrast to the 'I' subject position presented by Leon de Kock, this chapter seeks to tease out the other subject positions involved in the translation partnership. Meintjes draws on e-mail conversations with South African authors, public debates and other fora to narrate the emotional traces left behind by translation. She does this through the eyes of the writer and the translator.

Asking open-ended questions of her respondents she affords the writers and translators space to be reflexive and thus builds a co-constructed account of their views on being translated. Roland Barthes's (1974) notion of readerly and writerly texts, and his categories of *texte de désir, texte de plaisir* and *texte de jouissance* are used to understand the differing responses and attitudes of various authors which, she concludes, can be ascribed to their different understandings of the nature of their texts and to the emergence of different loyalties in the translation process.

Shifting to a discussion of the cultural in translation, Tajudeen Surakat examines the translatability of elements of Yoruba verbal art, or oral culture, into a predominantly literary, written language such as English. His contribution focuses on the translation of a section of verse from a prose narrative by Olu Owalabi which is set during the Nigerian Civil War of 1967–70. The work includes a number of incantations, praise poems and proverbs, all of which pose specific problems for the translator. Surakat discusses the various strategies available to the translator and the cultural difficulties involved, and ultimately suggests ways in which the loss of meaning can be minimized. Surakat provides an overview of Yoruba verbal art forms, which are commonly used by elders, orators and priests to embellish and adorn their speech. In his analysis he takes a broadly ethnolinguistic approach, drawing on systemic functional linguistics, linguistically-oriented translation theorists such as Newmark and Nida, and on more recent concepts such as Appiah's thick translation and Venuti's discussions of foreignization and domestication, visibility and invisibility. Surakat suggests two possible translations for each line of verse, broadly based on either a semantic or communicative approach. He concludes that of the two main art forms discussed here, praise poems and incantations; praise poems are 'easier' to deal with, largely because of the elements of religious culture involved in incantations. This chapter opens up a number of possibilities for future research on the translation of verbal art or orature, not only from Yoruba to English but also from languages in other regions of Africa.

The next chapter again focuses on the translation of a particular form of language, rooted in a specific culture and influenced by the mother tongue of the writer. Charmaine Young analyses translations of works by the Senagalese writer, Ousmane Sembène. Sembène is a native Wolof and Bambara speaker but chooses to write in French. He writes according to the linguistic and literary norms 'imposed' upon him by the French colonial authority, but he also appropriates this by representing the symbols, practices, idiosyncrasies and cultural uniqueness of his own society through particular stylistic and linguistic choices. This results in the emergence of a 'third culture' in the French text. Young believes that through a compromise between the techniques of domestication and foreignization the translation of post-colonial literature and its inherent otherness can serve to resist the conventions of the colonial encounter. Three texts are taken as examples, *Le docker noir* (1956), *Les bouts de bois de Dieu* (1960), and *Xala* (1974), together with their three translations by Schwartz (1987), Price (1970) and Wake (1976) respectively. The analysis concludes that differences in the approaches of the three translators either serve to 'release' or obscure the third culture in translation. Her findings confirm her original hypothesis that it is only by integrating domesticating and foreignizing strategies in the same translation that the third culture can be preserved in these kinds of texts.

In Chapter 7 Judith Inggs tackles a different genre of literature, that of the translation and rewriting of South African folktales primarily aimed at children. The story of the publication of these folktales in English, starting from the 1860s through to the present day, is discussed in terms of mediation, appropriation and imposition and traces the changing attitudes of transcribers, translators, rewriters and retellers over the last 150 years. Early writers introduced fairies, pixies and elves into the hot, sunny, South African landscape, unable to let go of the supernatural beings of their own childhoods. Attitudes towards the tales and towards the peoples among whom the tales originated were ambivalent or even patronising, assuming a distance between the reader of the English retellings and the Other of the source texts. By the 1980s such attitudes had changed, at times approaching reverence for a pre-colonial African paradise, which framed the way in which the tales were packaged and presented. New trends indicate the attempt to pursue a project of national unity and identity. One particularly interesting trend is the writing and translating of contemporary versions of tales by black South African storytellers who continue the tradition of storytelling in their own language as well as in English. A possible approach for new translations or collections is to produce hybridized texts in which difference is synthesised into something that might further the ongoing project of national unity.

Continuing with the topic of writing and translating for children, this time with an educational slant and focusing on children's literature as such rather than folktales, the chapter by Haidee Kruger also deals with hybridized translation strategies. This chapter sets out some practical and theoretical considerations for studying the translation of children's literature in the South African educational context. It provides a background to the practical uses and functions of (translated) children's literature in this context and within South African society as a whole. In particular, it focuses on the relationships between the various discourses that constitute South African society, and the function of translation broadly (and the translation of children's literature specifically) within this interplay of discourses. The tension between domestication and foreignization is particularly relevant. Most approaches to the translation of children's literature propose target-text oriented strategies such as domestication, localization and cultural adaptation to make the translated text as accessible as possible to the target-language child reader and to facilitate identification. However, in the multicultural South African context, where a great deal of emphasis is placed on intercultural tolerance and understanding, foreignizing translation approaches may well have a role to play. Kruger explores this tension in relation to the translation of children's literature and suggests that the situation in South Africa problematizes distinctions between the domestic and the foreign, producing hybridized translation strategies and requiring hybridized approaches to translation. Thus Kruger argues that domestication and foreignization are more usefully understood as divergent but complementary sets of strategies and that the constant interplay between them serves various functions.

Chapter 9 is concerned with another area of translation studies in an African context, that of appropriate and useful forms of training translators in multilingual countries. Ileana Dimitriu provides a fresh and insightful analysis of teaching paradigms during a period of transition, when social identities are undergoing profound shifts and identity practices can be deciphered from the ways people position themselves through language. Her research into translation and shifting identities is informed by broad post-structuralist, non-essentialist, views of identity as a multiple, mutating and flexible category, and by what is referred to as a semiotic construct that is influenced by its specific access to different identity-building resources. Where 'first-world' and 'third-world' coexist, as in a number of African countries, Dimitriu suggests that trainers need to be open to experimenting with less established forms of teaching translation. She sees translation in South Africa as playing a crucial role in civil life, and translators as central in integrating diverse communities, both culturally and linguistically. In order to equip them to do this Dimitriu proposes that the teaching and practice of translation should be viewed as a form of social, cultural and critical text-intervention. A modular approach to the teaching of translation is suggested which would provide flexibility in terms of adapting to contemporary challenges in education and the shifting identities of a society still in transition.

The final two chapters in the collection reflect on the use of spoken-language interpreting at tertiary level in South Africa. Both the universities used as case studies in these two chapters are historically Afrikaans-speaking universities which use interpreting services to provide greater accessibility. Parallel-medium teaching is one way of challenging the powerful role of English in tertiary education and provides a possible model for other universities, especially historically black universities. The findings of these two studies are for that reason of particular relevance in South Africa and other multilingual countries. The contribution by Marlene Verhoef and Johann Blaauw examines the characteristics of the various modes of interpreting used in teaching and learning and provides a typology of the interpreting genre as developed over the past four years by the North-West University in South Africa. Although the simultaneous mode of interpreting is used in classrooms it has become apparent that the educational interpreter's socio-communicative function, normally associated more with community interpreting, cannot be ignored. It concludes, on the basis of their longitudinal research data, that the type of interpreting used is a role-determined type of community interpreting using the simultaneous working mode. In their contribution, Anne-Marie Beukes and Marné Pienaar report on the use of simultaneous interpreting (using whispered interpreting equipment) as an alternative to parallel-medium teaching. Simultaneous interpreting is discussed as a language policy management mechanism in the context of the changing linguistic needs of students at South African tertiary institutions, using the University of Johannesburg as a case study. Interestingly, they conclude that the use of simultaneous interpreting in the tertiary context is not always feasible or appropriate and that its implementation needs to be understood and examined in relation to the motives and objectives of rendering such a service.

In conclusion it should be said that most of the chapters in this volume are contributions from South African academics despite our best efforts to obtain as wide a range of contributions as possible from the whole of Africa. This is a matter of some concern since it is a reflection of the continued problems around resources, communication and international exchange experienced by academics in other African countries and indicates the urgent need to establish a research programme to promote translation studies and research throughout the continent. The collection nonetheless reflects the many different vantage points from which translation and interpreting are being approached in an African context as well as pointing the way forward to an increasing body of research.

Translation Matters: Linguistic and Cultural Representation

Paul Bandia

1

Chapter Outline

Introduction

The importance of translation in the shaping of world history and culture has not yet been fully accounted for by literary historians and cultural theorists. Since the major shift in paradigm known as the 'cultural turn' in the 1980s, most disciplines in the humanities generally acknowledge the extent to which today's global culture is predicated upon the movement and encounters of various peoples and cultures. In our current context of an ever-expanding globalization and the migration and relocation of peoples and cultures, translation assumes a broader definition beyond the mere passage from one language to another to include the various aspects of transnational and transcultural encounters that constitute the subtexts of contemporary global culture. Translation therefore, in its pragmatic and metaphorical conceptualizations, is an indispensable instrument in the creation and diffusion of cultures within the global community. It is with this in mind that this chapter seeks to highlight the role of translation in the writing, preservation and disseminating of the African worldview, and the representation of African culture on the world stage.

Pre-colonial representation[1]

There is no doubt that translation has played an important role in ensuring communication and exchanges between the numerous linguistic and ethnocultural groups on the African continent, as well as with the outside world. In fact, the practice of translation in the continent is as old as the act of communication itself, as translation has always been necessary for communication between the various peoples and ethnicities on the continent. Multilingualism has always been a fact of life for people here, and it is not unusual to see ordinary individuals who speak a variety of languages, switching from one to the other regularly in their daily activities. This has been the case throughout history, perhaps due to the fact that there are major language families, each made up of a great variety of languages that often share a certain degree of mutual intelligibility, as well as certain cultural traits. There is a great deal of movement or migration over large areas spanning many cultures and languages, for purposes of trade, settlement or perhaps a nomadic tradition, which necessarily involves a certain measure of cross-cultural interaction and translation. Given the continent's vast oral traditions and the many non-alphabetized languages, the writing of these cultures can be viewed in terms of translation from orality to writing (Bandia, 1993). Also, because many of the languages in Africa are without literary capital, translation has come to represent the principal means by which an African cultural space has been created in the international marketplace. Translation has indeed been at the centre of the construction of an African history over the ages, and as a key factor it has adopted as many postures as the changing political and cultural trends that have shaped the history of the continent.

Today's culture of modernity assumes precedence over tradition by celebrating writing over orality. Having proscribed African culture to the realm of orality, modernist thinking seems to view translation in Africa mainly as a consequence of the arrival of outsiders with fairly developed writing cultures. This may explain why most contemporary allusions to translation in Africa often take as a starting point the arrival of Arabic and European civilizations on the continent. Nothing could be further from the truth. There is documented evidence of the existence of many indigenous writing systems, as well as other mechanisms for intercultural communication and cultural transfer between various ethnic groups and peoples in pre-colonial times. The similarities between the cultures and belief systems of geographically distant groups on the continent, as well as various manifestations of syncretism or hybridity resulting from the meeting or fusion of these cultures, attest to the widespread movement of ideas across ethnic boundaries by means of translation and related forms of intercultural communication. It is however true that in pre-colonial times African cultures and worldviews were expressed through a predominantly oral tradition, which was handed down from generation to generation. Orality played a major role in the expression of African cultures, shaping the language and the various forms of enunciation that were conducive to an oral aesthetic. For instance, an important function in African oral narratives is to convey wisdom and knowledgeability, which are often expressed in traditional forms of enunciation such as wise sayings, proverbs and aphorisms and other oral narrative genres such as short stories, riddles, oratory, elegies or panegyrics, set forms of discourse with specific stylistic characteristics and manners of delivery (Finnegan, 1970; Vansina, 1985; Okpewho, 1992). In some instances, the understanding of these oral narratives would require what Roman Jakobson (1959) has described as 'intralingual translation', that is, a process of translation or interpretation within the specific language of expression. For instance, as wisdom and knowledgeability are the prerogative of the elders in some cultures, the young cannot presume to understand such expressions, let alone use them in the presence of elders. This in effect implies that the transmission of these ideas or aspects of wisdom must have been handed down to other generations over the ages through an inherent process of translation and interpretation. In other words, such expressions of wisdom are handed down to the young, and therefore survive from generation to generation, through an intralingual interpretation process. There is also an esoteric quality to some of these expressions of African tradition, which often require the direct intervention of a translator or what some have referred to as a 'professional linguist' (Danquah, 1928). In pre-colonial times, the 'professional linguist' was considered the official spokesperson, and the depository of the memory and heritage of his people, with a special talent for narrating their history and culture. In many African societies, the 'professional linguist' belonged to a long lineage of gifted orators, some of whom had worked in the courts of great monarchs in kingdoms such as Mali, Zimbabwe and Ghana. These professional linguists often enjoyed a privileged position in society and wielded a great deal of political power and influence given their proximity to the king. According to Danquah (1928: 42), the Ashanti linguist was expected to repeat the words of the king for the benefit of the king's subjects, thus enhancing the authority of the king, whose ornate and esoteric language was not accessible to his subjects and required the intercession of the linguist. In his role as translator, a competent linguist was expected to embellish the king's speech, enhancing its eloquence and adding a touch of humour or philosophical content without altering the message, and as a result earn praise and esteem for the king and himself. Among the ethnic groups who are today within the geo-political space referred to as francophone, the 'professional linguist' is generally known by the name *griot*. These 'linguists' were known for their mastery of several languages, and as translators-interpreters they helped to spread the poetry and culture of a people over vast territories in many languages and cultures. The *griots* are generally credited with the survival of many great African epic stories.

The highly esoteric language used by traditional chiefs and elders often required mediation to ensure communication between the rulers and the people. Interpreters were sometimes required to simplify the esoteric language used by members of secret societies, or to embellish speeches or orations given at public events such as sermons, libations, religious or wedding incantations. The language used at these ceremonies was governed by strict conventions of style and phraseology, including proverbs and wise sayings unknown to non-initiates. As mediators between the ruling class and the people, interpreters enjoyed a great deal of respect and a high social status in these highly organized and socially stratified societies. Yet, they also formed a class apart, which was sometimes shunned and highly mistrusted by the people.

Drum language is also an important means of communication in traditional society, and involves the translation of linguistic codes into musical notes (Finnegan, 1970). This kind of 'intersemiotic translation' (Jakobson, 1959) is made possible by the tonal characteristic of African languages. Drum language has the advantage of being able to communicate over great distances, to convene a village gathering or announce a great event, or perhaps to engage in a dialogue with a neighbouring village. It is indeed a form of instant messaging, which saves the time and effort often required by verbal or written communication in such traditional contexts.

Contrary to popular belief that writing was introduced to Africa by Arabs in the ninth century and Europeans in the fifteenth century, indigenous writing systems did exist and had enhanced translation activity in pre-colonial Africa.

Many scholars point to the existence of writing systems well before colonialism, citing the alphabetized cultures of the Nile Valley, the Nubian, Pharaonic, Meriotic, Ethiopian and Kush civilizations (Gérard, 1986). A writing system of pictograms was in use, and there are areas in the history of ancient Africa that have been reconstructed through the translation of such pictograms into Arabic or Latin alphabets. This kind of writing and translating in pictograms is still being practised in some parts of Africa, in spite of the presence of Arabic or Latin scripts. Mveng (1980) mentions the existence of such pictogram writing among the Akan, the Ashanti, the Adinkra and the Baoulé peoples of Ghana, as well as among the Bamileke and the Bamun in Cameroon and the Baluba and the Bakuba in Congo. The works of Cheikh Anta Diop (1955, 1974) deal with Ancient Egyptian hieroglyphic and Ethiopian Amharic writing which existed in Africa long before colonialism. Cheikh Anta Diop's extremely important work of translating and deciphering Ancient Egyptian hieroglyphics, carried out in his radiocarbon laboratory at the Institut Fondamental d'Afrique Noir (IFAN) in Dakar, gave us some insight into the African antecedents of Ancient Egyptian civilization. In spite of the controversy surrounding his work, Diop succeeded in establishing the link between African history, language and culture and the rich civilization of Ancient Egypt. These historical facts are of great significance for the foundation of translation as an important activity in the literary and cultural history of Africa.

Colonial encounter

European colonization added another dimension to the vibrant intercultural activity on the African continent. In addition to the horizontal translation and intercultural activity among Africans themselves, and to some extent including the Arabic tradition, there was now a vertical translation practice, based on unequal power relations, between European and African language cultures. In this vertical relationship, translation became much more than a mere exchange of cultures or texts, and assumed an ideological basis which determined and influenced the orientation of translation in the recording and transcription of African oral culture in European languages, as well as in the conveyance of Western civilization in African society. The European colonizer's romantic quest for the Other, the unknown and the exotic, could only be fulfilled through a systematic translation and appropriation of the African logos. Europe was in search of a pristine and unadulterated past, and therefore conveniently transfixed Africa in colonial representations of the continent in a distant and primitive era, which it held up to itself as the mirror image of a Europe that had not yet lost its innocence, but also as a reflection of the very opposite of European modernity. The historical significance of translation in the colonial era can be ascertained through the large-scale recording and transmission of African oral tradition, on the one hand, and the importation and imposition of the European worldview on Africa, on the other. The colonial era begins with the arrival of Europeans in the fifteenth century marked by the spread of the Slave Trade and includes the pre-independence period, which begins in the nineteenth century with the partitioning of Africa, and extends into the 1950s. The Portuguese are generally credited with the early European contact with Africa when they first arrived along the coast of Senegal in 1445. As soon as they established their presence on the continent they began to familiarize the locals with the Roman alphabet, and to translate the local literature into Portuguese. The translation of African literature into Portuguese reached its height in the nineteenth century. Early Portuguese Christian missionaries sought to provide a minimum of literacy to Africans, as the Jesuits, showing an interest in African languages, set up schools to teach Portuguese and Latin. Realizing that evangelization and conversion of the locals would be quicker through the use of local languages, the missionaries developed a more modern writing system for these mainly oral languages. They produced dictionaries, grammar books and catechisms in several local languages, and these works became the inspiration for the creation of a literary movement known as the 1880 Group (Hamilton, 1975). The group launched a bilingual (Portuguese-Kimbundu) journal entitled *O Echo de Angola* which had published the very first translations between European and African languages. A prominent member of the 1880 Group was the translator-terminologist, Joaquin Dias Cordeiro da Matta, who was the author of *Philosophia popular em proverbios angolanos* (Popular Philosophy in the Proverbs of Angola). It was a collection of Kimbundu proverbs and riddles translated into Portuguese, encapsulating some of the fundamental philosophical thought of the Angolan people. Da Matta also published a bilingual Kimbundu-Portuguese dictionary which was described as a monument of erudition (Hamilton, 1975: 15). However, these works, which could have laid the foundation for a thriving literature in African languages, failed to do so because of the ethnocentric and assimilationist attitudes of the Portuguese authorities who eventually sought to promote writing and literature in European languages.

The vertical or asymmetrical translation characteristic of European colonization was particularly evident in the area of religious translation. European interest in this area was dictated by a strong desire to spread Christianity, while obliterating African religiosity by consigning African belief systems to the realms of paganism. The Christianization of African peoples would become an invaluable control mechanism, ensuring rapid colonization and exploitation of African people. And as the saying goes: while the Africans were reading the Bible and worshipping the Christian god, the Europeans were busy spiriting African wealth and resources out of the continent. The writing and translation of African religions and belief systems served an anthropological need, designed to denigrate these religions for the benefit of Christianity. A selective translation process was devised that sought to minimize those elements of African religious belief that were in contradiction with Christian doctrine, and to establish parallels between African and Christian belief systems likely to enhance proselytizing and conversion. The introduction of Christianity and secular Western beliefs and values into African society required the mastery of indigenous languages, as well as an understanding of those elements of African culture that could be harnessed to establish the basis for an African Christian community. Hence, missionary colonialism practised an interventionist translation whereby elements of African oral literature were reconstructed to enhance their compatibility with Christian beliefs. For instance, there was a preference for creation myths that emphasized the monotheistic dimension of African belief (Austen, 1990). Interventionist translating also meant suppression or omission of those elements of African belief that conflicted with Christian values. Upon their arrival, European missionaries to Africa engaged in large-scale translating of religious texts in African languages in order to spread Christianity. The seventeenth century saw the first translations of the Bible into African languages. Nama (1993: 420) states that by 1658 the language spoken by the Ewe people (Republic of Benin) was represented in an important document, *Doctrina Cristiana*, a handbook for the missionaries. However, large-scale publications of Bible translations in African languages only began in the nineteenth century. These were enhanced by other publications in Krio, a creole language spoken by freed slaves who settled in Liberia and Sierra Leone. The freed slaves and their descendants had greatly contributed to the Christian evangelization that took place in West Africa (Gérard, 1986).

It is important to point out that Arab incursions in Africa were also marked by an important religious translation activity. Although Islam has been present in Sub-Saharan Africa since 800 AD, it was mainly spread through the Arabic language. Indeed, the spread of Islam was accompanied by the massive imposition of the Arabic language on the continent. A situation of diglossia thus developed whereby Arabic became the language of learning and prestige, used mainly for certain literate or literary purposes. However, the Koran was translated much later into some African languages like Hausa and Yoruba mainly for the benefit of the local population, and some Islamic texts were thus translated into Ajani, a variety of Yoruba written in Arabic alphabet, by *malams* (teachers or learned men). The influence of Islam is also prevalent in the Horn of Africa and in East Africa as a whole, where there has also been a curious mix of African, Christian and Islamic traditions.

Religious translation has had a significant impact on African culture and has helped shape the African worldview through a process of syncretism or a blending of disparate belief systems.

Anthropological translation was also widely practised in Africa and was quite instrumental in the construction of the history of the continent. This is another area where vertical translation mattered and where ideology and power differentials played an important role in the recording, transcription and disseminating of African culture. Anthropological translation was often carried out by colonial administrators regardless of their field of expertise, as commissioned tasks or simply out of personal interest. These recordings and translations were often carried out with the aid of native interpreters and informants who might not always have been competent or reliable. It was not always easy to grasp meaning as expressed in the oral tradition, and at times the oral narrative had to be performed by the native interpreter to ensure a more adequate transcription and recording by the Western anthropologist. Needless to say, some of the native interpreters-performers may not have been initiates or trained in the art, thus leading to inadequate recordings and results. The interpreters-performers were quite often natives who were subordinates of the colonial administration. Some of their performances were produced by command on the verandas or in the tents of colonialism (Austen, 1990: 3). Also, while the oral narratives were performed in the indigenous language, the translation was carried out by government interpreters who often had a poor command of the European idiom. The translation was then further edited by the administrator-author of the published text, without any indigenous text to control the translation or any sense of the actual performance situation. These colonialist efforts at transcribing and translating African oral literature were bound to be flawed as the language of translation was the European language of domination sustained by the modernist belief in the superiority of writing over orality. The actual transcriptions and translations themselves involved technical as well as ideological issues, and were highly influenced by the colonial administrator's assumptions about African primitiveness. The colonial administrators' main objective was to achieve absolute control of Africans, and they saw the study of indigenous literature as a valuable key to 'native psychology' (Austen, 1990: 2). As clearly stated by the French folklorist and administrator, F. V. Equilbecq (1972 [1913]: 22), 'It is necessary to know whom one wishes to dominate . . . These traditions are the supreme vestiges of the primitive beliefs of the black and, on this basis, deserve to be saved from oblivion' (quoted in Austen, 1990: 2). Generally, colonial anthropology practised a hegemonic discourse whose ultimate goal was the overt subjugation of Africans to colonial purposes.

The Berlin Conference (1884–85) and the partition of Africa laid the groundwork for the large-scale colonization of the continent. By 1890, Africa was carved into European spheres of influence without regard for natural or ethnic boundaries. The emergence of an African literature in Portuguese, English and French is the direct consequence of this scramble for Africa. The role of translation in the writing and disseminating of African cultures and worldview in colonial languages became evident during this era and was closely determined by the various colonial policies. It is generally believed that the Latin countries had a more assimilative approach largely conducive to translating into European languages, while the English, through a policy of indirect rule,[2] encouraged vernacular-language writing and translation either for proselytizing or as a manoeuvre to maintain control over colonial subjects by denying them access to a global language. Vernacular-language writing was eventually followed by an active translation activity in English that enhanced cultural exchange across ethnic boundaries and paved the way for African literature on the international scene. These differences notwithstanding, representations of Africanity in European languages had taken root, leading to the demise of the 'professional linguist' or *griot* who, once revered and feared for his political influence, was now reduced to a mere anthropological guide to the colonial master. The *griot* was now derided and denounced as a traitor for letting the colonizer in on the secrets and traditions of the people. By the end of the nineteenth century and the beginning of the twentieth century, a wave of liberal romanticism in Europe and a fascination with various forms of symbolism led to a rebirth of interest in the oral cultures and traditions of non-western societies (Horton and Finnegan, 1973). This in turn led to a frenzy of recordings, transcriptions and translations of African oral 'texts', which were at times poorly done by amateurs or deliberately adapted to meet the exotic needs (or tastes) of Western society. It was not until towards the end of the colonial period that African writers, who had been immersed in both Africa and European language cultures, began to render these oral 'texts' in some reliable and authentic form. This kind of representation of Africanness through the transcription, recording and translation of oral narratives has continued to flourish especially with the introduction of audio-visual technology.

Postcoloniality and the fate of 'Translated Beings'

Translation again played a significant role in writing and communicating African thought in the 1950s and 1960s, the years immediately before and after independence for many African countries. Religious translation by missionaries continued unabated, but a new form of translation, or writing as translation, began to gain ground as creative writers on the continent sought to represent their cultures and worldview in writing either in African languages or in European languages. European missionaries continued to learn and alphabetize African languages in order to carry out vernacular translations for the purposes of evangelization. The Bible (and other religious texts) was thus translated into some African languages, and among the pioneer translators were S. W. Koealle, J. F. Schon and the Nigerian Bishop Samuel Ajayi Crowther, known for his translations of the Bible in Ibo and Yoruba. It is reported that the Bible has today been translated into over 100 African languages. Evangelical groups and well-organized and subsidized groups such as The American Bible Association continue to criss-cross the continent, carrying out translations of Christian religious texts into African languages as well as into some locally derived hybrid languages such as Pidgin English (Nama, 1993).

Outside religious translation, literary translation began to flourish during this period carried out by writers who were well-versed in African oral tradition and who had a good command of the European language. As stated earlier, many recordings of African oral tradition made by European colonists and their native informants and colonial scribes were often inadequate or simply 'colonized' versions of such oral narratives. The new breed of African writers therefore wanted to set the record straight, as it were, and, to undo the errors of the past, took on the translation of some of these African oral narratives into European languages. Among these early writers were the

Senegalese poet, Birago Diop, known for his collection of short stories titled *Nouveaux contes d'Amadou Koumba* (1958), the Ivorian Bernard Dadié, author of *Légendes africaines* (1954), and also the Senegalese Léopold Sédar Senghor and his translation of the epic poem *Chaka le roi zulu*, and the legend of *Soundiata Keïta*. Senghor's efforts are generally credited with laying the groundwork for *Négritude*, one of Africa's best-known philosophical movements (Senghor, 1964). A similar movement was taking shape among anglophone writers, who seemed to have enjoyed greater latitude than their francophone counterparts in how much liberty they could take with their creative use of the English language. In West Africa, for instance, Amos Tutuola's *The Palm-Wine Drinkard and his Dead Palm-Wine Tapster in the Dead's Town* (1952) is considered to be one of the earliest attempts at translating African oral narratives in the context of creative writing in English. Tutuola's novel draws heavily from Yoruba mythopoetics and oral culture, and some have characterized the novel as a form of literal translation of Yoruba oral discourse, rendered in an elementary English which had the effect of enhancing the novel's aesthetic appeal to some readers. Another attempt at writing and translating Yoruba oral culture is Daniel O. Fagunwa's transcription in Yoruba, *Ogboju-ode ninu igbo Irunmale* (The Skilful Hunter in the Forest of Spirits, 1938), which was subsequently translated into English by Wole Soyinka as *The Forest of a Thousand Daemons: a Hunter's Saga* (1982) and thus brought to national and international prominence. Gabriel Okara boldly admits to translating or transliterating from his native Ijaw language into English in crafting his novel, *The Voice* (1964). He explains his writing strategy by insisting on the need to overcome the inadequacy of the English language to capture and express the Ijaw language culture and worldview.

Besides such direct fictionalized translations of oral narratives into European languages, there have been other, more creative uses of African oral aesthetics in European-language fiction by writers such as Achebe, Senghor, Soyinka and Ahmadou Kourouma. Regarding the novel, *Les soleils des indépendances* (Suns of Independence, 1968), Kourouma had no qualms about stating his indebtedness to the art of translation in expressing the Malinké worldview in French. Critics have referred to the language of the novel as a kind of Malinkization of French, thus recognizing the need to bend the French language in order to capture Malinké traditional discourse and culture.

In East Africa the cultural significance of translation is highly determined by the region's triple heritage, namely Africa, Islam and Europe. There is a variety of literatures in various local languages that express African thought and worldview. Although there is hardly any translation activity between African languages, there is indeed creative writing in indigenous languages such as Kikuyu, Baganda, Chagga, Acholi and Luo that have each developed their own distinct literature. The Ugandan Okot p'Bitek is well known for his translation of the poem 'Song of Lawino' in English, which he had originally written in his native Acholi. After a brilliant career as a writer of fiction in English, the Kenyan writer Ngugi wa Thiong'o resolved to continue writing only in his native Kikuyu, and subsequently translated his work into English. His novel, *Devil on the Cross* (1982) was originally written in Kikuyu two years earlier. A great deal of translation has gone on in this region between African languages and Arabic. Many writings in African languages have been translated into Swahili, a lingua franca created mainly out of the contact between Islam and Bantu civilization. The Afro-Islamic heritage as expressed in Swahili has been translated into English by scholars such as Lyndon Harries, James de Vere Allen, Ibrahim Shariff, Jan Knappert and others (Gérard, 1986: 1049). Translations have also taken place in the opposite direction, that is, from English into Swahili, and the famous examples are Julius Nyerere's (founding president of Tanzania and father of *Ujaama*, the philosophy of African socialism) translations of Shakespeare's *Julius Caesar* and *Merchant of Venice*. Given its status as a lingua franca, spoken by over 100 million people across a vast territory, Swahili has been described as a major language of transnational import that can very well nourish and sustain its own literature, and into which world classics can be translated (Mhina, 1970). Unlike other regions in Sub-Saharan Africa where there are hardly any local languages spoken across national boundaries, Eastern Africa enjoys the unique privilege of having its own locally derived lingua franca of international significance, which assumes the role that colonial languages play in other parts of the continent.

In more recent times, in the context of neo-colonialism and rampant globalization, translation has continued to play a major role in the representation of the African worldview, culture and artistry on the world stage. Africanity enters and travels the world through translation, both in its pragmatic and metaphorical sense of migration, diaspora and displacement of cultures towards the global cultural centres which, as pointed out by Pascale Casanova (2004), seems to be the fate of minority cultures in the current context of globalization. Translation necessarily implies writing or communicating to the Other, the foreigner outside the purview of the source culture. African writers and intellectuals assert African identity in the global cultural space through translation. Translation therefore becomes the means for writers on the periphery to deal with the distance and decentring imposed upon them by hegemonic cultures. According to Casanova, translation here would include:

> adoption of a dominant language, self-translation, construction of a dual body of work by means of translation back and forth between two languages, creation and promotion of a national and/or popular language, development of a new writing, and symbiotic merger of two languages. (2004: 258)

These are all strategies conceived in terms of a continuum and movement adopted by dominated writers to counter literary and cultural domination by the centre.

Cultures of orality

In contexts where national languages are primarily endowed with oral traditions, there is as a consequence a lack of literary capital which must be overcome through writing in languages of international import. This is indeed the case of writers from societies that have long been under colonial domination, whose languages are not recognized in the global literary space, and for whom bilingualism and translation become an indispensable condition of existence. For these writers from marginalized cultures located outside the centre, translation is viewed not merely as an exchange between languages but as a principal means of access to the international literary space, a form of consecration or what Casanova has referred to as 'littérisation' (2004: 136), that is, the means by which a text from a literarily deprived nation comes to be acknowledged worldwide. The representation of the African worldview through translation can be construed as a double-edged sword as on the one hand it propagates Africanness on the world stage and on the other it highlights the power differential involved and the dominance of the centre. Pius Ngandu Nkashama alludes to this ambivalence when he critically, and perhaps grudgingly, discusses the central role of translation in assuring the consecration of African writers:

> The failing of African authors has often been to believe that a literary text has value only if it has been accredited as such by a magnanimous West . . . It is as though an author in an African language objectively attains literary status only from the moment that he produces a text in other languages, in this case those of

the colonizer. . . A moral credit can be granted him on the basis of translations duly authorized in the world. (1992: 24–30; quoted in Casanova, 2004: 136)

Viewed in the context of a desire for an African literature in African languages, Nkashama's argument is well-founded; however, it also stands to reveal the deep frustration of African writers regarding the inevitability of translation in the construction of a world-class literature. One might also argue that translation is indeed indispensable at all levels of creation including the representation or writing of oral culture in indigenous languages, the movement from orality to writing being a form of translation. The importance of translation for postcolonial writing has been well-established. In fact, Salman Rushdie sees an inherent act of self-translation in writing, particularly writing as practised by dominated or displaced writers. He states:

The word 'translation' comes, etymologically, from the Latin for 'bearing across.' Having been borne across the world, we are translated men. It is normally supposed that something always gets lost in translation; I cling, obstinately, to the notion that something can also be gained. (1991: 17)

What can be gained in translation is the possibility of framing the worldview of an analphabetic culture in a literate language, and the potential for its dissemination on a global scale. Translation is an indispensable intermediary or go-between that bridges disparate literary worlds. Unfortunately, its role in the conceptualization and dissemination of knowledge has not been fully accounted for by contemporary literary and cultural history. There is a kind of cross-pollination of ideas across nations and civilizations that is ensured through translation. African thought and culture has thus contributed immensely to the movement of world culture, and has in turn borne the traces of other major cultures.

Translation played a major role in the construction of a literary heritage for many nations going through decolonization in the twentieth century. Though an ambiguous enterprise – which can confer international recognition but at the same time minimize authenticity by imposing universal norms – translation has provided the mechanism for shaping specific minority discourses within global, hegemonic languages. African writers have conveyed African culture in colonial languages by creating a new idiom through the writing of oral tradition. While working within the colonial, metropolitan language, the writers resort to innovative practices that allow creative deviations resulting in a relatively unique language shaped by the oral artistry and cultural specificity of the African universe. In this way, their work becomes the repository of the African logos and history thanks to a creative process of writing-as-translation. According to Casanova (2004: 293):

> The *littérisation* of oral language makes it possible not only to manifest a distinctive identity but also to challenge the standards of literary and linguistic correctness . . . ; and also to provoke dramatic ruptures that are at once political and literary.

Besides asserting one's cultural heritage and subverting the legacies of colonialism, the writing and translation of orality ensures the preservation and dissemination of the African worldview in the global cultural space.

The African writer as translator

African indigenous literature comes to the world through translation and, like most writers from colonially dominated societies, African writers can be viewed as both translators and translated beings. Translation permeates African writing as even the representation of African oral tradition in writing is a form of translation and the expression of Africanness in colonial languages is generally achieved through an act of a translation. Having been put through political, linguistic and literary domination, these writers must inevitably deal with translation, and their bilingual existence can be seen as an embodiment of translation and an indelible mark of political domination. Writing in colonial languages is, for them, not a sign of submission but rather a means to counter the hegemony of a powerful and oppressive colonial métropole. These writers adopt several strategies, tantamount to translation, by which they strive to preserve their cultural difference on the international scene and counter the ethnocentrism and dominance of the metropolitan centre. By confronting the question of language, African writers conceive ways in which to affirm their difference in the colonial language. As linguistically dominated writers, they seek independence and freedom from colonial domination through the manipulation of language. Innovative linguistic strategies are deployed by these writers to distance themselves from the dominant language by creating either a local variety of the global language or a completely new language with its own literary potential.

In postcolonial contexts the writer has the choice to write either in a local vernacular and thus remain confined to a small literary space or in a global language accessible to a much broader readership. Faced with this dilemma,

African writers are forced to write in an adopted language imported through colonization, yet this allows them to champion the cause of their people on the world stage. For these writers, using the colonial language is hardly a matter of self-abnegation or a preference for the West, but rather a means to an end, that is, asserting their cultural identity globally. In fact, the younger generation of writers may no longer see the adopted colonial language as a language of domination. They have internalized the uses of this language, starting at a very young age, in more urban and multilingual environments where the colonial language is firmly part of the linguistic landscape. The younger generation of writers therefore are more likely to avoid the binarism or oppositionality of 'us' versus 'them', or 'colonized' versus 'colonizer', which is often realized in terms of the re-appropriation of the colonial language through the direct representation or translation of an African mythical past. These writers view the colonial language as part and parcel of their cultural heritage, which allows them access to the global literary space. In this context the colonial language is appropriated or deployed to counter neo-colonial, rather than colonial, forms of domination, which are manifested internally in terms of class conflicts between the people and the Western-controlled local elite. In the postcolony, language is heteroglossic, reflecting the plurality and the chaos of society resulting from economic and class discordance. The language of the neo-colonial postcolony is as a consequence hybrid, fragmented and diglossic in that it reflects the paradigm of class and power. As representation, the language expresses the plurivocality or the varied voices that need to be heard on the global stage. Representation of these multiple voices is tantamount to translating a hybrid, linguistically multilayered text from the periphery to the global centre. It is indeed the ultimate translation of already translated beings and universe, the postcolony being the invention and the negative cloning of the colonial métropole. In this respect, the hybridity of the postcolony recalls that of contemporary cosmopolitan global centres where migration and cultural relocation have also shaped a polyphonic and polylingual society reflective of class and power inequalities. These contexts by their very nature evoke translation and bilingualism as a fundamental condition of being. Translation therefore acts as a primordial instrument in the cultural representation of otherness. The representation of Africanness in these contexts is the result of a complex and non-binary translation practice whereby the African worldview is conveyed through a multiple translation process, while accounting for the condition of hybridity in the contemporary global space.

The relationship with the language of colonization becomes even more complicated given today's ecology of migration and diaspora. Many African writers now live in the colonial métropole or abroad in the global literary capitals, where the use of the colonial language is hardly a matter of choice but of necessity. The relocation of cultures due to migration and the proximity of cultures in the context of cosmopolitanism may result in the formation of hybrid cultures that call for new ways of relating to the metropolitan centre. The representation of Africanness in this context is far from being a direct translation of African oral culture for the benefit of an international audience. It is hardly a dualist or binary relationship between source and target cultures, but rather a complex one in which Africanity is just one aspect in a broader context of hybridity. The African writer's translation and representation of Africanness becomes therefore a movement from a relatively homogenous oral culture to a more heterogeneous or hybrid global culture. The writer therefore has to fashion an expression with the global language that fully accounts for African sociocultural reality, while acknowledging the already complex or hybrid nature of the receiving global culture. A good example of this new approach to the relationship of African orality to current cosmopolitan culture is Ben Okri's clever use of indigenous oral tradition to write about contemporary society rather than dwell in the past. Like writers of the older generation, Okri draws heavily from a mythical past in crafting *The Famished Road* (1991), but rather than simply projecting this past onto the global literary centre, Okri uses it in his novel to analyse contemporary society accounting for its multidimensional, cosmopolitan or hybrid reality. The writing of African orality therefore ceases to be a direct translation and representation of Africanness in a global language, becoming a non-binary and multifaceted representation of the African worldview within a more cosmopolitan global literary space. The writing of African orality paradoxically imposes a state of bilingualism, making it possible to be different linguistically and literarily in a global language that has become the medium of expression for a variety of peoples and cultures. Besides expressing a distinctive identity, writing orality allows dominated writers to challenge dominant literary and linguistic norms, as well as introduce literary practices that may test the limits of accepted cultural and literary practices within the dominant language. An interesting example of this is how African European-language writers are said to derive a great deal of authority from their oral narrative tradition to make liberal use of so-called obscene or vulgar language in their works. Obscenity is often used in well-known forms of expression such as proverbs, folktales and other traditional discourses, often paradoxically, to convey thoughts or ideas related to matters of great importance or in some cases for humour or derision. As dominated writers they may use obscene or vulgar language, perhaps to create humour, but mainly as a creative device to register the specificity of oral or traditional discourse. Chinua Achebe makes abundant use of this writing strategy in his novel, *Arrow of God* (1964), particularly in the scenes or passages dealing with the confrontation between the local population and the intruding colonialists. In the highly symbolic and premonitory battle of wits between the Chief Priest of Ulu and the Colonial Administrator, the local leader ridicules the white man by doubting his courage and brags about his own valour: 'I prefer to deal with a man who throws up a stone and puts his head to receive it not one who shouts for a fight but when it comes he *trembles and passes premature shit*' (Achebe, 1964: 179). To augment his sense of bravery and determination to resist the white man's authority, the Chief Priest states: 'If I had stolen his goat or killed his brother or *fucked his wife* then I might plunge into the bush when I heard his voice' (145). The Chief Priest's tough language is meant to enhance his authority and reassure his people of his determination to resist colonial encroachment. In the same novel the Chief Priest wraps foul language in formulaic expressions to warn his people against going to war: 'If you go to war *to avenge a man who passed shit on the head of his mother's father*, Ulu will not follow you to be soiled in the corruption' (27). In a light-hearted context the Chief Priest teases his friend, Abuekue, about greed: 'What do we say happens to the man who eats and then makes his mouth as if it has never seen food? ... *It makes his anus dry up.* Did your mother not tell you that?' (110). Vulgar language is used by an emissary in the following statement, to convey his appreciation of his hosts' hospitality: 'I am going out in the rain again. . . Washing my feet now would be like *cleaning my anus before passing excrement*' (184). These expressions of vulgarity are often direct translations from African oral discourse. They have the overall effect of asserting the African identity of European-language literature from the continent.

Language is therefore a primary force in the creation of literary space for dominated writers, whose relationship with language is one of translation. Asserting one's identity through an emphasis on linguistic difference in a global language is a way to subvert or challenge the unsavoury legacies of colonialism. It can indeed be said that contemporary global culture has benefited from the various cultural traditions around the world, and that translation has played a major role in the encounter between these traditions.

Notes

1. The first part of this chapter is an extended and revised version of a section which appeared in the *Routledge Encyclopedia of Translation Studies* entitled 'African Tradition' (Baker, 1998: 295–301).
2. Indirect rule was a (European) colonial policy, practised primarily by the British, in which local government was essentially left in the hands of traditional chiefs, subject of course to 'guidance' from the colonial authorities, who retained overall control of the colony's administration.

References

Achebe, Chinua. (1964), *Arrow of God*. London: Heinemann.

Austen, Ralph A. (1990), *Africans Speak, Colonialism Writes: Transcription and Translation of Oral Literature Before World War II*. Boston: African Studies Center, Boston University.

Baker, M. (ed.) (1998), *Routledge Encyclopedia of Translation Studies*. London and New York: Routledge.

Casanova, Pascale. (2004), *The World Republic of Letters*, trans. M. B. Debevoise, Cambridge, MA: Harvard University Press.

Dadié, Bernard. (1954), *Légendes africaines*. Paris: Seghers.

Danquah, Joseph B. (1928), *Gold Coast: Akan Laws and Customs*. London: Oxford University Press.

Diop, Cheik Anta. (1955), *Nations nègres et culture*. Paris: Présence Africaine.

— (1974), *The African Origin of Civilization: Myth or Reality?* New York: L. Hill.

— Diop, Birago. (1958), *Les Nouveaux Contes d'Amadou Koumba*. Paris: Présence Africaine.

Equilbecq F. V. (1972 [1913]), *Contes populaires d'afrique occidentale*. Paris: Maisonneuve et Larose.

Fagunwa, D. O. (1950 [1938]), *Ogboju-ode ninu igbo Irunmale*. CMS Bookshop, Lagos: Nelson.

— (1968), *Forest of a Thousand Daemons: A Hunter's Saga*, trans. Wole Soyinka. London: Nelson.

Finnegan, Ruth. (1970), *Oral Literature in Africa*. Oxford: Clarendon Press.

Gérard, Albert S. (ed.) (1986), *European-Language Writing in Sub-Saharan Africa, vols I and II*. Budapest: Akadémiai Kiado.

Hamilton, Russell G. (1975), *Voices from an Empire: A History of Afro-Portuguese Literature*. Minneapolis, MN: University of Minnesota Press.

Horton, Robin and Finnegan Ruth (eds) (1973), *Modes of Thought; Essays on Thinking in Western and Non-Western Societies*. London: Faber.

Jakobson, Roman. (1959), 'On Linguistic Aspects of Translation,' in R. A. Brower (ed.), *On Translation*. Cambridge, MA.: Harvard University Press, pp. 232–239.

Kourouma, Ahmadou. (1970) [1968], *Les soleils des indépendances*. Paris: Editions du Seuil.

— (1981) *The Suns of Independence*, trans. Adrian Adams. London: Heinemann.

Mhina, G. A. (1970), 'The Place of Kiswahili in the Field of Translation', *Babel*, 16, (4), 188–96.

Mveng, E. (1980), *L'art et l'artisanat africains*. Yaoundé: Éditions Clé.

Nama, Charles A. (1993), 'Historical, Theoretical and Terminological Perspectives of Translation in Africa', *Meta*, 33, (3), 414–25.

Nkashama, Pius Ngandu. (1992), *Littératures et écritures en langues africaines*. Paris: L'Harmattan.

Okara, Gabriel. (1970 [1964]), *The Voice*. London: Heinemann Educational Books.

Okiri, B. (1992 [1991]), *The Famished Road*. Cape Town: David Philip.

Okpewho, Isidore. (1992), *African Oral Literature: Backgrounds, Characters, and Continuity*. Bloomington, IN: Indiana University Press.

Rushdie, Salman. (1991), *Imaginary Homelands: Essays and Criticism, 1981–1991*. London: Granta.

Senghor, Léopold S. (1964), *Négritude et humanisme*. Paris: Seuil.

Tutuola, Amos. (1952), *The Palm-Wine Drinkard and His Dead Palm-Wine Tapster in the Dead's Town*. London: Faber & Faber.

Vansina, J. (1985), *Oral Tradition as History*. Madison, WI: University of Wisconsin Press.

wa Thiong'o, N. (1982), *Devil on the Cross*. Trans. from the original Kikuyu *(Caitaani mutharaba-ini)* by the author. London/Totowa, NJ: Heinemann, Barnes & Noble Books.

Cracking the Code: Translation as Transgression in *Triomf*[1]

Leon de Kock

2

This article has been braided from two main strands: first, my arguments probe the conditions that pertain to the project of literary translation in South African letters, both in the light of my own research into and observations of conditions in the field, and my own experience as a working translator, a participant in a domain that I regard as extraordinarily rich but also highly problematic. Second, the argument considers aspects of my own translation of Marlene van Niekerk's paradigm-busting novel, *Triomf* (1994, 1999a, 1999b, 1999c, 2004), as a case history which serves as possible corroboration of my arguments in the first part.

Translating in the seam

If writing in South Africa has historically been a vexed occupation,[2] then literary translation, too, has proved to be a hazardous engagement, a tightrope walk over a scene of daunting difference and blunt incommensurability. Translation, at some level, assumes that experience – if experience is the substrate of literature – is prior to, or at least adjacent to, or constitutive of, language (as language is arguably constitutive of experience); if this is the case, it follows that that divergent languages should equally well be able to express the substrate of experience, or recreate it, through translation, in translation's guise as a *mechanism* of transferring or recasting meaning from one language to another. To some extent, this view lies behind Walter Benjamin's fabulously appealing notion that there is higher-order 'pure language' that exists between the lines of all the Babelesque 'ordinary' languages, or mere operational languages, and that all such languages, including the original text in a situation of translation, are really engaged in the act of trying to approximate this higher-order register, this 'pure' expression of the experiential substrate.[3] So, in this way of seeing things, the translated text and the source text are to some extent equal contenders for an elusive, ever-beckoning goal of 'pure' expression. In this view, a writer's sense of experience, her reshaping of the phenomenal world into an imagined world via the coding of one language – the 'source' language – can just as well be recast in another language, the 'target' language. Both languages, in this view, are engaged in the act of approximating a higher ideal of expression, in Benjamin's terms. This is a theory that appeals to the perfectionist in me, and it accords with that sense, when writing, that one is engaged, à la Derrida, in a process of perpetual displacement, of using language as a trace, forever *tracking* the darting, fleet-footed, impossibly elusive prey of thought and being. However, taking a view of the South African literary topography, there are two immediate problems with the proposition that all languages are interchangeable, Babelesque currencies scattered and all awry beneath the superior god of meta-language. The first problem is presented by the case of literary expression – writing or orature – in which the experience relayed through language is *integrally* defined and captured by irreducibly localized expression, *sui generis*, giving it an ultra-thin translatability yield. The second is a literary scene, such as that in South Africa, in which the 'translation' of *experience* itself, not just the literary *representation* of that 'translation' of experience, the mute difficulty of *that* project – recasting perceived and re-imagined experience about others and otherness in a language other than that in which it arose – across different value systems, incommensurably divergent cultures, unevenly aligned epistemologies, opposing cosmologies and inconsistent worldviews, has historically been the core matter of the writing project itself. That is, in a setting of unresolved heterogeneity,[4] the translation of experience, the mediation of perception, and the static-ridden transfer of intercultural communication become the matter of a bigger, more problematic mode of translation.[5] This experiential and conceptual recasting of *modes of being* across languages is clearly a prior order of translation that precedes the sense and meaning we conventionally ascribe to the term. But the point must be made, because if, when we do literary translation in a situation such as this, the content of what we translate is already enmeshed in such prior acts of what I think of as modality translation, then the ordinary perils of mis-apprehension and mistranslation in the purely *literary* sense grow exponen-tially. When the mode and ontological substrate, and not just the style and the meaning, of the 'source' code is so difficult to translate that the term 'untrans-latability' potentially comes into play, then to translate in the regular sense of the term is to deal with a second order of difficulty, a second order of possible 'untranslatability'.

Both the problems sketched above can present very awkward conundrums in postcolonial contexts, rendering translation acutely problematic and rob-bing it of its more ideal cloak, in the classical sense, of elegant, neutral func-tionalism, since the choices made in its name ineluctably become potentially complicit in the unequal cultural trade-offs which are the stuff of colonial experience. However, if one is a postcolonial translator seeking to 'foreignize' the source text in the name of an unconcealed index,[6] a trace that exposes the epistemological violence of translation, then the South African scene becomes more engaging than many others. Yet at a more pragmatic level, speaking from the practising writer's keyboard rather than that of the theorist, if such a thing is possible, the problems of intercultural translation in South Africa remain perhaps less a gleeful opportunity for rupture and more a question of substan-tial difficulty, severely marking what strikes me as, still, the key purpose of lit-erary translation: to exchange literary meaning between different languages in a textual object which shows the highest equivalence of style, meaning, matter and form when read against the source text.

To cite a very prominent example of the problem I am sketching in the South African literary-cultural encounter: when, in the late nineteenth century, the German linguist Wilhelm Bleek and his sister-in-law, Lucy Lloyd, set out to record the stories and songs of an expiring Bushman culture by tran-scribing the utterances of /Xam communicants, prisoners they had extricated from hard labour on the Cape Town breakwater, they were taking on much more than they could possibly have imagined at the time. Bleek and Lloyd learnt the /Xam language from the mouths of their informants and they devel-oped an orthography. They then translated the songs and stories they had so collected into English, the famous archive of which runs to about 12,000 pages and is housed in the Jagger Library at the University of Cape Town. Retrospectively regarded, Bleek and Lloyd were engaged, imperfectly, clumsily, heroically and perhaps unwarily, in an act of experiential, cultural, cosmological and literary translation which, to this day, remains significantly defective. Defective not in the ordinary sense in which all translations are by definition subject to the possibility of near-endless improvement, but in the sense of incomplete, incommensurable with the source 'object' of meaning, and unable to convey anything even close to a 'full' capture of the source meaning in its own right, its own ontological domain, indeed succeeding only in offering mystifying but highly intriguing traces of a culturally inaccessible, disappearing mode of perception, experience and expression.[7]

Why should this be the case? In terms of a history of translation in South Africa, Bleek and Lloyd are an emblematic case of colonial liminality. Though schooled in positivist philology, with its hopeful promises of transparency and equivalence, Bleek and Lloyd were unable to make full sense of what they were transcribing and translating because they were unable to see it except through their own frames of understanding, and the framing semantics of an English that was, to put it bluntly, unschooled in Bushman cosmology and culture. This point has been argued convincingly elsewhere and does not need elaboration now.[8] The Bleek and Lloyd example is an abiding precedent for the Quixotic and highly problematic nature of intercultural translation in South Africa.[9] It sets the historical tone for the project of translation in the southernmost landmark of colonial Africa, at once utopia and dystopia, Le Vaillant's nymph-inhabited Arcadia, Van Wyk Louw's wide and sad land, Eugene Marais's 'Dark River', Dennis Brutus's place of 'Sirens Knuckles Boots', Thomas Pringle's scene of charity for a Bechuana Boy,[10] and it continues to resonate in acts of daily cultural exchange. Deeper acts of translation – borderline crossings, intermeshing identity-tagging, mutual ascriptions across linguistic and cultural confluences, imperfect couplings, experiments in hybridity, like tattoos on skin, marked on the bodies of people as much as on the texts of higher learning – these engagements have all been inscribed in the country's very nature as a 'seam', a cross-stitched fabric of 'quilted' subjectivities, interwoven but straining at the joints.[11] When such awkward acts of ethnographic or cultural barter are implicated in literary translation, then translation as a mode loses its innocence, loses any chance it had of positivistic clarity, resorting to a half-life of opaque representation instead. Examples of literary translation of historical note, following Bleek and Lloyd, in which the sheer torsion is arguably palpable, and can be felt in the peculiar texture of its rarefied and strained language, include Sol T. Plaatjie's rendering of Shakespeare into Setswana;[12] the many works of translating the Bible into indigenous South African languages;[13] the renderings of Bunyan's *Pilgrim's Progress* in African tongues;[14] A. C. Jordan's renowned translation into English of Xhosa oral-style short stories in *Tales From Southern Africa*;[15] H. C. Bosman's 'English' Marico Afrikaans (and their literal translations back into Bosman's own, careless and Anglicized Afrikaans);[16] the English *literary* translations of the Portuguese *experiential* translation of a seafaring encounter with the Cape, found in Camoens's *The Lusiads*;[17] the subsequent re-renderings of the Bleek-Lloyd/Xam archive by several English-speaking, contemporary South African poets, now translating from Bleek-Lloyd English to a re-interpreted, or at least rearranged, metrical register, for a contemporary South African rather than a late Victorian English palate;[18] and so the list goes on. All such examples arise from a need to bridge voids of understanding in a condition where the stakes are higher than mere literary appreciation, where, indeed, the very validity of countervailing forms of being and identity are at issue, their intrinsic nature and their transferability engaged in a value equation of material and immediate import. In the colonial project, and indeed in the postcolonial adventure, too, the lives of whole languages and literatures are at stake, their inner existence resisting the drift towards being miscast, misheard or misconstrued. Translation remains a currency of vital transmission, a cultural blood transfusion. Languages 'other' than the great South African lingua franca, English – where the bartering and trading of meaning most commonly occur – still need to speak their integrity, their otherness, in the Big Brother-language. The reasons should be obvious: English is now more than ever before a portmanteau – in the cyber-global world perhaps a Zip-file would be the more appropriate metaphor – a medium that takes writers into contemporary transnational channels of marketability and exposure. For translators working with South African texts in languages other than English, the historical burden of duty and conscience in the face of history is large. *Tradurre e tradire!*[19]

Translating a 'bastardized' text

How far can one go with language? How deep into the fissures of sensate being, the eyes that see, the ears that hear, the tongue that tastes and the processing apparatus that experiences phenomena and epiphenomena at first remove? This is the question that always strikes me when I set out on a project of extended novelistic translation. Speaking now not only theoretically but also as a working literary translator, writing up my *experience* of my own acts of translation,[20] I can record that it always feels, in the moment of embarkation, as if I have entered a kind of inter-zone, a place of great attraction and alluring power. It is a place where one potentially has the ability, in one's own hands, of creating a near-to-perfect simulacrum of imagined worlds, a character-infused 'multiverse'[21] of perception and experience, co-drifting down an imaginative stream with an author for whom one has the highest regard. As a translator, you have the choice, or the talent, or the determination, to do this in an elegant economy of expression, an adventurous foray into risky, inventive reshaping, making a *tour de force* – you hope and pray – of comprehensive capture and addition to value in literary language that is evocative, stylish, and accurate to a fault.[22] That is the mission. For me, this comes before any of the questions of political import. The project, writ large, is a sensuous challenge, an engagement that combines the best of one's experiential exposure, range of imaginative possibility, and verbal prowess, sifting through nuance and weighing up texture, rhythm and narrative flow. In the case of *Triomf* and its translation, this overall sense of challenge and opportunity quickly began to combine with the acutely problematic nature of the task at hand: how to speak in the flattened, over-spoken registers of modern South African English (SAE) and still convey the feel of a novel such as *Triomf*, a saga written in a scrupulously observed sociolect, a class and regional sub-code of Afrikaans, dumbed down from the pseudo-professorial registers of the Nationalist[23] politicians who created the area called 'Triomf' in the first place, and wrenched into the actual mish-mash of a colloquial, low-class, aggression-tinged, paranoiac, stained-by-ideology, bastardized-half-English idiom that is spoken in the house of Pop, Treppie, Mol and Lambert during the last days of Apartheid. These characters, who bear the ultimate legacy of Afrikaner nationalism, are a sorry group of disappointed travellers on the final leg of the 'Separate Development'[24] sortie, with little baggage left to carry except their own, overdetermined selves, forged in a frenzy of Nationalist 'self-determination' ('selfbeskikking'), and now they have internecine family incest as their inheritance, their final homage to a form of ideological self-consumption, nationalism taken to a catastrophic human extreme.

In the case of *Triomf*'s translation, then, there was an alluring sense of attraction just in the ability to set the scene, to disgrace English with a contortion of prose that speaks in its registers but simultaneously registers a calumny of its purity. That was the greatest appeal of all when I approached the task of translating the novel, then still regarded by many as untranslatable. Why should it be inimical to translation? The answer was simple: its Afrikaans was half-English already. The calculated bastardization of Afrikaans in the narration seemed impossible to 'translate', because, as it was, the original *Triomf*'s prose already consisted of a mish-mash of English and Afrikaans in a register that was surely *sui generis* – or so people thought. My initial, knee-jerk response went something like this: if so many of the Afrikaans sentences in the novel contained so many borrowed English words and phrases, functioning in the Afrikaans as a register of colloquialism, and now performing a transferred semantic function in the Afrikaans source text itself, then perhaps one could just reverse the process – write bastardized English sentences with an equal number of Afrikaans words and phrases, Afrikaans idioms and slang. But of course that would immediately defeat the purpose of translation, which is to foreswear any literal use of the source language at all, except perhaps in very occasional instances, followed by a glossary at the end of the text. However, it was clear from the start that this would be no mere instance of glossing a few foreign terms for local colour. *Triomf* was so peppered with explosive ruptures and assaults against the purity of Afrikaans, so many defacements of the pretty face of Afrikaans's grammatical propriety, that the thought of a glossary was simply far-fetched. Yet the possibility of reproducing the assault on 'purity' of language remained enticing, because soiling the bourgeois niceties of 'Algemene Beskaafde Afrikaans' (Generally Cultivated Afrikaans, the carrier of Afrikaans nationalism), was for the author of *Triomf* a deliberate political and novelistic strategy. For her, 'purity' had to be assailed at every level. 'Purity' of language, in the ideological stratifications that Afrikaans was subjected to under Apartheid, ran parallel to purity of 'group areas', purity of 'self-determination', the ban on 'mixed' marriages and 'mixed' love affairs, and it lay behind the 'cleansing' of Sophiatown to make Triomf. The 'triumph' of 'purity' came at the cost of lives and dignity; it ultimately impugned the dignity of Afrikaans, making it an enemy of its own, less purity-obsessed, dissident adherents. For Marlene van Niekerk, a disaffected, rebellious Afrikaner, writing in Afrikaans remained her only real choice, as it did for most mother-tongue authors, yet she felt compelled to use the language subversively, to turn it inside out and commit violence upon it in a raging assault on its tightly regulated modes of 'proper' expression and form. So a parallel assault on the modalities of English, in an English version of such an Afrikaans novel, was therefore not only enticing, it seemed compellingly necessary.

But how to do it? The problem seemed huge. Fortunately, I did not then see it quite as clearly as the above description might imply. The sense of challenge grew as I found myself making do with what came to hand, producing a first draft as a template upon which to begin relentless revision and reshaping. Throughout the translation's initial drafting, the author and I were working on the basis that the English *Triomf* would be published in South Africa by Jonathan Ball and Queillerie (which, in the end, it was), and that we could therefore assume an SAE readership. For me, this offered the partial 'solution' of assuming that most readers were at least acquainted with Afrikaans, and that my rendering could, therefore, to some extent break the rules of strict translation in the cause of a thematically motivated rupturing of formal 'purity', in the English version, too. In other words, if the original *Triomf* was a hybrid of Afrikaans with English, then my translation could, perhaps to a lesser extent, be a hybrid of English with Afrikaans. Many Afrikaans terms, idioms and phrases have, over the past two centuries or so, become part of SAE.[25] This led to the possibility that I might be able to renovate the stuffy registers of 'proper' English, which was a politically loaded act, too, given the hegemonic role that English has played through the many decades of missionary imperialism and race-based segregation in the country's history.[26] Yet this would need to be done carefully. The histories of English-based and Afrikaans-based race coercion were arguably comparable, but certainly not identical. In addition, the specificity of dissident Afrikaans rebellion against Afrikaans cultural and political strictures needed to be respected and, if possible, rendered in translation.

My instinct was to create the sense, in the translated work, of a milieu, a class-based 'atmosphere' in the language that could approximate working-class Afrikaans Triomf, sociologically speaking. I had grown up on the other side of Hurst Hill, which stands above Triomf/Sophiatown on the city-centre side, in the then-white area called Mayfair ('white', that is, apart from the shadow black servant population). In Mayfair, a similar social class to that in Triomf was complicit in a similarly race-laced compendium of vulgar behaviours, except for the fact that my own milieu had been formed within the registers of a streetwise, sloppy, slangy, degraded form of 'Joburg' English. It felt to me that the English sociolect with which I had grown up could almost serve as a register of translation for the Afrikaans vulgate in *Triomf*, since there was a sociological similarity: white communities, working class, racist, living in similar *actual* conditions, and physically proximate. It was a case of almost but not quite. I would have to rid my Mayfair-English of its strong Lebanese influences (arising from the substantial Lebanese community resident in Mayfair in the middle- to late twentieth century), and stain it more pointedly with

Afrikanerisms, local slang such as I also heard all around me, providing words like 'oke' and 'ou' for 'fellow' or 'chap', for example, and mixed English/Afrikaans usage such as 'ag don't sig man' ('sig' meaning hesitate or waver, 'ag' as in 'oh', an exhortation). The English I grew up hearing was full of impure bastardizations, containing a similar quota of the reprehensible and the vulgar to that found in Van Niekerk's novel, full of words such as *kafferboetie* ('kaffir-lover'), *moer* (multiple meanings: as a verb, 'biff him one', as a noun, 'vagina', 'sediment', among other meanings), *bliksem* ('bugger' as a noun, 'thump' or 'beat up' as a verb), and so on. Just as many English words formed part of the lexicon of the Afrikaans characters in the novel I was translating, so many Afrikaans words had helped form the lexicon of the English I had grown up speaking. I had a considerable arsenal of such terms and expressions, and I was eager to use them. It suited my own sense of narrative realism, my own feeling for the rough texture of the streets in which I had grown up. And the area in which I learnt such language upon my 'native' tongue was virtually contiguous with the actual Triomf. Many if not most of my fellow SAE-speakers would have heard the kind of language I intended to use, or they would be able to get the drift, especially in a novel where the drift was meant to be fairly violent and the grain of the language was never meant to be smooth.

The narrative possibilities for my translation were beginning to feel like a rich brew, an intoxicating cross-fusion of texture and idiom. The Afrikanerisms and occasional untranslated words would serve both to rupture the English text, spicing in the thematic element of impurity, and they would make the text *feel* Afrikaans, too, which was critically important – I wanted readers to read *through* the English into an Afrikaans world, imagining that they were in fact reading Afrikaans, hearing Afrikaans and experiencing an 'Afrikaans' world. So, to some extent, the text had to perform an act of illusionism. The possibility existed to create, with both losses and gains in the translated work, a *hybrid*, bastardized translation that I could only hope would eventually, additively, create a similar feel to that of the original, despite the problem that the English words and phrases already in the Afrikaans original served a trans-ferred, or transformed, semantic function as *part of Afrikaans sentences*, giving them a different contextualization and a new slant, and even though any sim-ple substitutions or reversals in the Afrikaans-to-English ratios of expression would be difficult and never a case of mathematical exactitude. It was a mas-sive task, and eventually it exhausted me quite comprehensively. The transla-tion went through countless drafts and a seemingly endless process of re-sculpting, with much advice from and negotiation with the author, but

eventually it simply had to be surrendered to the publishers, and to the intimi-
dating machinery of reception.

I propose, in the remainder of this essay (sections on internal defamiliarization and breaking the code, below), to discuss two particular aspects of this
case history. The section on internal defamiliarization deals with the implications of a need that arose in the process of translating, namely to create two
variant editions of the translated text. This brought about a situation in which
the aim of rupturing the purity of language used in *Triomf* could be achieved
both by means that were *external* to the English deployed, and by means that
were *internal* to it. The section on breaking the code deals with an instance of
what I call 'code-breaking', moments in the translation when I committed a
transgression of the core duty of translator, which is never to leave entire sentences untranslated. Such code-breaking, I will argue, illustrates certain complexities of translation in intercultural situations in which a *masala* or *bredie*
of languages is dished up by writers, who then want their works translated into
only *one* of the languages that went into the stew in the first place, insisting
(understandably) that the translator somehow retain the original flavour.

Both of the abovementioned aspects came into play when, after the first
few drafts of the translation had already been completed, news arrived that the
author's agent in London had secured a British publisher for the English
version of *Triomf* – the multinational group Little, Brown & Co. This news
threw the cat among the pigeons, suddenly and substantially changing the
entire picture from a translation point of view. I was called to a conference at
the author's house in Westdene, Johannesburg, in the course of 1998, and we
sat down to deliberate. What were we now to do, since all we had was a 'hybrid'
draft translation of the novel, surely unsuitable for international English
readers?

Initially, we resolved, with deep reluctance, to root out most if not all of the
Afrikaans words, phrases, idioms, curses and slang – meticulously beaded
arrangements of translation that I had painstakingly put together over a period
of about eight months – and find 'standard English' equivalents for them.
Needless to say, this came as an unpleasant shock to me. I was reluctant to give
up the project of translational hybridity upon which I had so ambitiously
embarked. Both the author and I were mindful of the need to keep the grainy,
grimy texture of the translated prose intact. But it now seemed that rupturing
the surface of linguistic purity, both an ideological and an aesthetic necessity,
would have to be performed via means other than the use of semantically
cross-infused Afrikaans terms that had either come into an SAE idiom over

time, or which we had thought we could implant into the English text for effect. The defamiliarization effect, as I like to think of it, was going to have to be achieved *within* the registers of English after all, not outside of it. This meant quite deliberately wrenching English for unfamiliar ways of expressing the outlandish Afrikaans semantic efflux everywhere on the riotous, scabrous surface of the original text.

So urgent did this task then seem to us, that Van Niekerk and I agreed I would move into the author's guest cottage, in the garden of her house, for at least a week, so that we could do intensive brainstorming on all the terms that showed up in jagged red underlining on my screen-display, words that the computer's automatic spell check was telling me were *not English*, or incorrectly spelled English. There were literally thousands of them. On the first night of my stay, I was struggling to sleep, distressed about the impending obliteration of my draft SAE translation, when I came up with a way of actually preserving the hybrid version of my translation while also changing it to 'standard' English. The idea was simple – make two texts! Simply by saving an extra copy under a different filename, and by using the CTR+SHIFT+F6 function, I could alternate between what would become the 'SA version' and a 'UK version', with both files open at the same time, turning the Afrikaans slang into an urban English patois for the UK version, but leaving most of it intact in the SA version. When I put this idea to the author the following morning, she agreed, albeit warily. This would create additional complexity to an already over-complicated situation, and it would also necessitate a very great need for keyboard acuity: I would need constantly to be aware of which version I was working in at any given moment. Forgetfulness and/or confusion could have quite serious implications. But if I could crack this ambitious task, then we might emerge with a unique case of deliberately divergent translations: one an 'externally' hybrid translation, for the South African market, and the other, for the UK market, a text whose hybridity and defamiliarization effects would have to be *internal* to the standard English we were now compelled to use, with a glossary for a select number of words which simply would not yield to any form of translation whatsoever.

Internal defamiliarization

So we sat together with heaps of manuscript paper, making handwritten changes, deciding on each highlighted word or phrase as we encountered them. I would do the transcription later, in the evenings, in some cases making changes only on the UK version, and in others (where the revisions seemed especially good, and where we made additional, incidental improvements) on both versions.[27] An example of a more straightforward kind can be found in Chapter 8, where 'Sies, Jannie!' in the SA edition (Van Niekerk 1999a: 135), becomes 'Sis, Jannie' in the UK edition (1999c: 164), and a paragraph or two down from this: 'They kiss. Wragtag!' becomes 'They kiss. Can you believe it?'. 'Sis' and *sies* are clearly very close, both of them expletives expressing disgust ('sis' being a widely used slang SAE alternative to the Afrikaans word *sies*), but *sies* carries a certain weight of vulgarity, a tinge of emphatic, unapologetic coarseness which is not nearly as pronounced in the somewhat more lightly expressed 'sis' in English. And 'wragtag', for the SAE-speaker, is a fairly well-known, guttural contraction of the word *waaragtig* in Afrikaans, meaning 'having the quality of truth, or truthfully'. The contraction, especially, with its double loading of gutturally expressible 'a' and 'g' sounds, communicates revulsion almost onomatopoetically, carrying for an SAE-speaker an instantly recognizable sound and feeling. This is largely lost in the bland UK version of this sentence, which I would classify as an example where translation entails a certain loss, and perhaps as a case where the translation fails to create the effect of 'internal defamiliarization'. Yet, such smaller examples of translational weakness (when measured against the spiced-up SAE version) are in a sense rescued by the general drift, the sheer narrative momentum, of Van Niekerk's powerful novel. It remains debatable to this day whether, in an example such as this, it might not have been a better idea to retain the foreign words even in the UK edition, relying on context for a sense of meaning, and thereby foreignizing the English text as well as sticking more closely to the original, which would have arguably been more consistent with the novel's overall thematic thrust. However, a policy decision was made, based on deliberations mutually and severally between translator, author, agent and publishers, extending beyond translator's ambit alone.

The term that arguably created the most anxiety around its translation is the near-unspeakable slang Afrikaans conjunction *meidepoes*. This term, probably one of the most racially loaded and offensive descriptors in the entire argot of Apartheid, combines a slang Afrikaans word for vagina, namely 'poes' (pronounced 'puss'), with the multiply resonant Afrikaans word *meid*, derived from *meisie* ('girl'), but signifying a 'coloured maidservant', according to one authoritative English-Afrikaans dictionary (Bosman et al. 1967). In common, racist usage, *meidepoes* combines the sense of a black or coloured woman with a large connotative reflux of disgust, centred metonymically on the female genitalia. There is stuff here for an entire dissertation on gender stereotyping, sexual and racial essentialism, and metonymic displacement. The author and I discussed the complexity and untranslatability of this word at length. Eventually, the simplest option was to use the term 'coloured pussy', but in a separate instance we came up with what was, for me, a fabulously suggestive alternative, namely 'toffee skirt'. While the term 'coloured pussy' gives one a deferred sense of the paradoxical, psychologically complex compound of desire and recoil contained in the conjunction of racial abuse and sexual licentiousness that *meidepoes* arguably represents, it lacks the contextual and semantic punch of the original. In context, 'toffee skirt', on the other hand (not an idiom in English), wrenches standard English out of its familiar idiomatic range of reference, allows a freer play of association, and evokes unexpected, lateral connections: 'skirt' combined with 'toffee' suggests a certain sticky, off-colour, licentious, possibly dirty, smudgy, low-class woman, especially given the colour and taste attributes, not to mention the texture, of toffee. Both appetite and surfeit, cheap attraction and recoil, are spring-loaded into that curious translational compound, 'toffee skirt', which for me is one of the best examples of the kind of 'internal' defamiliarization I have suggested is an attribute of the English in the UK version of *Triomf*. As the author and I worked through the SAE version, making idiomatic and semantic leaps from 'original' terms in the hybrid text to unusual and, at times, poetic switches and turns such as this, I began to wonder whether a strategy of internal defamiliarization wasn't, in fact, the more difficult, and the more ultimately rewarding, option than the slightly more literal hybridization of the translated text, such as I had fixed upon for the SAE version. I think this question remains open for debate. I do, however, feel fortunate in having both modes of translation, hybrid and internally defamiliarized, available in separately published editions.

Breaking the code

In Chapter 13 of *Triomf*, in my understanding of the novel a pivotal passage of narration, the novel's internal hybridity comes to the surface, spilling over into a crucially important dialogue involving a character called Sonnyboy and Lambert, the novel's child of incest. Lambert is a lumbering sociopath, emotionally and otherwise retarded, who was brought into being within the bosom of a family so indoctrinated into the ideologies of self against other that multiple, mutual incest becomes a logical imperative. Lambert is the grim, monstrous apogee of Afrikaner 'self-determination' taken too far: stunted, brutish, inbred, an epileptic 30-something subject to violent seizures, seeking love but not knowing any language for it other than the culturally and racially exclusive terminology into which he was born. The author's underlying theme: if you cut yourself off for long enough in self-constructed ghettoes, the result will be incest, on the real as well as the symbolic level. The *bloedskande* (incest) that for years has been a regular eruption in the Benade home in *Triomf*, is an analogue for the incestuous workings of the entire Nationalist machinery and the many perverse social symptoms it spawned over more than 40 years in South Africa. In the end, this 'caked up' (*saamgekoekte*)[28] system implodes; and it is brought down precisely by Lambert, the system's karmic instrument, so to speak, its self-produced nemesis and agent of destruction. Chapter 13 is critical because Lambert has a *real* encounter with otherness for what is probably the first time in his life. Up until this point, his social and interpersonal existence has been conducted from behind the distorting lens of an ideology which stigmatizes all instances of identity other than white Afrikaans.

In this chapter (entitled 'Lucky Finds'), Lambert is forced into communication with what might be described as *strong otherness*. But before this happens, he gets mocked and harried by his own kind, by members of the Afrikaner Resistance Movement (AWB),[29] in the form of two AWB adherents manning a stall in Lambert's neighbourhood. The AWB in 1994 was a militant, far-right group that tried, in various ways, to sabotage the 1994 democratic elections in South Africa. After escaping their mockery for his unwillingness to be their dupe, Lambert proceeds to the local dump, carrying a plastic municipal rubbish bag, R50 and six Spur (steakhouse) meal vouchers. He is looking for discarded plastic wine-bags, which he imagines he will use to store essentials such as petrol, in a hole he is digging under the surface of Triomf, for the family's escape to the 'North' when 'shit hits the fan' in the country (i.e. democracy). He is also on a mission to improve his home environment for the visit by a 'girl' promised to him by his devilish brother (father?), Treppie, for his birthday. However, once at the dump, he has a near-seizure and is saved from the grinding wheels of a dump-truck by Sonnyboy. This character, Sonnyboy, is irreducibly cross-hatched and 'impure' in Lambert's ideology. He is perhaps the book's most comprehensive 'South African' character. By contrast to the drubbing Lambert is given by the AWB men, his 'own kind', Sonnyboy not only saves Lambert's life, he also shows him kindness, and they find common ground with each other in the course of a conversation in which they smoke a dagga-joint (reefer of cannabis) together. Lambert initially goes into this engagement haltingly, but he eventually swops his R50 and six Spur vouchers for a revolver in Sonnyboy's possession, a pair of binoculars, and the *pasella* (free bonus) of an Mbira (*'umbira'* for Lambert), a hand-held musical instrument. By the end of the encounter, Lambert has been given a glimpse – not that he fully realizes this himself – of how an alternative South African conversation might shape up, and what kind of spirit it might be conducted in.

Sonnyboy is best allowed to introduce himself. These are the words used in the UK translation, in the passage in which he explains himself to Lambert:

> 'Look, that's how the dice fell for me here in Jo'burg. I'm a Xhosa, I come from the Transkei, and some of us are yellow.' He touches his face. 'That's why the bladdy Bushmen thought I was one of them, so I got a room in Bosmont right in among them. And they began talking real Coloured Afrikaans to me. So I got the hang of it on the sly, and I didn't say nothing, 'cause the less a Bushman knows about you, the better. It's a bad scene, the Bushman scene. They drink themselves stupid and then they rob and stab you and leave you for dead.' (Van Niekerk, 1999c: 275)

In the SA edition, this passage reads as follows:

> 'Kyk, daai's nou my luck in Jo'burg gewies, nè! Ek's 'n Xhosa, ek kom van die Transkei af. En ek's maar so.' He touches his face. 'Toe dag die Boesmans ek's ok 'n Boesman, toe kry ek 'n room in Bosmont tussen hulle. En hulle praat met my regte coloured Afrikaans. En toe leer ek maar so on the sly en ek sê fokol, want hoe minder 'n Boesman van jou af weet, hoe beter. Dis 'n bad scene, die Boesmanscene. Hulle lê dronk en suip en steel en steek jou met messe en goed.' (Van Niekerk 1999a: 227–28)

Apart from the four words outside of quote marks in this passage ('He touches his face'), the rest of it was left unchanged from its original form in the SA version of the translation. When I encountered this rare moment of utterly candid self-description in the course of the novel, it struck me as untranslatable in a sense that goes beyond linguistic or idiomatic untranslatability. I felt that Sonnyboy's description of himself *enacted* the hybridity of identity into which he had been inducted in the course of surviving outside of South Africa's white enclaves. Sonnyboy can talk Xhosa (and, in all probability, other indigenous languages, too), and when addressing Lambert he can adjust his lexicon to an Afrikaans in which he both mixes in English ('luck', 'on the sly', 'room', 'bad scene') and in which he distances himself from what he calls 'Coloured Afrikaans', a dialect he is telling Lambert he picked up 'on the sly' while pretending to be a Coloured as a result of the yellowish pallor of his 'Xhosa' skin. By contrast, Lambert can speak only Afrikaans and broken English. They are both low-life characters, and although Lambert *thinks* he is superior because he's white, the events of the chapter show that he is not, and that Sonnyboy is more resourceful, agile and in touch with the complexities of his shifting environment, not to mention a good deal more intelligent. If any character in *Triomf* is a 'true South African', it is Sonnyboy, culturally hybrid, linguistically diverse, street-smart and fully indigenized. His enunciations enact these characteristics. To some extent, Sonnyboy's very being – his irremediable hybridity, his means of survival – rests on the tip of his versatile tongue. To *translate* such a mélange of mixed speech into the pallid registers of 'standard English' struck me as a monstrous betrayal – *tradurre e tradire!* – a *denaturing* of the very fibres of Sonnyboy's necessary, irreducible specificity. If Sonnyboy stands in for an interracial South African self that proposes an alternative, to some extent, to single-stranded ethnic impositions and machinations of political identity, then how does one blandly go and strip him of precisely his multivocality in the name of translation? No, I would not do it. It went against the grain of everything I had been campaigning for, in the literary and teaching domain, in an attempt to break out from the ethnic prison in which I, too, had grown into adulthood in a white ghetto of Johannesburg. So I committed the first transgression of translation, which is to refuse to translate, insisting that my South African readers would understand at least part if not all of the mixed Afrikaans-English that Sonnyboy speaks in the passage quoted above. In literary terms, too, such a refusal to translate seemed significant in the South African literary and cultural set-up, because the passage in question, in my view, *is already a translation.* The very fibres of Sonnyboy's speech have been formed by the necessities of border-crossings, taking body and mind across boundaries, into unsettling and strange territories, translating experience into new forms of speech in very different tongues and idioms, as the generational journey from country to city and vice-versa is made, recasting both older and newer forms of experience in evolving vocabularies and tongues, resulting, in the end, in series of what one might call 'interlanguages', the above passage being a fine example of one of them. It should be easy to understand, in view of such a history, such an achievement, why rendering a passage like this in English was never going to be a simple matter of what is ordinarily understood as 'translation'.

However, while I had my way in the SA edition, the UK edition could not countenance a whole paragraph of language that would be incomprehensible to its more conventionally English-speaking readers, and so we had to resort, as far as possible, to internal defamiliarization, in terms and phrases such as 'bladdy Bushmen', but in my view this entailed a loss, a casualty of translation that had to be made up, as far as possible, by contextual richness elsewhere in the chapter, and contextual information, both of which abound in Van Niekerk's patient, probing, rounded-out fictional prose.

Chapter 13 contains code-breaking of another sort that deserves consideration here. The dialogue between Lambert and Sonnyboy is shot through with switches of language – from Sonnyboy's mixed urban patois to Lambert's degraded Afrikaans to Sonnyboy's own form of 'black' Afrikaans to Lambert's broken English to Sonnyboy's own turns of English – so that translating their dialogue became an act of meta-translation. I say 'meta-translation' because it forced into the forefront an awareness of the double layer of implied voice in a translated text. When a character like Lambert speaks in a translator's English (target language), both the reader and the translator implicitly understand the character 'actually' to be speaking Afrikaans (source language). This means that the reader – and this naturally includes the translator, a reader first and foremost of both texts – reads 'through' the translated text as one would look through a pane of glass, or a lens. The text serves to focalize the 'actual' content, which is behind the glass of the lens, so to speak. So when one reads Lambert saying:

> 'Shuddup with that noise! Shuddup. It's fuckenwell eleven o'clock at night! What the hell do you people think you're doing?' (Van Niekerk 1999c: 103)

one imagines him actually saying something that, if you could understand the source language, would read like this:

> 'Sjaddap met daai geraas! Sjarrap! Dis fokkenwel elfuur in die nag! Wat de hel dink julle doen julle!' (Van Niekerk 1994: 96)

This comforting meta-sense of the real content, in a different language, 'behind' the surface of the translated text, such as I feel a definite sense of when reading Constance Garnett's English translation of *Crime and Punishment* (possibly because of what strikes me as the 'Russian' awkwardness of her English register), this consoling illusion of actually reading a foreign language, and hearing Russian characters speak their Russian selves *through* the transparent pane of a known language, this great art of translation, is shattered when one's characters start speaking the 'foreign' language *and* the known language in the same dialogue! This is analogous to Raskolnikov diverting into *real*, broken English in the midst of his Russian-rendered-into-English dialogue. How does one then distinguish the *real* (broken) English he is speaking from the 'English' (actually Russian) he is speaking through the translator's code?

Such a problem becomes even more acute when the register of translation itself deliberately approximates a kind of 'broken English' anyway, in its seeking for the feel of the Afrikaans original. To make things further complicated from a translation point of view, the dialogue also contains Sonnyboy spicing in bits of Afrikaans into his English, which Afrikaans bits I left unchanged in the SA edition of the translation. The following scene, from the SA version of the translation, presents text that exhibits many of these elements. It contains whole passages of dialogue in a mixed register of English and Afrikaans, and it features both translated narrative description and untranslated hybrid dialogue text. To make these salient features clear, the words and sentences which appear in Sonnyboy's impure Afrikaans – that is, entirely untranslated text in the SA edition – are here rendered in bold text. For clarity, the UK translation of the Afrikaans that is here (i.e., in the SA translation) left intact in Sonnyboy's speech, appears in square brackets immediately following the relevant bit of untranslated Afrikaans (in the SA version). Text in italics indicates Sonnyboy and Lambert's actual English usage (i.e. text appearing in the original Afrikaans version of *Triomf* in English). So, **bold** = untranslated Afrikaans in the SA version, *italics* = English usage in the Afrikaans original text; square brackets = UK version's translation of language left untranslated in the SA English version; regular font = text translated from Afrikaans into English. The section of narrative quoted below occurs just after Lambert's near-seizure and Sonnyboy's rescuing of him from the wheels of a dump-truck:

> Lambert wants to get up, but his back feels lame. He can't get up nicely.
>
> The kaffir presses him softly against his chest, back down again.
>
> *'It's okay, my bra.* **Ek check vir jou net lekker hier**. [I'm just checking for you here.] *Wait, sit, it's okay. Are you feeling better now? You faint or what?* **Daai** [those] *lorries nearly got you, my man. Flat* **gesqueeza** **was jy** *nearly, my bra,* [you were almost squeezed flat, my brother] *flat* **soos** *a* [like a] *pancake. But I watch out for you, my man. I pick you up, I bring you here. I give you Coke. I'm your friend, man.* **Moenie skrik nie.** [Don't panic.]
>
> *'I'm not your friend,'* he says. *'I want to go home now.'* But he can't get up.
>
> The kaffir stands up. He takes a big step backwards. He motions with his hands. This kaffir's full of sights.

'Okay! Okay! Okay! You're not my friend, hey, you are my boss, right? Big boss, **ja baas**. [yes boss, left as is in UK edition and glossed] **Ek's maar net 'n kaffer by die dumps, baas,** [I'm just a kaffir at the dumps, boss,] *okay? I catch* **flou** *whiteys here* [I catch whiteys who faint here]. *That's my job, yes? Here a whitey, there a whitey, faint. Faint left, faint right, faint centre, all day long. I'm the fainting boy, right?'*

The kaffir turns his back to him. From behind it looks like he's laughing. Then he turns around again.

'Okay? Relax, my bra, relax **net** [just relax]. *Boss, king, president, chief, caesar. Whatever. God in heaven, anything you want,* **ek sê** [I say]. *Any way you want it. At your service.* **Askies baas, asseblief baas, dankie baas**, [Excuse me boss, please boss, thank you boss] **ja baas, nee baas,** [yes boss, no boss, given in UK ed. as 'ja baas, no baas' in italics and glossed] *sorry boss that I live boss!'* The kaffir turns away again. His hands are in ['at' in UK ed.] his sides. He drops his head and makes little shaking movements.

'I did not mean that so, man. Thanks for your help, man, very ['many' in UK ed.] *thanks. I just must go home now, that's all. I'm not feeling right, you see.'* (Van Niekerk 1999a: 224–225)

In rendering the third-last sentence of this dialogue, I changed Van Niekerk's more standard English phrase, which appeared in English in the Afrikaans original, '[t]hanks for your help, man, thanks very much', to a phrase more deliberately broken '[t]hanks for your help man, very thanks' ('very thanks' being the literal word-order for 'baie dankie' and indicating an obviously broken-English idiom, so as to make it clearer in the translation that Lambert is *really speaking English* here, very bad English, rather than Afrikaans translated into English). However, the editors of the UK version clearly missed my point, assuming that I had written unidiomatic English, and changed 'very thanks' to 'many thanks'. (I had already surrendered to the text to the mercy of the publishers and their editors.) In the rest of Lambert's originally spoken English sentence, the word-order is sufficiently Afrikaans to indicate to the reader of the translation that, although he is reading English coming out of Lambert's mouth, it is not translated Afrikaans but original Lambert-English ('I did not mean that so, man …' = 'Ek het dit nie so bedoel nie …').

Looking now at the typeface medley of the passage quoted above, which offers a typographical analogue of the internal hybridity of *Triomf*, it strikes me that the novel's translation was, to some extent, an act of both translation as code switching and translation as code-breaking; further, that this necessity to *break the code* of translation arises in transcultural semantic zones which I prefer to see as best explained by the cultural dynamics of the seam, that ever-recurring limit condition of South African letters, a paradoxical site of simultaneous convergence and divergence, cross-stitched in a compulsive urge to conjoin that which resists easy conjunction, a rich textual seam that runs through the entire field like a ridge, a persistent, abiding mark of difference. If anything was the real point of translating *Triomf*, it was to hold this seam together in all its contradictory tension and its peculiar torsion, indeed to maintain it as the work's ultimate textual integrity. That was the real point of translating *Triomf*, the real triumph of the novel, and the great challenge of its rendering in English.

Notes

1. Van Niekerk (1994). This novel swept the boards in South Africa in the 1990s, claiming several major prizes, including the M-Net Prize and the Noma Award, and it is generally recognized as a major work of Afrikaans fiction, perhaps the definitive anti- as well as post-Apartheid novel in Afrikaans. The English version (Van Niekerk 1999a and 1999b, 2004, trans. Leon de Kock), won the South African Translators Institute Award for Outstanding Translation in 2000.

2. I have made this argument extensively in 'South Africa in the Global Imaginary: An Introduction' (2004).

3. Benjamin, Walter, 'The Task of the Translator'. In Benjamin 1992 (70–82). See also De Kock (2003) for further discussion of Benjamin in relation to the *Triomf* translation.

4. This point has been set out and extensively argued in De Kock 2001 (271–290).

5. See Stephen Gray (1989), in which he makes a case for the Southern African writer as, in essence, a 'translator' across different systems of meaning and identity.

6. Such as Lawrence Venuti (1995) and other postcolonial translation theorists would have us do.

7. For a broader discussion, see Skotnes (2001 and 2007). See also Bleek and Lloyd (1911).

8. See, for example, Skotnes (2001). See also Martin Hall (1998), and Loren Kruger's discussion (2000) of Hall's essay, collected in *Negotiating the Past: The Making of Memory in South Africa* (eds Sarah Nuttall and Carli Coetzee, 1998); of particular interest is the argument about how the language and narrative of one of the /Xam informants, //Kabbo, evades Bleek's positivist philology as well as the imperial project of conquest and subjugation led by the former Cape Governor, Sir George Grey, Bleek's patron.

9. The most accessible view of the Bleek-Lloyd project is via their book, *Specimens of Bushman Folklore* (Bleek and Lloyd 1911), which runs to 468 pages and demonstrates the attempt to 'archive' living (in this case, dying) oral narrative traditions.

10. For a discussion of Le Vaillant, see Gray (1979); Van Wyk Louw's famous line 'O Wye en droewe land' is from the verse drama *Die Dieper Reg* Van Wyk Louw 1947); Eugène N. Marais's 'Dark River' ('Diep Rivier', a symbol of death), is from the poem of the same name (in Marais 1925);

Dennis Brutus's poem 'Sirens Knuckles Boots' appears in *A Simple Lust* (Brutus 1973); for Thomas Pringle's famous poem, 'The Bechuana Boy', see Pereira and Chapman (1989).

11. See De Kock (2001) on the poetics of the 'seam' in South Africa and Harris (2006) on the idea of 'quilting' in the work and statements of Antjie Krog.

12. On Plaatje, see Willan (1996: 308). Plaatje translated four of Shakespeare's plays, two of which were published: *Diposho-phoso [Comedy of Errors]*, Morija: Morija Printing Works, 1930; and *Dintshontsho tsa bo-Juliuse Kesara [Julius Caesar]*, Johannesburg: Witwatersrand University Press, 1937. The two translations that appear to have gotten lost are *Much Ado About Nothing* and *The Merchant of Venice* (Willan, 1996: 308).

13. See Beck (1997) and Sanneh (1989).

14. See Hofmeyr (2004).

15. See MacKenzie (2002) on A. C. Jordan's translation of Xhosa oral-style tales. Mackenzie says: '[W]hat we are dealing with here is not the translation of one language into another (although this does come into it), but, more particularly, the shift from one ontological mode to another' (347).

16. See the collection of Bosman's extant Afrikaans short stories, collected in *Verborge Skatte* (De Kock, 2001).

17. See Gray's classic discussion in his *Southern African Literature: An Introduction* (1979, Chapter 1).

18. See Alan James (2001), Antjie Krog (2004), Stephen Watson (1991).

19. To translate is to betray! Cf. Simon Lewis, '*Tradurre e Tradire*: The Treason and Translation of Breyten Breytenbach' (2001).

20. Principally, Marlene van Niekerk's novel, *Triomf* (1999), and Etienne van Heerden's novel, *In Stede van die Liefde* (2007, MS).

21. On the idea of a 'multiverse', and on 'co-drifting', see Kenny (1985).

22. Such as I believe was achieved by Michiel Heyns in his value-enhancing English translation of Van Niekerk's big follow-up classic to *Triomf*, entitled *Agaat* (2004, 2006). See my discussion in De Kock (2007).

23. In the South African historical context, 'Nationalist' gains an added meaning, apart from the standard sense of the word 'nationalist', referring also to characteristics of the political ideology created by the National Party in South Africa, which ruled from 1948 until the 1990s transition to democracy. 'Nationalist' in this sense implies a particularly pronounced racial xenophobia, racial exclusion, outright racial discrimination and stratification, and cultural self-obsession.

24. 'Separate Development' was the 'respectable' term for Apartheid, conjured up by the ideology's architect, H. F. Verwoerd.

25. The best guide to which, in my view, is *A Dictionary of South African English on Historical Principles* (Silva et al. 1996).

26. See my discussion in *Civilising Barbarians* (De Kock 1996)

27. This process was discussed in De Kock (2003).

28. *Saamgekoekte* ('caked together') carries a particularly pungent connotation of hypostatized, hardened, stale and 'stuck' coagulation, an unhealthy and stale overconcentration of elements.

29. In Afrikaans, the 'Afrikaner Weerstandbeweging'.

References

Beck, Roger B. (1997), 'Monarchs and Missionaries Among the Tswana and Sotho', in Richard Elphick and T. R. H. Davenport (eds), *Christianity in South Africa: A Political, Social, and Cultural History*. Cape Town: New Africa Books, pp. 107–120.

Benjamin, Walter. (1992), *Illuminations*, trans. Harry Zohn. London: Fontana.

Bleek, W. H. I. and Lloyd, L. C. (1911), *Specimens of Bushman Folklore*. London: George Allen & Co.

Bosman, D. B., Van der Merwe, I.W. and Hiemstra, L. W. (1967), *Tweetalige Woordeboek*. -7 th edn. Cape Town: Tafelberg.

Bosman, Herman Charles. (2001), *Verborge Skatte: Herman Charles Bosman in/oorAfrikaans*, (ed.), Leon de Kock. Cape Town: Human & Rousseau.

Brutus, Dennis. (1973), *A Simple Lust: Selected Poems*. London: Heinemann.

De Kock, Leon. (1996), *Civilising Barbarians: Missionary Narrative and African Textual Response in Nineteenth-Century South Africa*. Johannesburg and Alice: Wits University Press and Lovedale Press.

— (2001), 'South Africa in the Global Imaginary: An Introduction'. *Poetics Today*, 22, (2), 263–298. (Special issue: 'South Africa in the Global Imaginary', ed. Leon de Kock, co-eds Louise Bethlehem and Sonja Laden). Reproduced in De Kock et al. (2004).

— (2003), 'Translating *Triomf*: The Shifting Limits of "Ownership" in Literary Translation, Or: Never Translate Anyone but a Dead Author'. *Journal of Literary Studies*, 19, (4), 345–359.

— (2007), 'Found in Translation' (essay on *Agaat* translation, interview with Michiel Heyns and Marlene van Niekerk). *Sunday Times Lifestyle*, 28 January, 18.

de Kock, Leon., Bethlehem, Louise and Laden Sonja (eds), (2004), *South Africa in the Global Imaginary*. Pretoria: UNISA Press and Centre for African Renaissance Studies; Leiden: Koninklijke Brill.

Dudek, Sarah. (nd), 'Walter Benjamin & The Religion of Translation'. *Cipher Journal* (online journal), Available at: www.cipherjournal.com/html/dudek_benjamin.html (accessed 20 April 2008).

Gray, Stephen. (1979), *Southern African Literature: An Introduction*. Cape Town: David Phillip.

Hofmeyr, Isabel. (2004), *The Portable Bunyan: A Transnational History of The Pilgrim's Progress*. Johannesburg: Wits University Press.

— (1989), 'Some Problems of Writing Historiography in Southern Africa'. *Literator*, 10, (2), 16–24.

Hall, Martin. (1998), 'Earth and Stone: Archaeology as Memory', in Sarah, Nuttall Sarah, and Carli Coetzee (eds), *Negotiating the Past: The Making of Memory in South Africa*. Cape Town: Oxford University Press, pp. 180–200.

Harris, Ashleigh. (2006), 'Accountability, acknowledgement and the ethics of "quilting" in Antjie Krog's *Country of My Skull*', *Journal of Literary Studies*, 22, (1/2), 27–53.

James, Alan. (2001), *The First Bushman's Path: Stories, Songs and Testimonies of the /Xam of the Northern Cape*. Pietermaritzburg: University of KwaZulu Natal Press.

Jordan, A. C. (1973), *Tales from Southern Africa*. Berkeley and Los Angeles: University of California Press.

Kenny, Vincent. (1985), 'Life, the Multiverse and Everything: An Introduction to the Ideas of Humberto Maturana'. Revised version of a paper presented at the Istituto di Psicologia, Universita Cattolica del Sacro Cuor, Rome. Available at: www.oikos.org/vinclife.htm (accessed 20 April 2008).

Krog, Antje. (2004), *The Stars Say 'Tsau': /Xam Poetry of Dia!Kwain, Kweiten Ta //Ken, /A!Kunta, /Han=Kass'o And //Kabbo*. Cape Town: Kwela.

Kruger, Loren. (2000), Review of *Negotiating the Past: The Making of Memory in South Africa* (eds Sarah Nuttall and Carli Coetzee, OUP, 1998), *Modern Philology*, 97, (4), 633–639.

Lewis, Simon. (2001), *Tradurre e Tradire: The Treason and Translation of Breyten Breytenbach. Poetics Today*, 22, (2), 435–452. (Special issue: 'South Africa in the Global Imaginary', ed. Leon de Kock, co-eds Louise Bethlehem and Sonja Laden). Reproduced in De Kock et al. (2004).

Mackenzie, Craig. (2002), 'The Use of Orality in the Short Stories of A. C. Jordan, Mtutuzeli Matshoba, Njabulo Ndebele and Bessie Head'. *Journal of Southern African Studies*, 28, (2), 347–358.

Marais, Eugène N. (1925), *Gedigte*. Cape Town: Nasionale Pers.

Pereira, Ernest, and Michael Chapman. (1989), *African Poems of Thomas Pringle*. Durban: Killie Campbell Africana Library; Pietermaritzburg: University of Natal Press.

Sanneh, Lamin O. (1989), *Translating the Message: The Missionary Impact on Culture*. Maryknoll, NY: Orbis Books.

Silva, Penny, Wendy Dore, Dorothea Mantzel, Colin Mueller and Madeleine Wright. (1996), *A Dictionary of South African English on Historical Principles*. Cape Town: Oxford University Press.

Skotnes, Pippa. (2001), '"Civilised off the Face of the Earth": Museum Display and the Silencing of the / Xam'. *Poetics Today*. 22 (2): 299–321. (Special issue, 'South Africa in the Global Imaginary', ed. Leon de Kock, co-eds Louise Bethlehem and Sonja Laden). Reproduced in De Kock et al. (2004).

— (2007), *Claim to the Country: The Archive of Lucy Lloyd and Wilhelm Bleek*. Johannesburg: Cape Town: Jacana, and Athens, Ohio: Ohio University Press.

Szabari, Antónia. (2001), Review of *In the Language of Walter Benjamin* by Carol Jacobs, *MLN*, 116, (3), German Issue 613–617.

Van Niekerk, Marlene. (1994), *Triomf*. Cape Town: Queillerie.

— (1999a), *Triomf*. Trans. Leon de Kock. Johannesburg: Jonathan Ball; Cape Town: Queillerie ('slang' version).

— (1999b), *Triomf*. Trans. Leon de Kock. London: Little, Brown & Co ('standard English' version).

— (1999c), *Triomf*. Trans. Leon de Kock. London: Abacus (paperback version of Little, Brown & Co ('standard English' version).

— (2004), *Triomf*. Trans. Leon de Kock. New York: The Overlook Press ('Standard English' version).

— (2004), *Agaat*. Cape Town: Tafelberg.

— (2006), *Agaat*. Trans. Michiel Heyns. Johannesburg: Jonathan Ball.

Van Wyk Louw, N. P. (1947), *Die Dieper Reg: 'n Spel van die Oordeel oor 'n Volk*. Cape Town: Nasionale Pers.

Venuti, Lawrence. (1995), *The Translator's Invisibility: A History of Translation*. London: Routledge

Watson, Stephen. (1991), *Return of the Moon: Versions from the /Xam*. Cape Town: Carrefour Press.

Willan, Brian. (1996), *Sol Plaatje: Selected Writings*. Johannesburg: Wits University Press; Athens: Ohio University Press.

Translational Intertexts in *A Change of Tongue*: Preliminary Thoughts

3

Frances Vosloo

Chapter Outline

Introduction

In her book *A Change of Tongue* (2003) Antjie Krog devotes a section to translation, called 'A Translation'. This section is introduced to the reader through five intertexts, all of which directly (or indirectly) relate to the concept of translation; all of which serve as possible spaces of interpretation – intertextual spaces of allusion where Krog and the reader venture, but also where the reader engages with Krog as writer and more specifically with her as translator[1]. In this chapter I approach one of these intertexts, namely a quotation from Gloria Anzaldúa's work (1999) as a representation of certain elements of Krog's own discourse on translation. I examine how the theoretical assumptions implied by this intertext are employed in this section of *A Change of Tongue*, and also address the issue of whether the intertext does indeed serve the function and purpose an explicit intertext is generally believed to serve.

Antjie Krog's writing oeuvre covers a variety of genre and subject matter ranging from her very first poetry volumes and her autobiographical[2] works to the various translation projects with which she has been associated. Krog has established herself as one of the most important poets in Afrikaans, her mother tongue, and in South Africa. While her primary genre remains poetry, she has, through politicized and autobiographical fiction writing, and through the translation of others' and her own work, moved beyond a purely poetic profile by directly engaging with other identities (i.e. languages) and different kinds of intimacy (genre, subject matter etc.). Almost 25 years after her début poetry volume, Krog started writing prose that was a mixture of autobio-graphical fact and fiction. She has also been involved in various translation projects of her own and others' works, including *Country of My Skull* (1998, translated from Afrikaans), *Domein van Glas* (2000, translated from *Een Mond vol Glas* by Henk van Woerden), *Down to My Last Skin* (2000, an anthology of Krog's translated poems), *Lang Pad na Vryheid* (2001, translated from Mande-la's autobiography *Long Walk to Freedom*), *Met Woorde soos met Kerse* (2002, translations of African verse), *Mamma Medea: na Apollonios van Rhodos en Euripides* (2002, translated from *Mamma Medea* by Tom Lanoye), *A Change of Tongue* (2003, translated from Afrikaans)[3], *Die Sterre sê 'tsau'* / *The Stars say 'tsau'* (2004, translations of English transcriptions of / Xam verse by Bleek and Lloyd), *Body Bereft* (2006, translation of *Verweerskrif*), and most recently Krog and André Brinks's English translations of Ingrid Jonker's poetry, *Black Butterflies: Selected Poems by Ingrid Jonker* (2007).

In all of these projects Krog has consciously and/or subconsciously engaged with principles of sociability, and objective (or subjective) structures that have become embodied, internalized and inscribed in the authors' and her own being (Vosloo, 2007: 72). Furthermore, in all or most of these projects Krog has made the seemingly difficult transition from writer/poet to translator or from translator to writer/poet. Maier (2006: 170) believes that contemporary writers conceive of their work in an international context, which has led them to discover 'the act of translation as a meaningful vehicle to deal with the definition of human existence from a global perspective'. This humanitarian view on translation is, however, somewhat generalized – perhaps over-general-ized – as far as individualized translators/writers are concerned. How exactly do writers reflect on the similarities between translation and all creative writ-ing, to echo Maier (2006: 170), and how do they grapple with the numerous challenges in conveying situations and trying to establish continuity and communication? One way would be to use translator-protagonists (or writer-protagonists or interpreter-protagonists as in *A Change of Tongue* and *Country of My Skull*) in writing, whom the writer (i.e., Krog) uses as a vehicle to express her own 'sense of man's [humankind's] situation in a post-modern society'

(Von Bardeleben, cited in Maier, 2006: 165). Another way would be to make use of intertextual references: to speak through prominent writers or scholars not only to reflect on broader social or humanitarian issues, but more specifically on the practice of writing (and, in Krog's case, translating) itself.

This is why I have chosen to focus on the notion of intertextuality in this chapter, specifically the quotation by Anzaldúa, which reads as follows: 'Until I am *free* to write *bilingually* and to *switch codes* without having always to be translated . . . my *tongue* will be *illegitimate*' (in Krog, 2003: 267, my emphasis). The choice of Anzaldúa is not a random one; her quotation offers exciting angles with which to approach not only translation issues raised by Krog,[4] but translation issues in general: autonomy, bilingualism,[5] translation as codification, speech, legitimacy, and so on. The rather metaphorical view on the dynamics of writing and translation as outlined in the above paragraphs is relevant, given that Krog devotes a whole section in her book to translation. She not only relates her own experiences of literary/autobiographical translation in the practical sense, she also uses fragments of her own and others' lives to illustrate difficulties in communication, and differences and similarities between cultures; in short, dilemmas related to translating others and the self.

Being a self-conscious writer (aware of her cultural and social position), Krog frequently makes the transition to a self-conscious translator. This transition is not a sporadic one, but rather a continuous and recurrent process where the acts of translation she engages in become metaphors: metaphors for identity, for empowerment of the self and others, and for the writing subject. One could argue that the apparent self-consciousness with which writers write (Arrojo cited in Maier, 2006: 165) should manifest in the way the writer exploits extratextual resources in his or her own text. In the following section I share some preliminary thoughts on how Krog's self-consciousness as writer and as translator manifest in 'A Translation'.

Intertextuality in *A Change of Tongue*

When one considers the possibility that translation (like writing) is an internalized or embodied experience;[6] that it is a meaningful vehicle to deal with human existence; that it is an expression of the translator's sense of humankind's situation in a postmodern society; and that it is a self-conscious act in shaping cultural and social conditions, then the use of intertexts by a writer becomes an attractive phenomenon. In *A Change of Tongue*, translated from the original Afrikaans version by Krog and her son, Krog relates her own and others' experiences of post-apartheid South Africa. The text has a fragmented structure and consists of six parts or sections that are combined with lyrical pieces or prose poems. The section 'A Translation' deals among other things with language (multilingualism, bilingualism) and articulation, cultural distance and transfer, belonging, identity and otherness. The section is introduced to the reader by five intertexts (from Christiane Nord, Jacques Derrida, Gloria Anzaldúa, Salman Rushdie and Anne Sexton, in that order) that serve as a preface, immediately engaging the reader of 'A Translation' with Krog's theorizing on writing and on translation as practice. What Krog as writer does is psychologically (and theoretically) prepare the reader for what he or she is about to read; to 'instruct' the reader as it were on how to read the text – in what framework to position and perceive the words and ideas. Provocatively, she asks us to consider her own particular act or acts of translatorship in relation to the quotations; however, this consideration does not necessarily imply that the reader has to categorically accept that Krog is in agreement with the writers she quotes.

Nord, exponent of a functionalist approach to translation, is quoted: 'translation is an intentional interaction intending to change an existing state of affairs' (Krog, 2003: 266). The focus in this quotation is on the intentionality of translation, the changing of a source text in order to accommodate the primary goal or *skopos*, namely communication with the target reader and target culture. According to Nord (1991: 7), both the source and target texts are culture-bound linguistic signs that are determined by the communicative situation in which they are supposed to transfer meaning. Translation is thus closely linked with language and culture, given that language not only has semantic value, but also culture-bound meaning. In the same breath as Nord and the other three intertexts, Krog quotes Derrida: 'for the notion of translation we would have to substitute the notion of transformation: a regulated transformation of one language by another, of one text by another' (Krog, 2003: 266). Derrida's metaphorical view on translation is symptomatic of his concept of *différance*, defined as 'the non-full, non-simple, structured and differentiating origin of differences' (Derrida, 1982: 11). Translation – both the process and the product – by implication, thus forms part of a 'chain of signifiers' (Derrida, 1982: 11), where there is no original or translation, no single meaning or *skopos*; rather the representation of the representation of signs, and the signs of a shifted and shifting presence. The question is whether Krog does indeed regard transformation as an all-inclusive notion for cultural transfer or cultural sensitivity.

The fourth quotation by Rushdie, which follows on the Anzaldúa quotation, reads: 'Having been borne across the world, we are translated men. It is normally supposed that something always gets lost in translation; I cling obstinately to the notion that something can also be gained' (Krog, 2003: 266).[7] Rushdie's reference here is to migration as translation; culture as translation; as *traductio* – carrying across (Sturge, 2007: 12). Again one can see how metaphorical Rushdie's notion of translation is: on the one hand he almost celebrates translation as cultural difference, and on the other hand he highlights the possibility (or fact, if one wishes) that the target language will almost always benefit from or be enriched with those linguistic and cultural elements that are present in the source text.

The last quotation, by Sexton, reads: 'I use the personal when I am applying a mask to my face' (Krog, 2003: 266). Whether Krog wants the reader to reflect in the same way on her own writing – in other words constantly to keep in mind that the personal and the collective, or the private and the public, are inseparable as Krog says of Mandela (276) – is worth exploring. The question that comes to mind, for instance, is 'how is the mask [what mask?] applied, and can one speak of a mask at all when writing becomes an unmasked, personal, private act?' The quotation also serves to remind the reader that the narrator is not necessarily Krog.[8] These issues, as well as questions regarding Derrida and Rushdie's quotations, might prove interesting not only from a translation perspective, but also from a comparative one.

Whichever way the reader receives these intertextual references, the question will always be what the writer, – that is, Krog – achieves by including not one, but five intertexts, and whether they all serve a definite purpose. How are the text itself and the intertexts constructed to create a purposeful link? Moreover, can 'A Translation' – the whole section – be read as an intertext of Krog's translation oeuvre in general? Can it be read as an intertext of her writing oeuvre? Perhaps these questions are pushing the concept of intertextuality too far, but by entitling part 4 of the book 'A Translation', this section must surely be seen as encapsulating or reflecting on Krog's translation interests. Has this text therefore become the medium through which Krog sheds light not only on her texts and translations, but also on her identity, her translational being? These questions add to the general problematic around intertextuality and its use in a translational context.

According to Neubert, 'a translation is not created from nothing; it is woven from a semantic pattern taken from another text, but the threads – the target language (TL) linguistic forms, structures, syntactic sequences – are new' (Neubert cited in Wallmach, 2006: 14). This quotation can be rephrased in an intertextual context to read: a translation is never created from nothing; it is almost always an intertext, woven from a whole network of other source and target texts, but the threads – the target language forms, the structures, syntactic sequences, cultural patterns, cultural frameworks, sociocultural settings – are new, transformed, changed. Deconstruction points out that writers (let alone translators) never create original texts – any literary text is an (incomplete) product of literary texts that precede the given text. This text, then, is not only text and context, but constitutes intertextuality (Tymoczko, 1995: 12). One could thus assume a deconstructive approach in 'A Translation', for Krog in effect deconstructs her own writing and her own translating by making other texts visible and giving voice to those authors. However, in contrast with poststructuralist conceptions of the 'death of the author', Krog as writer remains alive through being the translator of her own work.

It is within the above-mentioned frames of reference that one can address issues such as how one talks about translation, to echo Maier (1998) in her discussion of the practice of translating women's fiction. Or rather, how does the *translator* talk about translation and about his or her own translations? The translator can, for instance, choose not to articulate the decisions made in practice, and to let the text and the translated words reflect his/her approach; but he/she could also overtly articulate these decisions, which will ultimately reflect the consciousness with which the act of translating is or was performed. How exactly these decisions are overtly articulated is of course an important point for discussion: Is there a translator's note or introductory section, did the translator make use of footnotes, are there examples of explicitation within the text, and so on?

In order to explore the figure of the translator him/herself more fully, many more in-depth questions or agendas are required, but for the purpose of this chapter, I focus on the use of intertextuality as a mouthpiece of the translator. In the next section, the third quotation, from Anzaldúa is further explored and contextualized. To repeat, it reads as follows: 'Until I am *free* to write *bilingually* and to *switch codes* without having always to be translated . . . my *tongue* will be *illegitimate*' (Krog, 2003: 267, my emphasis). In the course of the discussion and analysis I touch on aspects that are highlighted by some of the other intertexts.

Anzaldúa contextualized

The quotation by Anzaldúa is taken from her book *Borderlands/La Frontera* (1987/1999), in which she examines the condition of women in Chicana[9] and

Latino culture on the US-Mexico border, giving the reader both a close-up and distanced view into a life of alienation and isolation as a 'prisoner in the borderlands between cultures' (Artist Biography: Gloria Anzaldúa. [Online]). The book is structured around essays and poetry and the merging of personal narrative and issues of language and anger, thereby immersing the reader in Anzaldúa's world. Anzaldúa uses *autohistoria* – a genre, visual narrative or critical discourse that goes beyond the traditional self-portrait or auto-biography and combines the writer's personal story with his/her cultural his-tory (Salvidar-Hull, 1999: 13). Yarbro-Bejarano refers to Anzaldúa's writing (writing by a woman of colour) as 'embodied theory', which emerges from 'the material reality of multiple oppression and in turn conceptualizes that materiality' (1994: 6).

Anzaldúa's ideological and personal motive for writing contextualizes the quotation used by Krog. It is evident that when Anzaldúa says '[u]ntil I am free to write bilingually' she makes a strong assertion to challenge and confront the languages of oppression. A number of lengthy passages in *Borderlands/ La Frontera* are written in un-translated Spanish, the language of the Spanish colonizers, among others, whilst other passages are written in English. What makes Anzaldúa's writing particularly interesting, is that she uses eight lan-guages (two variations of English and six of Spanish), thereby creating a strained reading of her texts – almost a reading of frustration and irritation. It is, however, these very emotions Anzaldúa has had to deal with throughout her life, as she has always been confronted with language as a border. It is not surprising therefore that language and the articulation of the *mestiza*[10] identity are essential features of her writing. The *mestiza* identity is reflected in Anzaldúa's shifting between different genres, points of view and languages in realizing her ideal of 'border crossing', where writing almost becomes a vehicle for personal freedom and political activism. She calls for a new consciousness: a new value system that will narrow or heal the divide between 'white . . . and colored, . . . male and female' and thus between 'us and them' (Anzaldúa, 1999: 80, 83).

This new consciousness is perhaps also symptomatic of the political and personal value system Krog strives to accomplish through her own writing. A further interesting aspect of Anzaldúa's writing is that she employs a bold and unapologetic approach to her poetry, and through this she takes the reader into her 'world of estrangement from every culture she could possibly "belong" to' (Artist Biography: Gloria Anzaldúa. [Online]). Yarbro-Bejarano (1994: 13) argues that Anzaldúa's 'belonging nowhere' is the result of a multiple identity which prohibits her from being completely 'at home'. She thus creates her home – a consciousness – through writing, and the text becomes a 'site of multiple voicings' (Alarcón in Yarbro-Bejarano, 1994: 13). To belong (anywhere) is not a static concept, according to Probyn (cited in Anderson, 2006: 131), but a 'matter of moving between different, though possibly overlapping sites'.

Salvidar-Hull (1999: 4) interprets Anzaldúa's bilingual strategy as manifestation of the language of feminist assertion – assertion against a patriarchal society, against man-made rules and supremacy. In the context of translation theory, feminist theory is concerned with the genderedness of readers, writers, translators and other actors in the field of literary production. But above all it is a way of dealing with or approaching issues such as language and identity by way of gender as a social construction (Wallace, 2002: 66). In her seminal work on translation and gender, von Flotow conceives of women as translations themselves, as engaging with multiple levels of discourse: 'Translation has long served as a trope to discover what women do when they enter the public sphere: they translate their private language: their specifically female forms of discourse . . . into some form of the dominant patriarchal code' (1997: 12). One can argue here that Antjie Krog has already entered the public sphere through writing poetry and prose, and that she, in the process of translating others' and her own work, extends her private language. Through translation Krog also moves between different spheres: between the spheres of poetry, prose, autobiography, biography, and drama.

Wallace (2002: 69), however, argues that the feminist influence on translation studies is more visible within its metatexts – the footnotes, prefaces, introductions, commentaries and, indeed, the intertextual references[11] – all of which represent a deliberate move away from invisibility,[12] away from submission[13] to the original. This move away from the source text is considered a manipulative act on the translator's part – a creative act one can almost argue – which inevitably enlarges the visibility of the translator. What, then, if the translator is the author – how much can the writer as translator manipulate his/her own work; how much more creative can he/she be when translating; isn't the translator always visible when he/she is also the author? These considerations are important in the context of bilingual studies.

Maier (2006: 168), in citing Arrojo, believes translators work with discourses they cannot fully control or decipher, and that they find it difficult not to interfere and not to leave the mark of their own history and individuality in every discourse they engage in. At the same time, when a translator does leave her mark on the target text, the text cannot categorically be labelled a feminist translation, although the text could still reveal an implicit feminist standpoint. Maier's view relates to von Flotow's (1997: 35) contention that each individual (gendered) translator leaves his or her own mark on the work, thereby threatening the authorship of the source text. Is it probable that Krog, in most cases the translator of her own work, threatens her source text, and consequently her authorship? Does she threaten her authorship by translating others' work? For many translators, translation is an emancipatory and highly politicized act through which they transgress interlinguistic exchange and transfer cultural reality into new contexts (Wallace 2002: 70) – an essential feature of feminist discourse. But the presence of these features in a target text does not necessarily mark the text as feminist. Since Anzaldúa's work is explicitly feminist, a feminist discussion is, however, perhaps legitimate in this context. Maier (1998: 103) reminds us that representation is inherent in translation, because to translate an author is also to represent that author in another language, another tradition. The translator therefore is not powerless, for such representation involves agency – the translator identifies with the author and for that reason determines his or her appearance, his/her voice in another language.

In the second part of Anzaldúa's quotation, she says, ' . . . and to switch codes without having always to be translated.' With these words she further voices the need or desire for linguistic autonomy – to write without having to be decoded, interpreted, translated. In a sense Anzaldúa makes a plea against translation at the same time that she recognizes linguistic diversity or rather 'reclaim[s] the ground of multiple Mestiza languages' (Salvidar-Hull, 1999: 8). The implication is that such a multilingual text does not easily admit the reader who does not fully engage with the linguistic demands of this 'border' language (ibid.). What is more, this border language breaks down all dualisms: 'I will no longer be made to feel ashamed of existing. I will have my voice: Indian, Spanish, white. [. . .] my woman's voice, my sexual voice, my poet's voice. I will overcome the tradition of silence' (Anzaldúa, 1999: 81). Her emphasis therefore is on the larger cultural critique of domination through language.

Anzaldúa ends her statement by saying that if she cannot write in many languages, if she constantly has to be translated in order to be understood, her 'tongue will [remain] illegitimate'; 'illegitimate' meaning that she would rather not speak, not write. In 'How to tame a wild tongue,' an essay on language in *Borderlands/La Frontera*, Anzaldúa records her rejection of silence (the wild tongue cannot be tamed, only removed) and the ways in which her own language is incorrect according to dominant non-Chicana norms

(Anzaldúa, 1999: 77). Her use of the tongue as metaphor for identity, among other things, relates to Krog's 'tongvis' (*sole*) motif in her Afrikaans poetry, notably in the volume *Lady Anne* (1989),[14] and her use of 'tongue' in *A Change of Tongue* and in the Afrikaans, *'n Ander Tongval*. The relation between Anzaldúa's use of the tongue metaphor and Krog's use seems too close to be coincidental, considering the fact that *Borderlands/La Frontera* was first published in 1987 and Krog's use of the metaphor dates back only to 1989.

Yarbro-Bejarano (1994: 7) is of the opinion that Anzaldúa's choice or use of the terms 'border' and *mestiza* problematizes the way her theory is applied by non-Chicana readers, critics and writers, that is, outside her specific historical and cultural experience. But such universalizing readings are situated in the postmodern context of demarginalization of marginalized people (colour, language) and larger questions of identity, such as new political identities and politics of articulation (Hall in Yarbro-Bejarano, 1994: 11). What Anzaldúa's text does is to demonstrate the communication between 'the contemporary awareness that *all* identity is constructed across difference and the necessity of a new *politics* of difference to accompany this new sense of self' (Yarbro-Bejarano, 1994: 11). What she essentially creates is a space, an in-between, 'third space'[15] as it were, that makes room for different dualities and contradictions to co-exist. It can be said that the creation of such a space or 'contact zone' provides the postcolonial translator or writer with a double role: he or she on the one hand introduces, manipulates and/or preserves foreign (source text) elements in a text that might be denser, more unfamiliar, and difficult to read so that the target reader struggles to reach the colonized. On the other hand, Wallace (2002: 71) argues, the postcolonial translator provides a space for the voice of minority cultures and their dominated silence.

Translation and changing one's tongue

In reading the Anzaldúa quotation in *A Change of Tongue* one is tempted to take the voice of Anzaldúa as the voice of Krog. The rationale for this is found in the similarities, albeit subtle, in the way both writers construct their writing and how they articulate their thoughts and beliefs. *A Change of Tongue* is autobiographical fiction articulated through lyrical prose poems and narrative prose, in which Krog uses both the first and third person and direct speech to communicate meaning. One is furthermore tempted to read Krog's text, especially in the light of the various intertexts she includes at the beginning of the chapter on translation, as poststructuralist or postcolonialist. According to

Anderson (2006: 121), who explores the relation between autobiography and the feminist subject and the idea that the former provides a productive space, autobiography may help to name the ongoing complexity of meaning and the subject. This complexity between meaning and the subject, Anderson feels, should be further explored in its relation to the construction of theory. She cites Diane Elam, who considers autobiography an 'impossible genre since "experience" can never be directly represented and all autobiographies produce fictions or figures in place of the self-knowledge they seek' (Elam in Anderson, 2006: 120). Another view on the position of truth (fact/fiction) is that of Felman, who is of the opinion that autobiography and theory sometimes come together within the same text, and when this happens, each acts as a 'form of resistance to the other, unsettling the claims to truth of both' (Felman in Anderson, 2006: 121). What is interesting in Felman's view is the possibility of theory and self-representation merging in one text.

Krog's merging of theory (Anzaldúa's embodied theory), autobiography (fact), and fiction is significant in the context of translation. Through her narrative account of the process of translating Nelson Mandela's *Long Walk to Freedom* (in which Krog was involved) and her conversations with the fictional translator, Christina, Krog embodies the debates in translation theory. Krog introduces Christina to the reader as a Swedish translation scholar (Krog, 2003: 270) and the uninformed reader might well take this to be a real person. Closer examination of the text suggests that Christina most probably represents the functionalist translation school as advocated by Christiane Nord. In my view there is without doubt a strong link between Krog's intertextual use of Christiane Nord at the beginning of the chapter and her character Christina.[16] These accounts are interspersed with an even more personalized account of a letter to her children about her visit to the Netherlands and the roots of identity and belonging. She writes: 'In the deepest kernels of our souls, ... Cherfontaine [Serfontein] and I still gave out the same vibrations, we knew and translated one another' (Krog, 2003: 268). In another account she relates an argument she had with black friends about identity, race, collective guilt, the changing of perspective, of words, of body language; the account ends with Krog saying 'But I want to ... / "Belong" is the word I want to say, but do not say ... ' (ibid.: 274). This longing to belong echoes Anzaldúa's, and one can clearly see how translation becomes a metaphor for change and the sharing of identity. In yet another short account Krog relates a scene at home where she (Krog, in the third person) uses her mother as instrument to demonstrate the possibility of change. When her father complains about the dull food, her mother says: 'If you want more colourful food, I can transform it' (ibid.: 275).

Krog's account of her involvement in the translation of Mandela's autobiography is used as a constant translational thread that serves as meta-commentary in the text. She quotes, for instance, Mandela saying 'One's language should never be a dead end [. . .] That is why I believe in translation: for us to be able to live together' (Krog, 2003: 267). Here Krog as translator uses another's (powerful) voice to echo her own belief. Mandela's contention echoes that of the Swedish translator, Christina, who, in the context of postcolonial translation and the perception of otherness, says 'translation is essential if we are to learn to live together on this planet. We have to begin to translate one another' (Krog, 2003: 270). If one were to refer back to Anzaldúa's rejection of translation, one senses a possible inconsistency in Krog's use of intertextuality. Or is Krog referring to Anzaldúa's allusion to the switching of codes as a prerequisite for becoming legitimate in terms of language and identity? Perhaps this switching of codes in a translational context alludes to the powerless languages that were once trapped in hybrid spaces or structures and are now given a voice, that are now 'writing back', as it were (Krog, 2003: 271).

In a rather long subsection (ibid.: 268–271) Krog uses the third person to articulate the character's (Krog) rationale behind translation. With the sentence 'On the plane home, she thinks about the whole notion of translation', Krog engages the reader to also reflect. What follows is a strong claim for translation into, but also from, weaker languages, as is the case in South Africa where 10 of the 11 official languages have to rely on translation in order to survive. In quoting Gerrit Komrij, Krog supports his view that one's language should be inclusive and receptive to translation of works from world literature in order to create an 'open-minded' society, and above all to keep the language(s) fit and strong (ibid.: 270). Again the emphasis on the importance of translation for maintaining identity and enriching a language might be read as contradictory to Anzaldúa's assertion in favour of non-translation. It does, however, resonate with Rushdie's contention that 'something can also be gained' in translation and Derrida's notion of translation as 'transformation' (Krog, 2003: 266).

However, in the South African context, English is very much the dominant literary language, and Krog rightly points out that good or even brilliant authors writing in Afrikaans or isiXhosa or Sepedi suffer from non-recognition in such a literary landscape, and that such writers might just as well not exist if they do not write in English or are not translated into English (ibid.: 269). And if they do not exist, their tongues become 'illegitimate', as it were. But Krog wants to be legitimate, and she struggles as a result between the desire to be read in English, since 'English has become the door to the Father' (ibid.: 270), and the fear of betraying her colonized, Afrikaans roots, where the 'Father' means recognition in the English literary system and internationally. This fear that Krog articulates corresponds with the conceptual chasm between 'domestic' and 'foreign' as monolingual poles, which in turn is symptomatic of what Lefevere (1981: 76) calls the '[r]omantic stress on the mother tongue as the primary material for literary creation'. Although this standpoint has long dominated the way translation and translation products have been perceived, translation has since become a vehicle that enables us 'to enter fully into the space of another'; however, '[t]he ability to recognize oneself in the image of a foreigner is only truly praiseworthy when one has autonomy to retain in the process', to echo Schlegel (cited in Robinson, 1997: 218–219). Krog's fear of betrayal can be linked with the essentially literary problem of a refusal (by the writer) to choose one or the other language – Afrikaans or English – for her self-translation between languages, and the specific ways she recreates a text in a second language, and adapts it to a new sign system, diverges radically from literary norms. Hokenson and Munson (2007: 160) attribute this phenomenon to the fact that, in the case of self-translation, 'the translator *is* the author, the translation is an original, the foreign is the domestic, and vice versa.'

From the standpoint of the native language, translation becomes an act of respecting – instead of annexing – the foreign as other (Hokenson and Munson, 2007: 144). In line with this view is Goethe's theory of translation as an 'opening out onto the world in order to distinguish foreign and non-foreign in oneself', since literatures are images of cultural others (Hokenson and Munson, 2007: 141). This seems to be true for Krog regarding her own poetry, but also regarding her initial move towards translation projects in which she takes the reader to this opening in order for him/her to experience a 'coloring of strangeness', as Humboldt describes it:

> a translation should have a certain coloring of strangeness over it . . . As long as one feels the foreign, but not the strangeness, the translation has reached the highest goal; but where strangeness appears as such, [and thus] probably obscures the foreign, the translator betrays that he is not up to his original. (Humboldt cited in Berman, 1984: 154)

But perhaps 'changing one's tongue' in a translational context also (or perhaps ultimately) entails deciding what the author, or what Mandela, for instance, wants to say to his readers – his Afrikaans-speaking readers. According to Krog's fictional character Christina, all this should inform the translator's decisions regarding style[17] and language (Krog, 2003: 275). When one calls to mind Anzaldúa's multilingual strategy towards the kind of language she, as a feminist and politicized writer, uses, in order to undermine or to address the very oppressors of that language, Krog's discussion around Afrikaans in this chapter is put in a new perspective. Krog says 'Afrikaans is and always has been a highly politicised language . . . [the dialects] imply a background or an unspoken political point of view. Your Afrikaans says who you are, where you come from and who you sided with in the past' (ibid.: 276). In her translation of Mandela's book she thus uses different registers of Afrikaans in order to accommodate different ranges, but especially to 'transform the language of apartheid into a language of coming together, to rid it of the vocabulary of power and retribution' (Krog, 2003: 278). Here, as elsewhere in this section on translation Krog uses Mandela's autobiographical persona as vehicle for conveying, at least in part, her own incentive and her own ideology of translation.

In the same way it can be said that the kind of English Krog employs in *A Change of Tongue* has an Afrikaans 'feel' to it – this is an approach she usually follows when translating her own poetry, so that the poem retains its roots in the Afrikaans [source language] structure. Krog emphasizes the fact that people should recognize the text as a translation; that they should not lose touch with the Afrikaans (Wasserman, 2000: 4). Here one clearly sees the foreignizing element of translation. In an interview with Britz (2000: 6) about others' translations of her work, Krog says she feels alienated from her poetry which is distortedly represented because the poems sound and read too English. When this happens, the reader does not read any foreignness in the target text and the reading experience therefore becomes too easy, too unconstrained. Krog thus wants to 'retain the echoes of the original in the translation' (Meyer, 2002: 6).

Concluding remarks

From the above discussion the similarities between the theoretical grounding of Anzaldúa's writing and that of Krog are evident. The use of Anzaldúa as an intertextual reference by Krog was examined in terms of how Krog's text – on a meta and textual level – justifies her use of the specific quotation by Anzaldúa and its implied meaning. In reference to Anzaldúa's employment of embodied theory, one can make the preliminary conclusion that Krog in general seems to be using the same kind of approach to her writing, especially her autobiographical/fictional writing. In this regard it is perhaps apt to refer to Klopper's (2004) reference to transformational grammar – a theory which in the first place distinguishes between an observable surface structure of language (sentence) and a deeper structure of language (i.e. the implicit knowledge or codes required to interpret the sentence), and, secondly, identifies the rules by which deep structures are translated into surface structures. What is interesting from a translation perspective is the deeper structure, the implicit knowledge or code that is required from the writer to interpret, to feel, to see, to create, and which may be translated as the internalized disposition of the writer and, consequently of the translator.

Klopper (2004: 9) further asserts that the subject who has no ability to articulate him/herself also has no existence, and translation therefore is about rendering 'language from one code into another . . . to interpret the subject of speech, to convey the necessity of language beyond its function as conduit of information, to affirm the translatability not only of language but also of self'. It is thus no coincidence that Krog, at the beginning of A Change of Tongue, includes an epigraph on the notion of transformational grammar, by means of which she introduces, in my view, translation as metaphor for transformation first and foremost.

In the prose poem positioned between the sections 'A Translation' and 'A Journey', the text suggests this translatability of the self. In this section the narrator is in silent conversation with what is possibly a metaphorical river. The river is addressed as 'you' (the linguistic antithesis of 'I'), and at some point the narrative moves into the first person, when the 'I' is introduced: 'I cannot bear the earth without you, and so I do not keep quiet. I talk to you. And a "you" always calls forth an "I"' (Krog 2003: 281). What one notices at this point in the text, is that Krog introduces a personal discourse – a psychoanalytic model – that is formed deep in the unconscious and ramifies to social and metaphysical discourse (Hokenson and Munson, 2007: 148). The innate 'I' and its infinite capacities of 'self-translation' in language, is what Krog is referring to. This, says Hokenson and Munson (2007: 148), is the 'native language as sole verbal mode of expression of the self and of representation of the world.'

Further on, the narrator says: 'How can I talk to you? You with your surface as warm as skin and your icy undertones? Do I need a special language? A new tongue? How?' (Krog, 2003: 282). What will this special language be? How will this new tongue sound? Is this language/tongue a supposed universal language – a combination of Afrikaans/ English/ indigenous languages in one text (as Anzaldúa does with Spanish and English)? Does a new tongue represent a new identity, and what does this identity look like? Perhaps the reference is to a new ethics of living in South Africa (as opposed to Mexico) – a new space, where language becomes a language of respect, of care, of reconciliation, of transformation, of peace.

What about Anzaldúa's desire to be free to write bilingually? How is this desire articulated by Krog in her text? And does Krog see language as a border? Does Krog, through her text, support the idea of linguistic autonomy, of writing without having to be translated? Krog certainly is in favour of bilingualism but at the same time she is positive about the necessity of translation as a vehicle for the survival of minority languages. Language thus functions not as a border, but as an interstitial space, a site of multiple voicings, a third space, as it were. In this space, and through writing, Krog, like Anzaldúa, creates a vehicle for personal freedom and, perhaps, political activism, albeit in a more implicit way than Anzaldúa does. But through translation, unlike Anzaldúa, Krog contributes to healing the divide between cultural and linguistic dualisms: between 'us and them', between 'white and coloured/ black.' Bhabha's theory (1994: 38) of an '*international* culture' that is based on the 'inscription and articulations of culture's *hybridity*' also suggests that a person (a translator) exists solely in the in-between spaces of cultures and languages; this space is the only possible site of translation. This is the site in which Krog locates herself when translating.

What one has to bear in mind is that 'A Translation' does not only function on the level of translation strategy and textual discourse, it also functions on a meta-level where Krog employs the concept of translation to convey ideas concerning transformation, change, and the merging of the individual and the collective in writing. When Krog's text is read and interpreted with Anzaldúa's intertext in mind, it becomes a site where Krog's voice as a woman, her sexual voice and her poet's voice resonate. It is at this point that the quotation by Anne Sexton ('I use the personal when I am applying a mask to my face') becomes particularly interesting, for the interplay between the personal and the collective echoes in her words, as well as the masking action that translation essentially is. When the translator is also the writer, and when the writer becomes the translator, translation certainly becomes a masked affair.

This chapter is by no means exhaustive in terms of the multiple readings of and views on translational discourse that are contained within the intertextual references in *A Change of Tongue*. Further research and a more in-depth analysis of the relations between all these intertexts would, in my opinion, prove extremely fruitful.

Notes

1. The intertexts function very much like the preface to a translation, where the reader is predisposed to read the text within a given critical paradigm or conceptual framework.

2. Courtivron (2003) calls this genre 'language memoirs', autobiographical accounts of bilingual peoples' experiences between different languages and cultures.

3. *'n Ander Tongval* was published in 2005, two years after the publication of *A Change of Tongue* (2003). The latter was translated from an Afrikaans draft, edited and published; *'n Ander Tongval* went through a process of re-translation (from the Afrikaans draft and the English text).

4. The intertext with its reference to writing 'bilingually' and switching 'codes' assumes particular relevance in the context of a 'language memoir' that reflects on *A Change of Tongue*, and functions very much like the preface to a translation, where the reader is predisposed to read the text within a given critical paradigm or conceptual framework. The works of the two writers are also imbued with a form of spiritual activism that makes the link between them more pertinent.

5. Bilingualism, especially in the context of self-translators, has always been neglected in translation studies, primarily because of conceptual problems: the bilingual text exists in two language systems simultaneously, and there is the question of how the monolingual categories of author and original apply (Hokenson and Munson, 2007: 2). Scholars in postcolonial studies are increasingly focusing on bilinguality as a cultural issue in diglossic conditions, but without enough emphasis on literary bilinguality.

6. The German Romanticist, Schopenhauer, stressed the dynamic relation between language and thought, and believed that translation opens new spaces in the individual, monolingual subject. The translator should, therefore, grasp the *spirit* of the language in order to understand the nation that speaks it. He said: 'one has truly internalised a language when one can translate not books but oneself into it, and thus without losing one's individuality can communicate in it immediately' (in Hokenson and Munson, 2007: 145).

7. The migrant narrator in Shame (Rushdie 1983: 24) says: 'I, too, am a translated man. I have been borne across'.

8. As Krog points out in the Acknowledgements: 'the "I" is seldom me, my mother and father not necessarily my parents, my family not really blood relatives, and so forth.' (Krog, 2003: 369)

9. Chicana (sing.) is the name of resistance, says Alarcón (cited in Salvidar-Hull, 1999: 15), that enables 'cultural and political points of departure and thinking through the multiple migrations and dislocations of women of "Mexican" descent'.

10. Women of white, Mexican and Indian descent.

11. Simon (1995: 110–117) argues for the translator's preface as a literary genre that is deeply and consciously rooted in the social and political dimensions of literary interchange. One can also include most other metatexts in Simon's description, for any conscious reflection or commentary necessarily entails an interchange of texts that lie outside the immediacy of the target text.

12. See Venuti (1995) for his discussion on the invisibility of translators versus their visibility. The move toward the translator's visibility can also be seen as essentially postcolonial, depending on the cultural and linguistic context.

13. Simeoni's (1998) discussion of 'submissiveness' as a universal component of translators' beha-viour claims there is little room for choice and variability in their actions.

14. See Viljoen (1991: 19) for a discussion of the tongue/'tongvis' motifs, as well as Krog's poem 'transparant van die tongvis' in Lady Anne (1989: 92).

15. According to Bhabha (Rutherford, 1990: 211) the 'third space' allows for other (political, cultural) positions to emerge and is therefore characterized by continual hybridity and identification.

16. Christina accentuates the importance of translation as an act of communication (Krog, 2003: 270) –an approach distinctively associated with functionalism; Christina uses the Bible to illustrate the importance of cultural exchange and cultural specificity (Krog, 2003: 270) – Christiane Nord is a notable Bible translator; and Christina advises Krog to keep the target audience (the function of the text in the target language) in mind whilst translating – 'what is it that Mandela ultimately wants to say, and what he wants to say to Afrikaans-speakers' (Krog, 2003: 275).

17. Genette, Deleuze, and others, focus on the individual writer's 'singular' uses of language in a text, and view the latter as a unity of linguistic and stylistic patterning. Style is thus seen as a 'sustained mode of using standard language, while shaping and unsettling it through individual choices in singular or unique ways' (Hokenson and Munson, 2007: 167). Genette, for instance, asserts the writer's style is transposed from version to version, whereby he/she achieves different linguistic embodiments while remaining distinctive; in the context of translation, the original is considered a hypotext, and the translation a hypertext.

References

Anderson, L. (2006), 'Autobiography and the feminist subject', in E. Rooney (ed.), *Cambridge Companion to Feminist Literary Theory*. Cambridge: CUP, pp. 119–135.

Anzaldúa, G. (1999), *Borderlands/La Frontera* (2nd edn). San Francisco: Aunt Lute Books.

Artist Biography: Gloria Anzaldúa. Available at http://voices.cla.umn.edu/vg/Bios/entries/anzaldua_gloria.html (accessed 14 September 2007).

Berman, A. (1992 [1984]), *The Experience of the Foreign: Culture and Translation in Romantic Germany.* Trans. S. Heyvaert. Albany, NY: State University of New York Press.

Bhabha, H. (1994), *The Location of Culture.* New York: Routledge.

Britz, E. (2000), 'Proses van heelword belangrik in Krog-werk', *Die Volksblad*, 23 October, 6.

Courtivron, I. de. (2003), *Lives in Translation: Bilingual Writers on Identity and Creativity.* New York: Palgrave Macmillan.

Derrida, J. (1982), *Margins of philosophy, trans.* Alan Bass. Brighton: Harvester.

Hokenson, J. W. and Munson, M. (2007), *The Bilingual Text: History and Theory of Literary Self-Translation.* Manchester: St. Jerome.

Jonker, I. (2007), *Black Butterflies: Selected Poems by Ingrid Jonker.* Cape Town: Human en Rousseau.

Klopper, D. (2004), 'Difference, displacement and translation. Re-inscription of Afrikaner Identity in Antjie Krog's *A Change of Tongue.* Unpublished paper presented at the *Transculturality in the Diaspora: Spaces, Cultures, and Identities Conference,* Bremen University, Germany, November 2004

—(2005), 'Krog vertel oor roetes tussen tale', *Die Burger*, 19 November, 14–15.

Krog, A. (1989), *Lady Anne*. Emmerentia: Taurus.

—(1998), *Country of My Skull*. Johannesburg: Random House.

—(2000), *Down to My Last Skin*. Johannesburg: Random Poets.

—(2002). *Met Woorde soos met Kerse*. Cape Town: Kwela.

—(2003), *A Change of Tongue*. Johannesburg: Random House.

—(2004), *Die Sterre sê 'tsau'. /Xam-gedigte van Diäkwain, Kweiten-ta-//ken, /A!kúnta, /Han•kass'o en //Kabbo. Gekies en Versorg deur Antjie Krog*. Cape Town: Kwela.

—(2004), *The Stars say 'tsau'. /Xam poetry of Diäkwain, Kweiten-ta-//ken, /A!kúnta, /Han•kass'o and //Kabbo. Selected and Adapted by Antjie Krog* . Cape Town: Kwela.

—(2005), *'n Ander Tongval*. Cape Town: Tafelberg.

—(2006), *Body Bereft*. Roggebaai: Umuzi.

Lanoye, T. (2002), *Mamma Medea: na Apollonios van Rhodos en Euripides*. Trans. Antjie Krog. Cape Town: Queillerie.

Lefevere, A. (1981), 'Translated literature: Towards an integrated theory', *Bulletin of the Midwest Modern Language Association*, 14, (1), 68–78.

Maier, C. (1998), 'Issues in the practice of translating women's fiction', *BHS*, 75, 95–108.

—(2006), 'The translator as *theôros*: Thoughts on cogitation, figuration and current creative writing', in T. Hermans (ed.), *Translating Others* (vol. 1). Manchester: St. Jerome, pp. 162–179.

Mandela, N. (2001), *Lang Pad na Vryheid*. Trans. Antjie Krog. Florida Hills, South Africa: Vivlia.

Meyer, S. (2002), 'The only truth stands skinned in sound: Antjie Krog as translator', *Scrutiny 2. Issues in English Studies in Southern Africa*, 7, (2), 3–18.

Nord, Christiane. (1991), Text Analysis in Translation. Amsterdam: Rodopi.

Robinson, D. (1997), *Western Translation Theory from Herodotus to Nietzsche*. Manchester: St. Jerome.

Rushdie, S. (1983), *Shame*. London: Jonathan Cape.

Rutherford, J. (1990), 'The third space. Interview with Homi Bhabha', in J. Rutherford (ed.), *Identity: Community, Culture, Difference*. London: Lawrence & Wishart, pp. 207–221.

Salvídar-Hull, S. (1999), 'Introduction', in G. Anzaldúa. *Borderlands/La Frontera* (2nd edn). San Francisco: Aunt Lute Books, pp. 1–18.

Simeoni, D. (1998), 'The pivotal status of the translator's habitus', *Target*, 10, (1), 1–39.

Simon, S. (1995), 'Translation and the will to knowledge: Prefaces and Canadian Literary Politics', in S. Bassnett and A. Lefevere (eds), *Translation, History and Culture*. London: Cassell, pp. 110–117.

Sturge, K. (2007), *Representing Others: Translation, Ethnography and the Museum*. Manchester: St. Jerome.

Tymoczko, M. (1995), 'The metonymics of translating marginalised texts', *Comparative Literature*, 47, (1), 11–24.

Venuti, L. (1995), *The Translator's Invisibility: A History of Translation*. London: Routledge.

Viljoen, L. (1991), 'Die teks as transparant: Antjie Krog se *Lady Anne* binne die Suid-Afrikaanse werklikheid', *Stilet*, 3, (2), 19–31.

Von Flotow, L. (1997), *Translation and Gender: Translating in the 'Era of Feminism.'* Manchester: St. Jerome.

Vosloo, F. (2007), 'Inhabiting the translator's habitus: Antjie Krog as translator', *Current Writing*, 19, (2), 72–93.

Wallace, M. (2002), 'Writing the wrongs of literature: The figure of the feminist and post-colonialist translator', *The Journal of the Midwest Modern Language Association*, 35, (2), 65–74.

Wallmach, K. (2006), 'Feminist translation strategies: Different or derived?', *Journal of Literary Studies*, 22, (1/2). Available at: www.thefreelibrary.com (accessed 21 May 2008).

Wasserman, H. (2000), 'Afrikaans vibreer van genade – Krog', *Die Burger*, 24 October, 4.

Wolf, M. (2006), 'The female state of the art: women in the "translation field"', in A. Pym, M. Shlesinger and Z. Jettmarová (eds). *Sociocultural Aspects of Translating and Interpreting*. Amsterdam: John Benjamins, pp. 129–141.

Yarbro-Bejarano, Y. (1994), 'Gloria Anzaldúa's Borderlands/La Frontera: Cultural studies, "difference," and the non-unitary subject', *Cultural Critique*, 28, 5–28.

How Translation Feels[1]

Libby Meintjes

Chapter Outline

Human beings do not see things whole; we are not gods but wounded creatures, cracked lenses, capable only of fractured perceptions. Partial beings, in all the senses of that phrase. Meaning is a shaky edifice we build out of scraps, dogmas, childhood injuries, newspaper articles, chance remarks, old films, small victories, people hated, people loved

(Rushdie, 1991: 12)

How does a writer respond to the translator's competing claims for creativity and originality? At what stage does the writer hand over the creative baton to the translator and where is a line drawn (or not) to mark transgression and/or betrayal? As translators are we conscious of the impact of translation on those most intimately affected by the process? Is it possible to *narrate* the emotional traces left behind by the work of translation? If writing is a metaphorical act of translation, bringing with it a sense of absence and loss, does translation exacerbate this sense of loss (cf. also Paul Ricoeur's likening of translation to Freud's concept of the work of 'memory' and 'mourning' 2004: 8)?

This chapter is an attempt to narrate these traces through the eyes, primarily, of the writer but also to some extent through the eyes of the translator. To allow a natural process of reflexivity, I have felt it important to let go of the complex space that I as researcher and translator occupy and to avoid further 'muddying' (Albouezi and Pahl 2007: 3) the writer's reflections on the process of translation by introducing theoretical and critical approaches to translation. By asking opened-ended questions such as: 'What is your response to being translated?' and 'How does it feel?', I aimed to give the participants 'space to be reflexive' and thus to use their responses to build a 'co-constructed account' (ibid.) of their views on being translated. On starting out on this research, I was expecting to come across intractable opinions, frustration and dissatisfaction with the translation process. However, my expectations of uncovering hard-line responses, such as Vera Nabokov's public burning of translations of Vladimir Nabokov's books outside Stockholm in July 1959 (Kaplan, 2003: 1), were firmly disappointed.

The desire to probe the experiences of writers of translation arose from a desire to understand how South African writers understand the concept of translation and reflected on it in relation to their work as well as from a sense that they 'handle' the translation process very differently. Some writers have their works translated;[2] and some of these writers translate the works of others.[3] Some writers have translated their own works[4] and still others write 'in translation' in English,[5] thus sidestepping some of the dilemmas involved in the translation process.

Historically, this decision of black writers, more particularly, to write in English dates back to the African Authors Conference held in Johannesburg in 1936. At the Conference these black writers 'chose to regard English as the vehicle of an inclusive 'national' literature' (De Kock, 2001b: 393), a move that could be misinterpreted as a form of 'internal colonialism' (399) but which rather represented a clever rhetorical sleight of hand aimed at using the very colonial discourse around the *civil imaginary* to their own ends (cf. De Kock, 2001b).[6] There is therefore a relatively long-standing tradition for African writers to write in English, notwithstanding more overtly oppositional (postcolonial) stances adopted by writers, such as Ngũgĩ wa Thiong'o, who advocate writing in the mother tongue,[7] the latter position having found little favour among current South African writing. South African writers have therefore continued in a tradition that has them writing translation out of their work, in one way, and back into their work in another by stretching the English language to include the 'foreign', to represent an otherness which might normally only be associated with translation.[8] This resonant hybridity of the text is not, however, necessarily restricted to African writers as all South African writing is an intricate admixture of South Africa's languages, woven with the themes, tropes and figures that make it, in some way at least, representative of South African literature, of the 'seam' De Kock uses to refer to the 'site of joining together that also bears the mark of the suture [...] unavoidably bear[ing] the mark of its own crisis' (De Kock, 2001a: 276, see also De Kock in this volume). This image of the seam is also a beguiling metaphor for translation which attempts to join and yet retain the mark of its difference.

The question that arises is whether these differing levels of engagement with translation impact on the attitude of writers to translation? The writers considered in the present article represent a range of current South African writing. In drawing on their experiences I have taken advantage of public discussions at public events, such as writers in conversation at *Die Boekehuis*, Melville, Johannesburg (2005) and the *Cape Town Book Fair* (2006). The writers considered in this chapter include (in alphabetical order): Imraan Coovadia[9] (translated writer: *The Wedding* (2001) and *Green-eyed Thieves* (2006c)); Michiel Heyns (translated writer: *The Children's Day* (2002), *The Reluctant Passenger* (2003), *The Typewriter's Tale* (2005) and *The Bodies Politic* (2008), and translator of Marlene van Niekerk's *Agaat* (2004)) for which he and Van Niekerk were awarded the Sunday Times Fiction Prize in 2007)[10]; Zakes Mda[11] (translated writer: *Ways of Dying* (1995), *Heart of Redness* (2000), *The Madonna of Excelsior* (2002), *The Whale Caller* (2005) and Cion (2007); Lewis Nkosi[12] (translated writer: *Underground People* (2002), *Mating Bird* (2004a), and *Mandela's Ego* (2006a)); and Marlene van Niekerk[13] (translated writer: *Die Vrou Wat Haar Verkyker Vergeet Het* (1992), *Sprokkelster* (1997), *Triomf* (1994, 1999a, 1999b), *Agaat* (2004, 2006a) and *Memorandum: – Verhaal met Skilderye* (Van Niekerk and Van Zyl 2006a and 2006b)). The authors were consulted primarily in their capacity as writers. However one of these writers, Michiel Heyns, is also the translator of Marlene van Niekerk's *Agaat* (2006a) and gave some input as a translator. I have drawn on the writing of two other South African writers on translation, either in terms of their experiences of being translated (J. M. Coetzee, author of numerous books, notably *Disgrace* (1999) for which he won the Nobel Prize in Literature in 2003, and translated writer) or of translating (Leon de Kock, author of *Blood Song* (1997) and *Gone to the*

Edges (2006), and translator of Marlene van Niekerk's *Triomf* (1999a) for which he won the South African Translators' Award for Outstanding Translation (*Triomf*) in 2000. Other writers have been consulted in a more peripheral manner. Although the concern of this chapter is primarily with the responses of South African writers to *being* translated, it does briefly examine *writing in translation* in South African works before moving on to a more detailed description of responses to translation.

Salman Rushdie speaks with particular authority as someone who engages in his writing in *translating* worlds and perceptions. His words, quoted at the start of this chapter, encapsulate the difficulties facing translation and translators. Writings and interpretations of writing are refractions of experiences, 'the scraps, dogmas' and 'childhood injuries' (Rushdie, 1991: 12) which make up our lives and are constitutive of our understanding. As these imperfect Rushdian beings, we strive to make sense of our own and other worlds by constructing tenuous and transient 'edifices' of meaning (ibid.). Understanding the lived experiences and thoughts of others is difficult enough without compounding the complexity of the task by adding the dimension of translation. How do we remain true to our translation project when the lenses through which we see and understand the world, art, literature – in sum life – are so distorted by our own perceptions?

It is the realization of the enormity of the task facing us as translators that brings us up short in the face of a fundamental paradox of translation. Translation is both an attempt to overcome difference and yet to carry over what is different. The line between appropriating and misappropriating other worlds is a fine one. It is a human characteristic to make accessible, to domesticate (Venuti, 1998) the 'textual space of the Other' (Da Silva Matte, 1996: 228), to make it ours. The risk inherent in this appropriation is that we fail in the second, far more unyielding, aspect of the translation enterprise, which is to carry over what is different. While the act of translation aspires to reproduce sameness/identity in relation to the 'original', that task is doomed to failure since the very nature of translation is, in part, to make difference understandable. Deconstruction has pointed to this fundamental *crisis of identity* in the act of translation – translation's fatal flaw is to be, at one and the same time, *Other* and *not Other*. *Other* in the sense that it represents the foreign (the *Other*) carried over into the target system and that it is inevitably different to the source text, and *not Other* because it cannot transport the *Other*, complete and whole, and because it can never be the *Other*. Antoine Berman has referred to this conundrum of translation as the trial of the foreign (*l'épreuve de l'étranger*) (1984); J. M. Coetzee refers to 'the necessary imperfection of translation' (2006). What does this tell us about translation? That it is a complex, difficult and sensitive task subject to hermeneutic and critical inquiry (Steiner, 1995)? Above all it tells us that translation is an activity that, by its every act of interpretation, produces uniqueness and difference. Translation, like all forms of creative writing, is subject to the intertextual: no writing is fully original; no writing carries a singleness of meaning, leading us to conclude that there is possibly no such thing as an *original*, except in referential terms for the purposes of identification. In this sense we can, following Gayatri Spivak (1998: lxxxvi), say that translation is just another 'version of intertextuality'. Octavio Paz argues, along similar lines, that:

> Each text is unique, yet at the same time it is the translation of another text. No text is entirely original, because language itself is essentially a translation. In the first place, it translates from the non-verbal world. Then, too, each sign, each sentence, is the translation of another sign, another sentence. This reasoning may even be reversed without losing any of its force and we may assert that all texts are original because every translation is different. To a certain extent every translation is an original invention and thus constitutes a unique text. (Paz, 1986: 1)

We find ourselves returning therefore to the idea that translation, too, is original, different and unrepeatable,[14] existing, like the original, both in its uniqueness and inevitable reference.[15] This understanding of translation leads us to anticipate a number of ways in which a writer may find translation uncomfortable. The most important of these would be the potential clash of two unique and creative texts, both spinning off in different directions in a complex chain of connotation, intertextuality and *différance* (Derrida, 1998).

The partnership

Writing (experienced) as an expression of self[16] has the potential to engender competitiveness around originality and ownership, and protectiveness and resistance from the writer, at least in an initial moment, because translating opens up the space for tensions around the inevitable difference and loss in conveying the foreign, which is also the self of an other. The writer is not necessarily the only partner to feel dispossessed. Translators feel entitled to 'latitude and a free hand' (De Kock, 2003), to have a claim on the text and may feel disempowered in the face of authorial claims. This chapter explores the responses of writers and some translators to this *travail de deuil* (mourning of inevitable loss), in which the translator seeks to carry out Paul Ricoeur's 'rescue operation' (*sauvetage*) (cf. Ricoeur, 2004: 8 in his reference to Freud).

The act of translation brings into being a relationship 'between two partners', the foreign (the text, the writer and source language) and the intended reader (the text, the translator and the target language), with the translator occupying the 'uncomfortable position of mediator' (Ricoeur, 2004: 8–9).[17] There arise, as a matter of course, issues of loyalty and betrayal within this partnership and herein 'resides the trial' to which Antoine Berman refers. The inevitable uncertainty, imprecision, and ambiguity of translation, the non-repeatability of texts, their readings and interpretation(s)[18] have implications for this partnership between writer and translator. Translation becomes a 'serious' business (cf. Derrida, 1998) not only in the Derridian sense of translation as a metaphor but also in the sense of translation as praxis which traverses our lives as we negotiate the business of translating ourselves for others (cf. Hoffman, 1990).[19]

The reader

In addition to the competing claims of the writer and translator, we have the competing claims of the texts, and more specifically, in the instance of translation, of the claims of the target text behind which stands the target audience, the reader. The mirage of the intended reader, as partner in this process, beckons the translation with enticing promises of new readerships and intellectual exchange. The relationship between the foreign and the target text therefore also calls for investigation. Walter Benjamin (2000: 15) suggests that the idea of an '"ideal" receiver' detracts from our understanding of art:

> since all it posits is the existence and nature of man as such. Art, in the same way, posits man's physical and spiritual existence, but in none of its works is it concerned with his response. No poem is intended for the reader, no picture for the beholder, no symphony for the listener.
>
> [. . .]
>
> But do we not generally regard as the essential substance of a literary work [. . .] the unfathomable, the mysterious, the 'poetic', something that a translator can reproduce only if he is also a poet?

Benjamin is clearly referring here to what Roland Barthes (1974) has described as 'writerly' texts (*texte de jouissance*). When the writer has his or her eye on something more writerly, more 'unfathomable' and 'mysterious', the writer's focus is not on the reader, but on something that is both more distant (the unfocused, distant gaze) and more immediate (the text). In this case, the translation is not done for 'the reader's sake' but for the sake of the text (and, I suppose, we can say in some sense for the writer him or herself as the model reader). This understanding goes some way to easing the tensions between writer and translator by focusing attention on the so-called original. Although we may have established a primary loyalty, we have not entirely disposed of the notion of readership. We need a sleight of hand to allow the translator to don the mantle of the 'model reader' (Eco, 1979), who, as interpreter of both 'original' and 'translation', occupies the space in between, becoming a 'palimpsest writer',[20] replacing, rewriting and interpreting the 'original'.

If more 'writerly' texts are not written for an audience as such, other 'readerly' texts are written specifically for a particular kind of readership (Barthes, 1974). Roland Barthes' 'readerly' texts refer in particular to consumer or popular literature (examples of which are crime and detective fiction, romance fiction, chicklit literature, westerns and science fiction), a literature which appeals more to a mass audience (Cawelti, 1976; Meintjes, 1989) than do other forms of 'unfathomable' and 'mysterious' literary production (Benjamin, 2000). The focus of such literature is quite explicitly reader-oriented. In this case the partnership loyalty becomes more focused on the relations between the 'original', its 'translation' and the 'target reader'. Barthes' distinction between 'writerly' and 'readerly' texts is useful in understanding the different responses of writers to the translation process, as we see below.

Umberto Eco (1994) ascribes three reasons to writers' lack of interest in the translation process: lack of 'linguistic competence' in the languages of the translated text, lack of 'faith in the literary value of their works' with a desire 'only to sell their product in as many countries as possible', and prejudice (1994) of which he gives two 'equally despicable' examples of overweening ego (a belief in one's 'inimitable genius' that simply has to 'suffer' translation 'as a painful political process to be borne until the world has learned his language') or '"ethnic" bias' (a belief that the response of 'readers from other cultures' is unimportant) (1994). Of course, there is always the possibility that writers simply do not understand what is at stake in translation, believing that translation is something that *just happens*. I would nonetheless like to believe that writers, through their experiences of the difficulties of writing, have a far more sophisticated understanding of what is involved in 'writing' translations. Barthes' 'readerly' and 'writerly' texts and his categories of *texte de désir, texte de plaisir* and *texte de jouissance* make it possible to capture a more nuanced understanding of the relationship between a writer and translation.

Writing for the reader

Although linguistic competence and lack of faith in literary value both play a part in the attitudes of some writers, a more real assessment would be that writers are very much aware of the reader-oriented nature of their texts. It would be fair to say that Margie Orford, (author of *Like Clockwork* (2006a))[21] is more concerned about audience and the representation of social themes than about literary quality. Orford's writing belongs to the newly emerging South African crime novel genre.[22] In its social commentary, it is reflective of her research in the area of human trafficking, depicting the burning issues of violence against women, drugs, and sex slavery facing South African society:

> I think we are in a state of civil war against women and children and the perpetra-
> tors of violent crime are overwhelmingly male. There is a sense of unbridled
> misogyny and entitlement. (Rutter, 2008)

In discussing her response to being translated, Orford (2006b) expressed the opinion that the quality of her writing differed from that of writers such as Zakes Mda or Marlene van Niekerk and that the 'risks' were therefore 'not as great'. What kind of risk can we be talking about but the risk of loss (of value – whether this be literary or other)? Orford (2006b) articulated her view of translation simply as gain: translation provides an opportunity for a broader readership, greater recognition and financial rewards (factors echoed by a number of other writers). Although she did not say so in as many words, Orford's assessment of her writing derives from a particular understanding of the nature of her text, which is explicitly reader-oriented with a bias toward social commentary. Writing for the reader, Orford would not appear to antici-pate translational problems, and translation appears in fact more 'feasible', less arduous than the translation of writerly texts because the focus is on what the reader wants, not so much on the text.

Writing in translation

For various reasons, historical, as we have seen, but also largely to do with audience and publics,[23] many African South African writers have elected to write in English rather than in their mother tongue. These writers use an adopted language in their own particular ways to convey the cadence and tone of their own languages and cultures, to represent their own lives and communities. In this sense their writing is already a form of translation (Gyasi, 1999: 2 and Bandia in Chapter 1 of this volume).

An amusing courtroom scene in Lewis Nkosi's *Mandela's Ego* (2006a), where Simon Gumede, court interpreter and sartorially debonair man about town(ship) is interpreting for Sigebengu, a character accused in a case of common assault, reflects this 'translation', not only through the language used but in the communication of different worldviews ...

> NATIVE COMMISSIONER (hearing a case of common assault): Ask the Accused, how does he plead, guilty or not guilty?
>
> SIMON GUMEDE (interpreting): The Big Baas asks, how do you plead, guilty or not guilty?
>
> SIGEBENGU (the Accused): *Hhawu! Baba, Nkosi yami!* The One Whose Ears Are So Translucent They Allow The Sun To Shine Through!
>
> NATIVE COMMISSIONER: What is it? What is he saying?
>
> SIMON GUMEDE (trying to suppress a smile): Your Honour, he says, 'You Whose Ears Are So Translucent They Allow The Sun'...
>
> NATIVE COMMISSIONER: (cutting Simon short): Never mind all that. Ask him, how does he plead, guilty or not guilty? And instruct the Accused not to waste the time of the court. He must first plead. Guilty or not guilty? That is the law.
>
> SIMON GUMEDE (to the Accused): The Big Baas asks you not to waste the time of the court. What he wants to know is: Are you guilty or are you not guilty of striking the complainant with a kierie and nearly splitting his head in two?
>
> ACCUSED: *Hhawu! Nkosi yami!* My Lord! All I wish to say is, it was a fair fight. The man insulted me. He called me names. *Msunu kanuoko! Root of your mother!* Is what he said. He [. . .]. (Lewis Nkosi, *Mandela's Ego*, 2006: 88–90)

As an interpreter or scholar of translation studies one might shudder at the transgressions in the interpreting process (and this is not an unfair representation of what happens in a South African court room). However, what is of interest here is the translation of different world views.

Translation, in a more literal sense, already stands in the text in – the Zulu *Hhawu! Baba, Nkosi yami!* followed by what the reader presumes to be the translation in the text, 'The One Whose Ears Are So Translucent They Allow The Sun To Shine Through!'. Translation is, however, present on other levels too. For example, the way the honorific is set out graphically with the unusual use of capitals and the poetic and other-worldly expressiveness of the phrase both reflect a different kind of discourse and emphasis. To this we can add the humorous juxtaposition of respect 'The One Whose' with the comical representation of the Accused's perception of whites as these strange creatures 'Whose Ears Are So Translucent They Allow The Sun To Shine Through!' that represents cross-cultural perceptions in a particular way. The formulation both represents another language, cultural expression and tradition and 'translates' these cross-cultural perceptions.

Another form of translation lies in the depiction of the cross-cultural encounters between the various personae. For the Magistrate, well-versed in the guiding principles of law, and for anyone who has some understanding of the fact that there are different conventions of behaviour in different contexts, it may well be feasible to state that they are not guilty while being fully aware that they did in fact strike someone on the head. According to Lewis Nkosi (2004b and 2006b), this is extremely difficult for a Zulu to do because a Zulu is morally bound to acknowledge his (or her) wrongdoing from the start. So Sigebengu feels the need to state what he has done wrong but also to give reasons for his behaviour. He cannot simply deny his wrongdoing by pleading not guilty – hence the reluctance and inability to answer the Magistrate's question with a simple yes or no answer.

We are presented with a cameo of cultural differences. First, the Magistrate finds the interpreting process frustrating and obstructive. Second, Simon Gumede, as the only agent (Thompson, 1984) in the proceedings to have access to both cultures and languages, cannot help enjoying the power and the humour of the situation. He inserts bits of additional information, sometimes to clarify, but at other times simply because he can and it is in his nature to do so. Third and finally the Accused simply applies himself earnestly to the task of being true to himself, his values and his self-protection.

Both the writers considered under the rubric of 'writing in translation', Zakes Mda and Lewis Nkosi, had very few reservations about being translated and gave no indication that they followed the translation process at all closely.

Although Mda takes care to review his own work and sends chapters or sections of his works in progress to his personal group of readers for comment (2006), he has few qualms about letting go of his works for translation into other languages.[24] In response to a question about the role of his editor or editors, he spoke of his resistance to advice from his editors to change material in his books to suit the audience, more specifically an international audience.

Mda is emphatic that his readers are not 'morons', unable to understand different worlds, different contexts even if they are not familiar with them. This would imply that he would also be resistant to a 'domesticating' approach (Venuti, 1998) to the translation of his works. Despite his strong views on the inviolability of his texts, Mda is not interested in the translation process per se, and plays no part in the selection of his translators,[25] believing that 'the publisher knows best'[26] (Mda, 2006). From this one can infer that he believes he has no role to play in the translation process. He claims to have no emotional or intellectual response to having his works translated and not to have read those translations which are in languages he knows, although he spends a considerable amount of time working with actors in the production of his plays in different languages (ibid.).

Despite his indifferent attention to the translation process as such, Mda is positive about translation in general terms because it exposes his writing to 'other cultures' (ibid.). There is therefore both satisfaction at the idea of 'others' reading his works and of reaching a broader readership, which is in line with his decision to write in English. Responses elicited at a much earlier stage of this research from Lewis Nkosi (2004b) were not dissimilar.

Since both Mda and Nkosi are already involved in the translation of ideas, perspectives and cultures in their writing, the idea of translation presents no dilemma for them. Although the fiction of Mda and Nkosi cannot be described as readerly texts, both writers are aware of the audience (albeit in a different way) and the depiction of the foreign as they write. Translating across languages therefore does not present the formidable challenge it does for some writers.

Writing for the text

Coovadia

Some of Mda's and Nkosi's thoughts are echoed by Imraan Coovadia (author of *The Wedding* (2001) and *Green-eyed Thieves* (2006c)) who, when asked to comment on his response to being translated, said: 'It's interesting. I'm not very resistant to it, or especially controlling of the final result. Perhaps I'll grow to be . . .'. Being translated is therefore a relatively new experience for Coovadia who has yet to consider its full implications. He expresses mild concern about the potential untranslatability of some English variants he uses in his novels – such as 'Durban, Indian, Johannesburg, outdated, 1960s' English and 'English simulations of other languages (Gujarati, Afrikaans)' (Coovadia, 2006b). But while Coovadia appears on the face of it to be relatively trusting of translators, his faith in them is not complete – as can be inferred from his comment that he is not sure that the translators have even noticed that he uses variants of English (ibid.).

In Coovadia's case, too, the writer is seen to have little control over the translation process. Translators are selected by the publisher and, because Coovadia does not understand the languages into which he has been translated (Hebrew and Italian), he feels that he has very little to say about or influence over the translation product.

When asked what he felt were the risks of writing and, by extension, of translation where one sets 'in motion certain forces of which you are not the master – forces of language, forces of the unconscious' (Van Niekerk, 2006a), Coovadia agreed that writing 'demands risk-taking' but that translation was a 'much longer-range kind of risk' because you never know *how* you have been translated unless you are conversant with the language of translation (Coovadia, 2006b). The loss of control over his work was nonetheless set off against the more positive and practical benefit 'in which the career and trajectory of your book is extended . . . and I think most writers like to keep an eye on that. It's more *social and extensive* in character: who's reading my book in Estonia? What do the Nicaraguans think of it? Is there some budding young Telugu poet who can *borrow something* from what I've done?' (Coovadia, 2006 my emphasis).

For Coovadia translation represents an excitement, a potential for exploring how others relate to his work, and it is the concretely expansive and intertextual nature of it that excites him. His focus is on the writerly, intertextual text capable of transcending borders and circulating ideas outside the confines of the supposedly global language that is English.

Marlene van Niekerk

Coovadia's excitement resonates with the excitement experienced by Marlene van Niekerk:[27]

> And from rejoicing in the gift held within all languages, namely its generosity to become divinely unmoored from mere functionality, in this sense one can say that the translator is for the writer like the god Hermes is for the traveller. Translators are divine tricksters, falling into your business and whisking it with their own wings! (Van Niekerk, 2006b)

Others have articulated the same idea from the perspective of the reader, seeing translators as 'priests who mediate' the readers' 'relationships with the literary gods' (Peder Zane, 2006).

Van Niekerk's response to the issues of translation signal a very different preoccupation with translation and the relationship it has with her own writing in Afrikaans. In a series of chain interviews on *LitNet*, an Afrikaans online journal cum discussion forum, Van Niekerk (2006c) echoed the Derridean notion of works 'calling' for translation. For her translation means 'being part of a 'conversation'' and literary works in a certain tradition 'call upon and towards each other'. She believes it incumbent on writers of all languages, but more specifically Afrikaans, to:

> grow up and sit ourselves down and write works of science, social analysis, anthropology and fiction that would feed and (dis)play and gentle the Afrikaans language to such a degree that the works themselves call for translation, and help to create a dynamic of eager communicative exchange with other cultures and experiences. (Van Niekerk, 2006c)

Van Niekerk's 'calling' metaphor blends writing, translation and intertextuality, and is a mix of the theoretical, the pragmatic and the affective. Like Derrida she does not see this call or cry as pure but as one that is sometimes distant and strained but full of potential. She likens it to Proust's 'finely fangled sensitivities and elaborate "onion peeling"' (Van Niekerk, 2006b). There is a movement backwards and forwards, to the past, and to the future, in which she sees translation as making the sound of this 'call … audible', even as it distorts it (ibid.).

In Van Niekerk too, therefore, we find an understanding of the 'social and extensive' character of translation (Coovadia, 2006b). She articulates more clearly, however, the notion that 'translation sometimes realizes potentialities of the text which were not visible in the "original"', something which she finds 'very compelling' (Van Niekerk, 2006b). It is clear that for Van Niekerk translation is a supremely original and creative act, defined by its intertextuality.

Michiel Heyns

Michiel Heyns, formerly Professor of English at the University of Stellenbosch in South Africa, is both a writer and the translator of what has been referred to by some critics as the great South African novel (Brownlee, 2006), Van Niekerk's *Agaat*. Heyns, a South African academic who teaches English literature, is Afrikaans-speaking but writes in English and also translates into English.

His novels *The Children's Day* (2002) and *The Reluctant Passenger* (2003) have been translated into Afrikaans and French respectively. His two most recent works are *The Typewriter's Tale* (2005) and *The Bodies Politic* (2008).

Strangely for such an acclaimed translator, Heyns feels 'oddly distanced' (2006b) in his relationship to the translation of his own works. He was involved in the translation of *The Children's Day* in the sense that he reviewed the Afrikaans translation, changing elements such as the use of idiom but most markedly 'loosen[ing] up the translation which was such a close translation'. He also engaged in discussion with his French translator, in fact more so than with his Afrikaans translator. Expanding on his sense of distance, Heyns was one of the few writers actually to broach the subject of ownership: 'in a strange way it doesn't seem like my own work any more, although of course I do ultimately judge it as a version of my work. [. . .] I feel proprietary but not possessive, if that makes sense' (Heyns, 2006b).

For the first time we see tensions around the ownership of the text surfacing. Heyns was also one of the few writers to articulate, and then only tangentially, a sense of loss and exclusion from the translation process, expressing the wish that he had had more influence over the translation process – not necessarily so much in relation to the translations themselves as in relation to the final product: marketing and the choice of the cover for the translations.

What emerges is not so much the invisibility of the translator, so familiar a concept in translation discourse, as the invisibility of the writer: the exclusion of the writer (whether through the writer's own wishes, as in the case of Mda, or not) both from the translation process and the final commoditization of the text in translation. Heyns' concerns about the marketing and packaging of his works can be related to the 'value' (Appadurai, 1996) ascribed to them through practical marketing decisions which are wrested from the control of the author. '[T]he literary text, far from functioning as an independent aesthetic object, circulates within a complex network of social relations and significations' (Frow, 1995: 145 and cf. Appadurai, 1996), making it subject to a politics of value that are outside the control of the author. Graham Huggan also writes about the 'trafficking [. . .] of culturally 'othered' artefacts' and of 'the institutional values that are brought to bear in their support' (Huggan, 1994: 412).

In keeping with this sense of proprietary or ownership/possession, Heyns speaks of the translator being 'wholly in the employ of the text, as it were, and a good translator subordinates his or her preferences to the quirks of the text' and of the fact that 'translation *should* be a cherishing, not an abuse.'[28] He gives as examples his own approach to translating Marlene van Niekerk's

Agaat, of having to give way to the idiosyncracies of her writing which are very different to his own. Heyns' focus on the text brings with it an understanding that transgressions will occur and hence a sense of loss and exclusion.

Having had the experience of writing, being translated, and translating, Heyns is deeply appreciative of the problems that present themselves in translation. A translator cannot be 'deaf to the tone' of the writing but at the same time needs to have some latitude in conveying that tone. His notion of being 'proprietary' without being 'possessive' encapsulates the amount of 'give' that an author needs to allow in the translation, and also reflects the kind of translation partnership that evolved between him and Van Niekerk while he was translating *Agaat*.

For Heyns, his translation of Van Niekerk's book *Agaat* is not the same book as the original but the result of co-operation between translator and writer and as such fully endorsed by Van Niekerk. Being Afrikaans-speaking, Heyns has real empathy and understanding for Van Niekerk's writing – and at the same time her writing resonated with his wide literary background so that he was able to recreate, and reproduce the referentiality of the text by creating other allusions in the English, drawing on the English canon of writers such as William Shakespeare, T. S. Elliot, Gerard Manley Hopkins, John Dunne, and W. H. Auden. A kind of sixth sense allowed him to relate both emotionally and intellectually to Van Niekerk's writing, by doing what both he and Van Niekerk describe as 'potentialising meaning' (Van Niekerk, 2006b and Heyns, 2006b).

In reading and translating Van Niekerk's work, Heyns found himself constantly returning to Eliot's *The Wasteland*. An example of this can be found in his translation of Van Niekerk's *liefhebbend* (fond, loving) in the Afrikaans, which encompasses everything 'feminine, an active enfolding of language' and which Heyns translated with a quote from Hopkins' *God's Grandeur*: ' . . . over the bent world broods with . . . ' (2006a).

In Heyns' translation of *Agaat* we find one of the most appealing images or synecdoches for translation. As Heyns draws on references in the English literary canon to translate the referentiality of the Afrikaans text, he is forced to populate the bookshelf of one of the central characters, Milla – with all the works he refers to – so new writings, different intertextual references are added, or replace and obscure others. Indeed his translation is not the same book, it stems from a different bookshelf. This repopulated bookshelf reflects both Heyns and Van Niekerk's understanding of the intertextual nature of translation; it is also emblematic of Heyns' focus on the writerly text in the translation process.

Leon de Kock

The final writer to be considered is Leon de Kock, the translator of Van Niekerk's *Triomf*, and a poet in his own right, as well as an academic. Here we examine only his experiences as a translator. He opens one of his articles[29] on the subject with the following:

> Literary translation is a curiously double-edged process. It is a noisy, difficult, messy and vertiginously unstable practice, yet it conventionally aspires to the appearance of seamless certainty, to a weirdly silent, humming invisibility. (De Kock, 2003: 345)

Leon de Kock confesses to starting out with the hubristic idea that 'translation was a secondary form of writing, a derivative act in [the] service of a higher order of originality' but found the whole experience to lead him to the rather humbling realization that 'literary translation is a comprehensively engaging creative act'. Initially he says, 'I wanted to become part of that novel's recreation. I wanted to write that novel.' So it is interesting that he starts off in his negotiations with the author saying things like: 'I made it clear to her that I would need to have a lot of latitude and a free hand' but ends up seeing things from a very different perspective:

> in this negotiation [. . .] the self – in this case, two selves – are impelled by an Eros-like drive to find their very life-affirmation in the making of, and association with, a particular creative object. However, and this is the exquisite paradox in the matter, in order to allow the event to happen at all, both writers have to give up their exclusive claim to the text. (De Kock, 2003: 349)

In claiming ownership of the translation, De Kock initially experiences something akin to 'the feeling of "pure language"' (cf. Benjamin, 2000): '[b]etween the two languages there seems to exist a metalingual, or conceptual, understanding of the content, a kind of Platonic ideal form similar to Benjamin's sense of "pure language"' (De Kock, 2003: 349). In ironic amusement at himself, De Kock reconfigures Benjamin's translator who liberates 'the language imprisoned in a work' as a kind of freedom fighter, the swashbuckling 'hero translator, who must break jail and liberate the temporarily reconfigured version of pure language back into multilingual general possession'. But alas, reality sets in all too soon, When 'the *real* world of publishers, agents and contracts' (ibid., emphasis mine) heaves back into sight, the conventional notion of sole ownership cuts the ground from beneath the feet of our hero. 'This "real world"', says De Kock, 'has entirely seen off the poststructuralist challenge [to writerly ownership], if it ever noticed the beast in the first place' (2003: 350) and the translator is forced to reassess his position.

What is interesting about De Kock's comments is the transition from the sense of control of ownership to that of dispossession and invisibility. While working on the translation, the translator has a sense of power, but once the 'real' world sets in, everything 'collude[s] to force the translator back into the shadows' (De Kock, 2003: 350). It takes one simple query from the editor about the use of Afrikaans words in De Kock's translation from the editor of the international publishing house, Little, Brown and Company, to shift this balance of power. It was, according to De Kock, 'the equivalent of pulling a single thread in the text loose' (ibid.). What the editor asked in effect was for the translator (and the author) to switch his focus from the text to the reader. This seemingly simple request had the effect of 'catapult[ing]' them 'out of [their] respective senses of possessing or owning the text', making them aware for the first time of 'third-party expectation, third-party evaluation, and, worst of all, the possibility of third-party censure' (De Kock, 2003: 350). The moment the focus changes from the text to the reader, the translator of a writerly *texte de jouissance* (De Kock, 2003: 349) with all its (selfish) erotic and satisfying pleasures, is thrown into disarray, and he is dispossessed. Forced to acknowledge that ownership does not vest solely in the translator or the author and that there are other parties claiming proprietary rights, the translator has to deal with divided loyalties. Where before only the text and the best interests of the text had to be taken into account, the translator's loyalties are now divided across any number of vested interests – readers, editors and publishers – and this opens the door to concerns about the opinions (critics, reviewers, etc.)

Both the translator and the author/writer become prey to invisibility, to the politics of value and to the commercial exploitation of their creative works as commodities within the larger social semiotic, labelled by Huggan as the 'postcolonial exotic' (1997: 412).

Conclusion

Discussions with writers have shown that the translation process is far less fraught than anticipated:

> Perhaps the Pure Language does not exist, but pitting one language against another is a splendid adventure, and it is not necessarily true, as the Italian saying goes, that the translator is always a traitor. Provided that the author takes part in this admirable treason. (Eco, 1994: 12)

It is also clear that the responses to translation are largely dictated by the nature of the texts. The more readerly the text the less interest is displayed in the translation process. The most obvious reason for this is that in the case of a readerly *texte de désir*, there is no real divided loyalty. The nature of the text is not in dispute: to give pleasant, undemanding enjoyment. All those involved work towards achieving that common goal of catering for the desires of the consumer because in simplistic terms everyone is satisfied: the author because s/he sells more; the publisher and editor for the same reason and because their business grows; the readers because they get what the want and expect; the translator because the work is quick and less demanding.

Investment in the translation project, as in the case of Eco and Van Niekerk, generates its own excitement and rewards in terms of the possibilities of the new writerly *texte de jouissance*: 'you dance with your translator as you dance with your own unconscious' (Van Niekerk, 2006b). Dispossession occurs when the author and the translator are called upon to switch their allegiances from the text to the reader and when the translator is displaced from his or her role as the model reader inhabiting the same space, insofar as this is ever feasible, as the text.

An interesting case is presented by those writers whose writing already represents a form of translation. There is a temptation to categorize their writing as *texte de plaisir*, falling in between the *texte de désir* and *texte de jouissance*. I think this would be unfair. Although the writers discussed in this chapter tend to accept the translation process as something inevitable and manageable, this is because they have already imposed a form of 'self-translation' (cf. Hoffman, 1990 and Besemeres, 2002) on their readers, relying on the readers' ability and willingness to stretch their imaginations to do justice to the text. Rather than their attitudes reflecting a lesser sense of the writerly nature of their work I would like to believe that, occupying the 'liminal' or 'interstitial' space 'between' (Bhabha, 1994) competing imaginaries, they are undaunted at the prospect of doing the same across languages.

Notes

1. I am grateful to Zakes Mda, Lewis Nkosi and Margie Orford for being so willing to engage in discussion at various fora. I was also exceptionally fortunate to have direct e-mail 'conversations' with a number of these authors and I would like to acknowledge the thoughtful contributions from Imraan Coovadia, Michiel Heyns, and Ivan Vladislavić. I would also like to express my special appreciation to Marlene van Niekerk who took time from her busy schedule to consider my requests and my questions and who never fails to inspire.

2. Examples of these writers would be Ivan Vladislavić, Marlene van Niekerk, Zakes Mda and Lewis Nkosi.

3. Translators referred to in this article are Michiel Heyns and Leon de Kock. There are obviously many others who could be mentioned.

4. The self-translators referred to in this article are Mark Behr and André Brink. Another example would be Dalene Mathieu.

5. Examples of these are Sello Duiker, Antjie Krog, Zakes Mda, Phaswane Mphe, Nic Mhlongu, Njabulo Ndebele, and Lewis Nkosi.

6. De Kock argues powerfully that apparent submission by African writers and leaders at that time should be seen to contain 'the seed of a richer sense of discursivity – a greater appreciation of the plenitude of the social – [. . .]' (2001b: 408) and that 'the campaign for civil rights was taken up symbolically as a contest over the publicly held *terms* of the civil imaginary. Black South Africans did not fight *not* to become colonial subjects, they fought to *become* colonial subjects in the public realm, the *res publica*, in the fullest possible sense, and they did so in the image of the unalloyed imperial promise. In the process they sought to hold to eternal shame the shoddy colonial compromises inflicted in the name of the civil imaginary.' (403).

7. Ngũgĩ wa Thiong'o, while writing in his mother tongue, Gĩkũyũ, translates his works into English.

8. Bill Ashcroft et al. prefer to denote this subversion and estrangement of standard British English by use of the term 'english' or 'englishes' in the lower case (1989: 8).

9. Both *The Wedding* and *Green-eyed Thieves* were shortlisted for the Sunday Times Fiction Award (in 2002 and 2007 respectively). *The Wedding* has been translated into Hebrew and Italian.

10. This is the first time the prize was awarded to a translated work and jointly to the translator and original author.

11. Mda received a special merit award in the Amstel Playwright of the Year Award for *We Shall Sing for the Fatherland* in 1978; the Amstel Playwright of the Year Award for *The Hill* in 1979; the M-Net Book Prize for *Ways of Dying* in 1997 (which was also awarded the Olive Schreiner Prize and shortlisted for the CNA Prize and Noma Prize); the Commonwealth Writers Prize: Africa and Sunday Times Fiction Award (2001), the Hurston/Wright LEGACY Award for Fiction (2003), Africa Regional Commonwealth Writers' Prize, Africa Region (2001) for *The Heart of Redness*; and *Cion* shortlisted for the Commonwealth Writers' Prize Best Book Award, Africa Region.

12. Nkosi is chiefly known for his critical and scholarly writing. *Mating Birds* (1982) met with critical acclaim and has been translated into ten languages. *The Underground People* was shortlisted for the Herman Boesman Prize.

13. Van Niekerk was awarded the Eugène Marais Prize and Ingrid Jonker Prize for *Sprokkelster* in 1978; the M-Net Prize, CNA Prize and Noma Prize for *Triomf* in 1995; the LitNet Dopper Joris-Oskar prize and the UJ-Prize for Agaat in 2004 and 2005 respectively, as well as the Hertzog Prize for Prose and the C.L. Engelbrecht Prize for literature for *Agaat* in 2007.

14. As a translator I am all too familiar with the experience of returning to my translations and questioning earlier decisions. This process is important because it is about re-interrogating the original (source text) and my *original* interpretation. My re-reading of the translation makes it

a different text. Just as it is not possible to return to the same original, it is impossible to return to the same translation since neither is 'immutable' (Da Silva Matte, 1996: 231).

15. A practical consequence of this *inevitable reference* can be seen in the translation of Marlene van Niekerk's *Agaat* (2006) by Michiel Heyns, more specifically in the 'translation' of Milla's bookshelf (cf. p. 78).

16. A recent panel of contemporary South African writers (2008) reading and discussing their writing were virtually unanimous in describing the process of writing as something that was so inherently part of who they were that it was impossible *not* to write. Imagine the difficulty in handing over something that is so personal to someone else to refashion, even if this refashioning is in another language. (Writers included Chris van Wyk, author of *Shirley, Goodness and Mercy,* popular performance poet Lebo Mashile, Niq Mhlongo, author of *Dog Eat Dog*, Craig Higginson author of *The Hill* and Heinrich Troost author of *Plot Loss*).

17. Deux partenaires sont en effet mis en relation par l'acte de traduire, l'étranger – terme couvrant l'oeuvre, l'auteur, sa language – et le lecteur destinataire de l'ouvrage traduit. Et entre les deux, le traducteur qui transmit, [. . .] C'est dans cette inconfortable situation de médiateur que reside l'épreuve en question. [The act of translation in effect brings into being a relationship between two partners, the foreign – term covering the work, the author, his/her language – and the intended audience of the translated work. And between the two, the translator who transmits [. . .]. It is in this uncomfortable position of mediator that the trial in question resides.] (my translation).

18. Gayatri Spivak has described translation as the 'relation between two palimpsests' (Spivak 1998: lxxxvi).

19. Eva Hoffman's autobiographical *Lost in Translation: A Life in a New Language*, published in 1990, is a poetic and moving account of the 'self-translation' that colours lives in a constantly globalizing world.

20. See endnote 18. The translator as writer replaces or 'erases' the source text to allow a new text to emerge which still carries with it the mark of the previous text, just as the source text carried the mark of previous texts within it.

21. Margie Orford's venture into crime literature has been followed by the more recent *Blood Rose* (2007). *Like Clockwork* has been translated into Afrikaans, and Czech, Dutch, German and Russian translations will be published in 2008.

22. This is not to say that there is no history of the genre in South African literature. One well-known author that springs to mind is James McClure, author of, among others, *The Steam Pig* (1971), *The Caterpillar Cop* (1972) and *The Gooseberry Fool* (1974). More recent writers include Richard Kunzman, Deon Meyer and Mike Nicol.

23. The complex question of audience and public(s) falls outside the scope of this chapter but it is possible to point rather rapidly to the small South African reading public as one of the reasons that writers seek to write for a wider, global (English-speaking) audience. The African-language reading public in South Africa is even smaller than the English-speaking one and the reasons for this are also largely historical but complicated by current language attitudes in the country.

24. So far two of Mda's novels have been translated into French: *Ways of Dying* (1995) as *Le pleureur* (1999) and *The Madonna of Exelsior* (2002) as *La madone d'Excelsior* (2004). The latter novel has also been translated into Italian as *La Madonna di Excelsior* (2006b). Given his popularity, his books are likely to be more translated in the future.

25. Mda's French translator is same person who translates J. M. Coetzee into French – Catherine Glen-Lauga.

26. The role of publishers in, for example, choosing translators, providing (or not) translation briefs, and dictating changes in terms of audience can be decisive in shaping the translation (without them necessarily exercising any quality control over the translation as such), as can be seen by the effect that the publisher's intervention had in the case of De Kock's translation of Van Niekerk's *Triomf* (see below in this chapter). The role of publishers is not discussed in any detail here but readers are referred to Lawrence Venuti (1995) and Peter Fawcett (1995).

27. Van Niekerk is best known as the author of *Triomf* and *Agaat*. Both novels have met with national and international acclaim. *Triomf* has been translated from Afrikaans into English, Dutch and French, and *Agaat* from Afrikaans into English.

28. In the course of interviewing various writers and translators about translation I was made aware of just how easily we can be caught up in our own theoretical worlds. A conclusion to one of the questions I put to my interviewees was: 'Many would say that translation is a form of abuse. How would you respond to that?' This is not a question that would surprise many translation scholars and yet the answer I received from Imraan Coovadia was: 'I would say that they've never been abused.' The response was a sobering one.

29. De Kock resumes this discussion of translation in Chapter 2 of this volume, entitled: Cracking the Code: Translation as Transgression in *Triomf*.

References

Alboueži, Khadeegha and Pahl, Kate. (2007), 'Dilemmas of translation and identity: Ethnographic research in multilingual homes'. Available at: www.ling-ethnog.org.uk/documents/OU_meth_sem/ Kate_ Pahl.rtf (accessed 7 November 2007).

Appadurai, Arjun. (1996), *Modernity at Large: Cultural Dimensions of Globalization*. Minneapolis, MN: University of Minnesota Press.

Ashcroft, Bill, Griffiths, Gareth; and Tiffin, Helen. (1989), *The Empire Writes Back: Theory and Practice in Post-colonial Literatures*. London and New York: Routledge.

Barthes, Roland. (1974), *S/Z: An Essay*, trans. Richard Miller. New York: Hill and Wang.

Benjamin, Walter. (2000[1923]), 'The task of the translator: An introduction to the translation of Baudelaire's *Tableaux Parisiens*', in Lawrence Venuti (ed.) *The Translation Studies Reader*. London and New York: Routledge, pp. 15–25.

Berman, Antoine. (1984), *L'épreuve de l'étranger, culture et traduction dans l'Allemagne romantique*. Paris: Gallimard.

—(2000), 'Translation and Trials of the Foreign', in Lawrence Venuti (ed.) *The Translation Studies Reader*. London and New York: Routledge, pp. 276–289.

Besemeres, Mary. (2002), *Translating One's Self: Language and Selfhood in Cross-Cultural Autobiography*. Oxford: Peter Lang.

Bhabha, Homi K. (1994), *The Location of Culture*. London: Routledge.

Brownlee, Russel. (2006), Michiel Heyns *(The Typewriter's Tale)* in conversation with Russel Brownlee on aspects of his work. Cape Town Book Fair. Monday 19 June 2006.

Cawelti, John G. (1976), *Adventure, Mystery and Romance: Formula Stories as Art and Popular Culture*. Chicago and London: University of Chicago Press.

Coetzee, J. M. (1999), *Disgrace*. London: Seeker and Warburg.

—(2006), *Speaking in tongues*. Available at: www.theaustralian.news.com.au/printpage/0,5942, 17924843,00.html (accessed on 15 June 2006).

Coovadia, Imraan. (2001), *The Wedding*. New York: Picador.

— (2006a), *The Impact of Islam on our Writing - Discussion with Ray Jacobs, author of 'Confessions of a Gambler' & Imraan Coovadia, author of 'The wedding'*. Moderator: Chris van der Merwe. Cape Town Book Fair, Monday 19 June 2006.

— (2006b), e-mail responses to questions on translation. Received 28 June 2006.

— (2006c), *Green-eyed Thieves*. Roggebaai: Umuzi

da Silva Matte, Neusa. (1996), 'Translation and Identity', *Meta*, 41, 2, 228–236.

De Kock, Leon. (1997), *Blood Song*, Cape Town: Snailpress.

—(2001a), 'South Africa in the Global Imaginary: An Introduction'. *Poetics Today*, 22, (2), 263–298. (Special issue: 'South Africa in the Global Imaginary', ed. Leon de Kock, co-eds Louise Bethlehem and Sonja Laden).

—(2001b), Sitting for the Civilization Test: The Making(s) of a Civil Imaginary in Colonial South Africa. *Poetics Today*, 22, (2), 391–412. (Special issue: 'South Africa in the Global Imaginary', ed. Leon de Kock, co-eds Louise Bethlehem and Sonja Laden).

— (2003), 'Translating *Triomf*: the shifting limits of "ownership" in literary translation or: never translate anyone but a dead author', *Journal of Literary Studies*, 19, (3–4), 345–359.

— (2006), *Gone to the Edges*. Pretoria: Protea Book House.

Derrida, Jacques. (1998/1976), *Of Grammatology*, trans. Gayatri Chakravorty Spivak. Baltimore: Johns Hopkins University Press.

Eco, Umberto. (2003), *Mouse or Rat? Translation as Negotiation*. London: Phoenix, Orion Books.

— (1994), 'A Rose by Any Other Name', trans. William Weaver, in *The Guardian Weekly*, January 16 1994. Available at: www.themodernword.com/eco/eco_guardian94.html (accessed 28 June 2006).

1979. *The role of the reader: Explorations in the semiotics of texts*. Bloomington, IN: University of Indiana Press.

Fawcett, Peter. (1995), 'Translation and Power Play, *The Translator*, 1, (2), 177–192.

Frow, John. (1995), *Cultural Studies and Cultural Value*, Oxford: Clarendon Press.

Gyasi, Kwaku A. (1999), 'Writing as translation: African literature and the challenges of translation', *Research in African Literatures*, 30, (2), 75–88.

Heyns, Michiel. (2002), *The Children's Day*. Johannesburg: Jonathan Ball.

— (2003), *The Reluctant Passenger: A Novel*. Johannesburg: Jonathan Ball.

— (2005), *The Typewriter's Tale*. Johannesburg: Jonathan Ball.

— (2006a), Michiel Heyns *(The Typewriter's Tale)* in conversation with Russel Brownlee on aspects of his work. Cape Town Book Fair. Monday 19 June 2006.

— (2006b), e-mail responses to questions on translation. Received June 2006.

— (2008), *The Bodies Politic.* Johannesburg: Jonathan Ball.

Hoffman, Eva. (1990), *Lost in Translation: A Life in a New Language.* New York: Penguin

Huggan, Graham. (1994), 'The Postcolonial Exotic: Rushdie's Booker of Bookers', *Transition*, 64, 22–29.

Kaplan, Alice. (2003), 'Translation: the biography of an artform', *Mots Pluriels*, 23 March 2003. Available at: www.arts.uwa.edu.au/MotsPluriels/MP2303ak.html (accessed 23 November 2007).

McClure, James. (1971), *The Steam Pig.* UK: Gollancz.

— (1972), *The Caterpillar Cop.* UK: Gollancz.

— (1974), *The Gooseberry Fool.* UK: Gollancz.

Mda, Zakes. (1995), *Ways of Dying.* Cape Town, New York: Oxford University Press.

— (1999), *Le pleureur*, traduit par Catherine Glenn-Lauga. Paris: Dapper.

— (2000), *The Heart of Redness.* Cape Town: Oxford University Press.

— (2002), *The Madonna of Excelsior.* Cape Town: Oxford University Press.

— (2004), *La madone d'Excelsior*, traduit par Catherine Glenn-Lauga. Paris: Editions du Seuil.

— (2005), *The Whale Caller.* Johannesburg: Penguin.

— (2006), *Zakes Mda, author of the 'Whale Caller', open discussion with visitors to the Cape Town Book Fair.* Cape Town Book Fair. Monday 19 June 2006.

— (2006b), *La Madonna di Excelsior*, traduzione dall'Inglesi di Maria Baiocchi e Anna Tagliavini. Roma: Edizioni e/o.

— (2007), *Cion.* Johannesburg: Penguin.

Meintjes, Elizabeth. (1989), *The Cultural Semiotics of Detective Fiction: The Translation of a Popular Genre.* Unpublished doctoral thesis. University of the Witwatersrand, Johannesburg.

Nkosi, Lewis. (2002), *Underground People.* Cape Town: Kwela Books.

— (2004a (1982)), *Mating Birds.* Cape Town: Kwela Books.

— (2004b), Lewis Nkosi in Conversation. Die Boekehuis, Melville Johannesburg: August 2004.

— (2006a), *Mandela's Ego.* Roggebaai, South Africa: Umuzi.

— (2006b), *At last we can smile – Fred Khumalo, author of 'Touch my blood' and Lewis Nkosi, author of 'Mandela's ego'.* Moderator: Kole Omotoso. Cape Town Book Fair, Monday 19 June 2006.

Orford, Margie. (2006a), 'Conversation at Cape Town Book Fair'. Monday 19 June 2006.

— (2006b), *Like Clockwork.* Cape Town: Oshun Books.

— (2007), *Blood Rose.* Cape Town: Struik Publishers.

Panel Discussion of Contemporary South African Writers (2008), 'Readings and Responses to Issues'. Facilitated by Professor Michael Titlestad. Johannesburg, University of the Witwatersrand, Thursday 3 April 2008.

Paz, Octavio. (1986), 'On Translation', UNESCO Courier. Available at: www.findarticles.com/p/articles/mi_m1310/is_1986_May-June/ai_4375052 (accessed 28 June 2006).

Peder Zane, J. (2006), 'Novels found in translation', book review. *New Observer*, Wednesday July 5 2006. Available at: www.newsobserver.com/308/story/414694.html. (accessed 5 July 2006).

Ricoeur, Paul. (2004), *Sur la Traduction*. Paris: Bayard.

Rushdie, Salman. (1991), *Imaginary Homelands: Essays and Criticism 1981-91*. London: Granta Books.

Rutter, Karen. (2008), 'South Africa's Crime Wave – in Bookstores', *Time*, Wednesday April 2 2008. Available at: www.time.com/time/world/article/0,8599,1727386,00.html (accessed 5 April 2008).

Spivak, Gayatri. (1998 (1976)), 'Translator's Preface to Jacques Derrida's *Of Grammatology*', corrected edition, 1998. Baltimore and London: John, Hopkins University Press, pp. ix–lxxxvi.

Steiner, George (1995), *After Babel: Aspect of Language and Translation*. Oxford: Oxford University Press.

Thompson, John B. (1984), *Studies in the Theory of Ideology*. Cambridge: Polity, Berkeley University of California Press.

Van Niekerk, Marlene (1992), *Die Vrou Wat Haar Verkyker Vergeet Het*. Pretoria: HAUM-Literêr.

— (1994), *Triomf*. Quellerie.

— (1997), *Sprokkelster*. Kaapstad: Human & Rousseau.

— (1999a), *Triomf*, trans. Leon de Kock. Johannesburg: J. Ball.

— (1999b), *Triomf*, trans. Leon de Kock. Johannesburg: Little Brown and Company.

— (2004), *Agaat*. Kaapstad: Tafelberg.

— (2006a), *Agaat*, trans. Michiel Heyns. Kaapstad: Jonathan Ball Publishers.

— (2006b), E-mail responses to questions on translation. Received 24 April 2006.

— (2006c), 'So it is a risk this business of writing', Interview with Marlene van Niekerk conducted by Hans Pienaar. *LitNet*. Available at: www.oulitnet.co.za/nosecret/van_niekerk_pienaar.asp (Accessed February 28 2006).

Van Niekerk, Marlene and van Zyl, Adriaan (2006a), *Memorandum: – Verhaal met* Skilderye. Kaapstad: Human & Rousseau.

— (2006b), *Memorandum: A Story with Paintings*, trans. Michiel Heyns. Cape Town: Human & Rousseau.

Venuti, Lawrence. (1995), *The Translator's Invisibility*. London, New York: Routledge.

— (1998), *The Scandals of Translation: Towards an Ethics of Difference*. London, New York: Routledge.

Problems and Prospects of Translating Yorùbá Verbal Art Into Literary English: An Ethnolinguistic Approach

5

Tajudeen Surakat

Chapter Outline

Introduction

One significant feature of contemporary black African literature, whether written in the indigenous or European languages, is the incorporation of traditional verbal art forms such as proverbs, incantations, and praise poems (Tutuola, 1952; Achebe, 1958, 1964; Ṣoyinka, 1963, 1965; Alkali, 1984, 1997). Scholars have also rekindled interest in the collection, transcription, translation, and analysis of these oral genres (Lindfors and Owomoyela, 1973; Finnegan, 1977; Ọlatunji, 1984; Sheba, 2006). Famous Yorùbá writers such as D. O. Fagunwa (1903–1963), Adébáyọ̀ Fálétí (b. 1935) and Olú Owólabí (b. 1936) have produced several literary works which are embellished with *orin-ìbílẹ̀* (folksongs), *ìtàn-àbáláiyé* (folk-tales), *ọfọ̀/ògèdè* (incantations), *oríkì/orílẹ̀* (praise poems), and *òwe* (proverbs). In order to make these creative writings accessible to a wider audience, efforts have been made – and are still being made – to render them in Indo-European languages, particularly English and French (Bamgbose, 1974; Surakat, 1988). The translations have met with varying degrees of success. In some instances, it has been claimed that translating oral art forms is very difficult, if not impossible, especially when the languages concerned are culturally and typologically divergent (Beier, 1970; Onwurmene, 1981; Surakat, 1985, 1987; Innes, 1990; Okpewho, 1990). It is against this backdrop that this chapter examines the translatability of elements of Yorùbá verbal or oral culture (or orature) into the language of a predominantly literate, literary culture. The main objectives of this chapter are, in essence, i) to give a systematic account, informed by linguistics and translatology, of the various options and strategies open to a translator of Yorùbá verbal art into English; and ii) to discuss cultural problems in rendering Yorùbá orature into literary English and suggest ways of minimizing loss of meaning. By implication, language is subsumed under culture as in E. A. Nida's (1975a) ethnolinguistic approach (see below). The data used here are taken from a Yorùbá prose narrative by Olú Owólabí (1980) which deals with the Nigerian Civil War of 1967 to 1970. The 'creative realism' portrayed in the work marks a radical departure from the 'Fagunwa School' which is more preoccupied with fantasy, fairy tale, and the supernatural. More important is the fact that the source language (or SL) text, *Ẹni Ọlọ́run Ò Pa*, contains several elements of Yorùbá oral tradition such as proverbs, praise poems, incantations, songs, war chants, and so forth. The text is only one of the eleven plays and prose narratives authored by Owólabí, a prolific Yorùbá writer of his generation. Several lines of praise poems and incantations from the first chapter of the text are analysed below (Owólabí 1980: 2–3; see also Surakat, 1987 and 2007).

The Yorùbá people, verbal art forms and the SL text

Yorùbá designates both the people and language of a predominantly West African ethnic group, found mostly in the South-West region of Nigeria, but also in the Republics of Benin, Togo, and Ivory Coast. In Nigeria alone, with a population of about 140 million, there are more than 20 million Yorùbá people found mainly in Ọ̀yọ́, Ògùn, Oǹdó, Èkìtì, Òṣun, Kwara, Lagos and Edo States. Yorùbá is one of the three major ethnic and linguistic groups in Nigeria, while (native and non-native) speakers of the language are found all over the country. Although farming is the major traditional occupation, Yorùbá people are also active in fields such as education, arts and crafts, and trade and commerce. The Nobel Laureate, Wọlé Ṣóyínká, a well-known writer, playwright and translator, is of Yorùbá extraction. Various religions are found among the Yorùbá people, including Christian, Muslim and traditional religions. The Yorùbá language belongs to the Benue-Congo (hitherto classified as Kwa) of the Niger-Congo language family and it is one of the few African languages which has been studied extensively, not only in Nigeria, but also in American and European institutions. Traditionally, oral poetic genres are valued among the Yorùbá. Every speaker – an elder, orator, or a priest – uses verbal art forms to adorn and punctuate their talks and speeches. There are several of these verbal art forms:

(a) *Oríkì* and *orílè* (praise poems or panegyrics) are mainly eulogistic compositions, constituting the most popular of all the Yorùbá oral poetic genres. Every god or deity, individual, clan, tree or herb, and animal, has a praise name. Chanters of praise poems may be both professional and amateur. For instance, an *Ọba* (king) has a palace bard whose duty it is to chant royal praises to calm the nerves or boost the ego of the king especially on formal or ceremonial occasions.[1] At the same time, a mother may sing praises in honour of her beloved child, to serve as a morale booster, or to depict the virtues/attributes of the child. Praise poems are also heard on festive occasions when *griots* or professional praise-singers chant in return for some token from the subjects of their compositions. There are different categories of panegyrics depending on the object of praise: lineage, town or clan praises *(orílè)*, and praises for traditional rulers, chiefs, noblemen, dignitaries, as well as the common man *(oríkì)*. All Yorùbá divinities and deities have praise names, as do plants, animals, and even abstract and non-living things (Beier, 1970; Finnegan, 1977; Ọlátúnjí, 1984).

Yorùbá panegyrics can also be categorized as either formal or informal. Most praises for traditional rulers, clans and deities are formalized. Children who are born with particular characteristics or in strange, abnormal circumstances also have formalized praise poems (e.g. twins, triplets, those born with the umbilical cord twisted around the neck, etc.). According to O. Ọlátúnjí (1984: 87), the linguistic and stylistic features of *oríkì* and *orílè* include a: '...high incidence of nominalization, preponderance of kinship terms, multiple references to the subject (of praise), multiplicity of oblique references to historical and/or mythical events, fluidity of structure and content'. *Oríkì* and *orílè* can be combined, an example of which is found in the SL text where a few lines of *oríkì* are followed by lines of *orílè* (lines 1 and 2, 12 and 13–17 in the SL text below). Although they do not have exact equivalents either in classical or modern European poetry, they share in spirit certain features of the Epic and Ode (Ògúnbòwálé, 1970: 149–150).

(b) *Ọfọ̀* or *ògèdè* (incantations) refer to words that are chanted according to a formula, and are believed to be magically effective in manipulating people and things, both natural and supernatural. *Ọfọ̀* can be used to hypnotize human beings and animals so that they behave in conformity with the pronouncements of the chanter. It can be used to invoke either protective or destructive spirits, for certain effects as requested by the chanter. It is believed that *ọfọ̀* can change or alter the order of natural events such as 'making' or 'stopping' rain. The traditional Yorùbá believe that all animate and inanimate things have secret codes or primordial names, and whoever knows these secret names can control or hypnotize their bearers. Incantations can be either beneficial or malefic. The main features of *ọfọ̀* are: the invocation, problem-statement, assertion (positive, negative, and conditional), appeal or prayerful request (or application), repetition of certain phrases or lines, and symbolic word-play. The incantatory lines examined in this chapter are regarded as beneficial in that they are intended to protect Àlàbí (the subject of the poem) from evil, and invoke supernatural forces to protect him against the dangers of war. The most common features of the lines consist in assertions, prayerful requests, and phrasal repetitions.

The Source Language Text (SL) by Owólabí (1980) is titled *Ẹni Ọlọ́run Ò Pa*, and literally translates as: 'He whom God does not kill (shall not die)'. It is a story based on the operations of the Third Marine Commando in the riverine and Delta regions during the Nigerian Civil War of 1968–1970. The plot is simple and straightforward, presenting events chronologically and revealing the bravery and military exploits of the hero (Col. Bayọ̀) and his soldiers, right from the port of departure through the battle scenes. The story contains Yorùbá poetic genres such as praise poems, incantations, songs, proverbs. It makes allusions to traditional myths and legends, and also includes borrowings from other languages and cultures such as Hausa, Arabic, Igbo and English (see also Surakat, 1987).

The story opens with the soldiers and their family members at the port of embarkation. The atmosphere is emotionally charged. Noise and cries fill the air: wives bidding their husbands farewell and parents praying for their sons to return home safely. Some recite verses from the scriptures while others chant incantations. When the ship is about to set sail, a Yorùbá man from the city of Ìsẹ́yìn shouts his son's name (Àlàbí) and then chants the lines (which form the data for this chapter) in verse form. In other words, the story up to this point is in prose, while the chant by Àlàbí's father is a single stanza verse of 21 lines. These lines are here reproduced as in the original text (Owólabí, 1980: 2–3)

1. Àlàbí Ògún, ọmọ Ọlọ́pọndà   (*oríkì*, personal + *orílẹ̀*, lineage)
2. Ọmọ Ọlọ́pọndà Baba eégún   (*orílẹ̀*, lineage/clan)

3. Àlubọ̀ lọwọ́ ń lọ sẹ́nu   (incantation)
4. Àgègé kì í gòkè ọ̀pẹ kó má sọ̀   (incantation)
5. Àfèrèmòjò kì í bá wọn kú ikú àjọkú   (incantation)
6. Gologínní ni adìẹ ń bọ̀ oko èèmọ́   (incantation)
7. Dandan ni kí o bọ̀ wá bá mi   (incantation)
8. Àsínlà ni ti àgbọ̀nrín   (incantation)
9. Ọjọ́ àgbọ̀nrín bá sín lọjọ́ ikú rẹ̀ yẹ   (incantation)
10. Bí a bá dáná igún   (incantation)
11. Ẹyẹ mí̃ì là á fi sun   (incantation)
12. Àlàbí ọmọ Ọlópọndà   (*oríkì*)
13. Ọmọ Onísẹyìn ọmọ Ẹbẹdí   (*orílè̩*)
14. Ọmọ Ẹbẹdí mọkọ   (*orílè̩*)
15. Ìlú Ẹyọ kìkì è̩gàn   (*orílè̩*)
16. Ibi ojú ńbú ni tó ju ẹnu lọ   (*orílè̩*)
17. Bèèrè o tó wò ọ́   (*orílè̩*)
18. A kì í gbọ́lkú (sic) ọmọ gúnnugún   (incantation)
19. A kì í gbọ́ rírùn ọmọ àkàlàmàgbò   (incantation)
20. A kìígbó (sic) àrùn ọmọ ológbò   (incantation)
21. Tóó, o ó ó lọ, o ó bọ̀ ni o   (incantation, prayerful request)

Translatology, ethnolinguistics and the problems of translation

This chapter supports a scientific, multi-disciplinary treatment of translation and takes a broadly ethnolinguistic approach to the translation of Yorùbá verbal art. Ethnolinguistics is here understood as synonymous with 'anthropological linguistics' and 'linguistic anthropology' (Senft, 2007: 80). The following is a useful definition for our purposes:

> [ethnolinguistics] is the study of language as a cultural resource and cultural practice . . . with the general goal of providing an understanding of the multifarious aspects of language as a set of cultural practices, that is, as a system of communication that allows for interpsychological (between individuals) and intrapsychological (in the same individual) representations of the social order and helps people use such representations for constitutive social acts. (Duranti in Senft, 2007: 80)

Decisions on how to translate are often made based on what the translator considers to be relevant to the target audience, leading Ernst-August Gutt to assert that the relevance theory of communication is adequate for explaining all translation matters, so that there is no need for a separate translation theory. In relation to issues of equivalence, fidelity or faithfulness, Gutt (2000: 123) states that ' . . . the different ways in which people have translated at different times in history can be attributed to differences in what the translator believed to be relevant to his contemporary audience'. However, as Kwame Appiah has argued, in certain contexts and certain specific types of literature, relevance becomes irrelevant. He cites examples of Akan proverbs to show that mutual recognition of the use of such proverbs 'cancels literal intentions' and that, like metaphors, proverbs do not mean only what they say (Appiah, 1993: 422).

A further trend in the discussion of the role of translation and translators in globalized societies and economies is the position recently championed by Venuti (1992, 1995) in his discussions of 'foreignization' and 'domestication' in translation, and the 'visibility' versus the 'invisibility' of the translator. Central to this discussion are issues of hegemony and dominance vis-à-vis language and cultural identity as observed in translation particularly in the advanced capitalist societies (see also Robinson, 1997, and references to Schleiermacher, 1813, and Benjamin, 1923 cited in Rollason, 2006).

Foreignization is a method of translation which aims to retain traces of the translated text, whereas domestication moves a text closer to target cultural and linguistic values. Venuti (1995) highlights the fact that translators become invisible when they render a text in a fluent, natural and elegant style (as in domestication) such that the receptor audience cannot tell whether they are reading a translation or an original work, whereas foreignization makes the translator much more visible. Venuti is in favour of foreignization and visibility in certain contexts, advocating a policy of resistance, which:

> assumes an ideology of autonomy, locating the alien in a cultural other, pursuing cultural diversity, foregrounding the linguistic and cultural differences of the source-language text and transforming the hierarchy of cultural values in the target language. (Venuti, 1995: 308)

Although the validity of Venuti's position concerning political domination, economic exploitation, acculturation and language endangerment may not be in contest, Venuti's approach has not gone uncriticized. For example, Christopher Rollason (2006: 4) questions the need for any such polarity in an increasingly global society, and Rita Oittinen (2001) points out that Venuti's dichotomies do not adequately cater for different categories of readers and why they read. Rollason (2006: 4) quotes the Italian translation scholar Dora

Sales Salvador (2004) who suggests that 'in the contradictory yet complementary dialectic between exoticizing (foreignizing) and familiarizing (domesticating), the ideal solution would be to find a medium term, an in-between space, respecting otherness but able to transmit and communicate to the target culture'. Rollason then adds that:

> [i]nevitably and whatever ideological position assumed, there will be a continuum; inevitably, any translation in practice will combine one and the other strategy in the interests of intelligibility and, indeed, of selling the book and finding and keeping readers. At the same time, though, a given translator will certainly prefer to use one method more frequently than the other. . . . (ibid.)

In essence, the translation of the source text discussed in this chapter will unavoidably contain, in varying degrees, instances of foreignization and domestication, visibility and invisibility. The 'literal', 'semantic' and 'communicative' translation techniques drawn from Peter Newmark which are adopted here in fact to some extent reflect Venuti's dichotomies of 'fluency' versus 'resistancy'. However, the paramount concern is how to achieve effective communication or intelligibility (with and by the target audience), and fidelity to the original text and author, as far as practicable, given that English and the Yorùbá languages and their cultures are typologically and genetically unrelated.

The academic exercise in translation described in this chapter is mainly concerned with demonstrating that cultural gaps between SL and TL may create particular translation difficulties, and impede effective communication between the translator and the target audience. Consequently, there is a need to suggest measures for surmounting the problems, or at least to minimize the loss of meaning. Within the context of linguistic/cultural universalism and relativism, Nida's (1975a) ethnolinguistic approach is suitable for discussing linguistic and cultural problems in translation (Surakat, 1987; Sa'Adeddin, 1990). In his 'Linguistics and Ethnology in Translation Problems' Nida treats translation problems as cultural, subsuming language under culture. He considers that translation problems may be 'conveniently treated under: i) ecology, ii) material culture, iii) social culture, iv) religious culture, and v) linguistic culture' (Nida, 1975a: 68).

Ecological factors (climate, vegetation, flora and fauna, topographical and physical relief features) influence the thinking or behaviour of the inhabitants of a given geographical zone, and are also reflected in the language of the region. For example, Yorùbá does not have satisfactory 'equivalents' for different types of snow or even for the four seasons of the temperate regions, or for plants and animals that are restricted to that climatic zone. Aspects of material culture (especially in scientific or technical texts) can also pose translation problems between African and European languages due mainly to gaps in scientific and technological advancement. Most African languages, for instance, do not have indigenous lexical items for 'ship', 'airplane/jet', 'grenade' or 'bomb' and therefore make use of paraphrase, amplification and circumlocution. However, material culture is more dynamic than non-material, which explains why 'borrowing' and calque or loan translation often occur (Surakat, 1985, 1987; Fawcett, 1997).

Cultural untranslatability involving traditional practices, social organizations, and systems of social control arise chiefly in the areas of kinship terms, marriage systems, and social classes (e.g. Chieftaincy, Age-grades, etc.). Religion falls under non-material culture; and according to Nida (1975a) features of religious culture pose the most perplexing translation problems. The translator has to contend with both concrete and abstract phenomena – deities, objects of worship, incantations, mystical beliefs, and so on (Surakat, 1987). However:

> the phase of culture in which the greatest number of translation problems arise is the linguistic one (because) translation from one language to another involves, in addition to the other cultural problems, the special characteristics of the respective languages. (Nida, 1975a: 74)

The various translation problems under 'linguistic culture' are treated under phonological, graphological, syntactic, morphological, lexico-semantic and stylistic features (see also Nida and Taber, 1974: 106–119; Surakat, 1987: 33ff). Catford (1965) and Bassnett (1980) also provide examples to illustrate linguistic and cultural problems in translation. Cultural untranslatability occurs, in the words of Catford (1965: 99): '. . . when a situational feature functionally relevant for the SL text is completely absent from the culture of which the TL is a part'. For example, translating the simple French expression *Bon appetit* into English poses a cultural problem, not because approximate, or even exact, words for the French expression are not available, but because the convention surrounding *Bon appetit* is not found in English: 'Exact translation is impossible: 'Good appetite' in English used outside a structured sentence is meaningless. Nor is there any English phrase in general use that fulfils the same function as the French . . . '(Bassnett 1980: 22). In a situation where an SL cultural item has no TL equivalent 'the solution adopted by most translators would be to transfer the SL item. . . into the TL text, leaving its contextual meaning to emerge from the co-text, or else explaining it in a footnote' (Catford, 1965: 100).

Appiah's concept of 'thick translation' is particularly applicable in the translation analysed here. Appiah refers to a particular type of literary translation as an 'academic translation'. In this context he proposes a 'translation that seeks with its annotations and its accompanying glosses to locate the text in a rich cultural and linguistic context' (2000: 427). He links such translation to the teaching of literary translation and introducing American students to Akan proverbs in order to show their complexity and to 'invite them . . . to a deeper respect for the people of pre-industrial societies' (428).

In the context of the Owólabí text discussed here, a working definition of interlingual translation is adopted, conforming to Eugene Nida and Charles Taber's (1974: 12): assertion that 'translating consists in reproducing in the receptor language the closest natural equivalent of the source language message; first in terms of meaning, and secondly in terms of style' (see also Nida, 1975b: 33ff; Catford, 1965: 1 and 20; Newmark, 1981: 7). This definition allows for the fact that absolute equivalence or correspondence between source language (SL) and target language (TL) texts is not always achievable. It also accommodates 'loss of meaning', 'compensation' or 'negotiation' even though it emphasizes 'dynamic equivalence': translating such that the TL version yields a similar effect on its target audience as the original did on the source language audience (cf. Venuti, 1992, 1995).

In terms of translation techniques, Newmark's (1981) framework is applied. However, the principle of textual equivalence (semantic or communicative translation) is preferred to that of formal correspondence (interlinear or literal translation) because the latter approach is insensitive to contexts of utterance and culture. According to Newmark (1981: 63), the interlinear technique is a process in which:

> [t]he primary senses of all words in the original are translated as though out of context, and the word-order of the original is retained. The main purpose is either to understand the mechanics of the source language or to constitute a pre-translation procedure for a complicated SL text.

This is what Dryden refers to as 'metaphrase' (Steiner, 1975: 254). In contrast, in the literal technique, ' . . . the primary senses of the lexical words of the original are translated as though out of context but the syntactic structures of the TL are respected' (Newmark, 1981: 63; cf. also Appiah, 1993). Newmark's distinction between semantic and communicative translation is well known, with the former focusing on the 'contextual meaning of the original' (Newmark, 1981: 63) and the latter on producing 'an effect as close as possible to that obtained on the readers of the original' (ibid.: 39). Semantic and communicative translation may be applied within the same text because there is an area of overlap. Both fall within the realm of 'free' translation, what Dryden calls *paraphrase* or 'sense for sense' translation although the semantic approach is considered more objective than communicative translation (see also Venuti, 1992 and 1995). In communicative translation, according to Newmark (1981: 42) '. . . one has the right to correct or improve the logic (of the SL text); to replace clumsy with elegant, or at least, functional syntactic structures; to remove obscurities; to eliminate repetition and tautology . . . '. A mild version of Dryden's *imitatio* is implied by communicative translation since it allows for license on the part of the translator to reinterpret, twist or adapt the original (SL) text to suit the receptor audience. However, a deliberate distortion or an extreme 'ideological revaluation' (Fawcett, 1997: 132) of the SL text by the translator may lead to what Surakat (1987: 27) refers to as 'propagandist translation'. This approach is avoided here. (cf. also Steiner 1975: 254–255; Kelly, 1979: 42; Bassnett 1980: 60). In the following section, each SL line is translated either word-for-word or literally as TL, and then followed by free versions (semantic and communicative) as TLa) and TLb).

Data presentation, analysis and discussion

SL1.	Àlàbí Ògún, ọmọ Ọlọ́pọndà
TL1,	(proper nouns) child (proper noun)
TL1a)	Àlàbí Ògún, the son of Ọlọ́pọndà
TL1b)	Àlàbí Ògún, offspring of Ọlọ́pọndà

SL2.	Ọmọ Ọlọ́pọndà Baba eégún
TL2.	child (proper noun) father masquerade
TL2a)	The son of Ọlọ́pọndà who is the father of the masquerade
TL2b)	Offspring of Ọlọ́pọndà father of the masquerade

SL3.	Àlọbó lọwọ́ ńlọ sénu
TL3.	to-go-come is hand going to mouth (when eating)
TL3a)	To and fro the hand goes to the mouth
TL3b)	Safely does the hand ply the mouth

SL4.	Àgègé kì í gòkè ọpẹ kó má sò
TL4.	(tool) does not go-up palm not to descend
TL4a)	Àgègé doesn't climb the palm without returning
TL4b)	If àgègé climbs the palm-tree, it must descend
SL5.	Àfèrèmòjò kì í bá wọn kú ikú àjọkú
TL5.	(animal) does not join them die death collective/togetherness
TL5a)	Àfèrèmòjò does not die a collective death
TL5b)	Àfèrèmòjò doesn't suffer a mass-death
SL6.	Gologínní ni adìẹ ṅ bọ̀ oko èèmọ́
TL6.	(ideophone) is fowl coming farm burr
TL6a)	The fowl goes through the burr farm unharmed
TL6b)	Neatly does the fowl pass through the burr
SL7.	Dandan ni kí o bọ̀ wá bá mi
TL7.	Compulsory is that you come back meet me
TL7a)	It's compulsory that you return to meet me
TL7b)	Surely you'll come back to me, safely
SL8.	Àsínlà ni ti àgbọ̀nrín
TL8.	to-sneeze-survive is for antelope
TL8a)	The survival sneeze is for the antelope
TL8b)	A sneeze of survival is that of the antelope
SL9.	Ọjọ́ àgbọ̀nrín bá sín lojọ ikú rẹ̀ yẹ
TL9	day antelope do sneeze is day death it miss
TL9a)	If the antelope sneezes, it escapes death
TL9b)	The day the antelope sneezes, it escapes death
SL10.	Bí a bá dáná igún
TL10.	if we make fire (for) vulture
TL10a)	When fire is made to burn a vulture
TL10b)	If fire is prepared to roast the vulture
SL11.	Ẹyẹ mîî là á fi sun
TL11.	bird another will we roast
TL11a)	Another bird will be burnt
TL11b)	It's another bird that falls victim
SL12.	Àlàbí ọmọ Ọlọ́pọndà
TL12.	(name) child (lineage)
TL12a)	Àlàbí the descendant of Ọlọ́pọndà
TL12b)	Àlàbí offspring of Ọlọ́pọndà

SL13.	Ọmọ Onísẹyìn ọmọ Ẹbẹdí
TL13.	child owner-(town) child (clan)
TL13a)	Descendant of the founder of Ìsẹ̀yìn offspring of Ẹbẹdí
TL13b)	Offspring of the Owner of Ìsẹ́yìn, offspring of Ẹbẹdí

SL14.	Ọmọ Ẹbẹdí mọkọ
TL14.	child (clan) know-husband
TL14a)	Descendant of Ẹbẹdí knows the true husband
TL14b)	Offspring of Ẹbẹdí who knows the real husband

SL15.	Ìlú Ẹyọ kìkì ẹ̀gàn
TL15.	town (clan) only contempt
TL15a)	The contemptuous town of Ẹyọ
TL15b)	A town of Ẹyọ which is riddled with contempt

SL16.	Ibi ojú ńbú ni tó ju ẹnu lọ
TL16.	where eye abuse one than mouth more
TL16a)	A place where facial expression curses more than words of mouth
TL16b)	A place where gaze speaks louder than voice

SL17.	Bèèrè o tó wọ̀ ọ́
TL17.	ask you before enter it
TL17a)	Ask before you enter it
TL17b)	Seek permission before you dare enter

SL18.	A kì í gbọ́ ikú ọmọ gúnnugún
TL18.	we do not hear death child vulture
TL18a)	We do not hear the death of the baby vulture
TL18b)	No one hears the death of the vulture-chick

SL19.	A kì í gbọ́ rírùn ọmọ àkàlàmàgbò
TL19.	we don't hear smelling child hornbill
TL19a)	We don't perceive the smell of the young hornbill
TL19b)	No one smells the stink of the hornbill-fledgling

SL20.	A kì í gbọ́ àrùn ọmọ ológbò
TL20.	we don't hear ailment child cat
TL20a)	We don't hear about the ailment of the baby-cat
TL20b)	No one hears the sickness of the kitten

SL21.	Tóó, o ó lọ, o ó bọ̀ ni o
TL21.	(ideophone) you will go, you will come (emphatic particle)
TL21a)	Surely, you'll go and come back
TL21b)	Indeed! You'll go and must return

At the macro (discourse and/or cultural) level, one major problem is that the Yorùbá *oríkì* or *orílè* is a genre which does not, as mentioned above, have an equivalent in classical or modern European poetry. The ode, epic or Homeric epithets are remote approximates of, but not identical to, *oríkì*. This clearly represents a gap between the western European and African cultures. Moreover, the literary semiotics of the modern European novel does not normally accommodate the use of panegyrics (such as *oríkì/orílè*), whereas African or Yorùbá literary works contain numerous forms of the genre.[2] In terms of 'dynamic equivalence', therefore, the English translation is more likely to appeal to an African than a western European reader. However, the content or meaning of the original should be discernible to both categories of the target audience.

There are also sociocultural difficulties in the translation of *oríkì* into English mainly because of allusions to legends and historical events unfamiliar to the average European. For instance, proper names such as Àlàbí, Ògún, Olópondà, Oníseyìn, Èbèdí, and Èyo have social relevance within the context of the poem, the significance of which is not contained in the TL version because there are no ready English equivalents. This means that the non-Yorùbá reader may not understand the cultural relevance of the panegyric. Again, this has implications for dynamic equivalence. If 'Yaqub' can be rendered as 'Jacob', 'Yusuf' as 'Joseph', 'Musa' as 'Moses', or 'Isah' as 'Jesus', it is because of certain similarities in the 'revealed religions'. But the traditional Yorùbá names in the SL text have a sociohistorical relevance which makes them culture-specific. *Àlàbí* (SL1 and 12), for instance, is a typical Yorùbá pet name or epithet for a male child who comes after two or more girls (Surakat,1987: 188). Literally, it means 'one who forms a division between births' (Abraham, 1962: 481). *Ògún* is a name associated with the clan or lineage of worshippers of the Yorùbá 'god of war and iron'. Hunters, soldiers or warriors, blacksmiths and others who use iron implements worship *Ògún* (ibid.: 456). Olópondà, Èbèdí, Oníseyìn, and Eyo are legends which can be meaningfully interpreted or deciphered only by those who understand the genealogy of Ìséyìn, a Yorùbá town in the present day Òyó State of South Western Nigeria, with a long history dating as far back as the Old Òyó Empire of the sixteenth century.

The first option for the translator is borrowing or 'loan translation' which implies transferring the SL items into the TL text. But this approach fails to convey the social and historical significance of the names. In order to compensate for the cultural gap, glossaries may be provided to explain the names, one of the strategies suggested by Appiah (2000: 427). But as Beier (1970: 17) observes, in ' . . . translating poetry from a very different culture, the problem often is that we have to suffocate the actual (TL) text in an entanglement of notes'. Although such notes provide additional information (through 'compensatory amplification' – see Malone, 1988; Fawcett 1997: 45ff) which enhances comprehension, they tend to divert the attention of readers, thus making the reading dull and cumbersome. If this is so, notes should be reduced to the barest minimum (at least to give relevant cultural information) (see also Catford, 1965: 100; Surakat, 1987). Borrowing or loan translation is consonant with exoticization or foreignization (Venuti, 1992, 1995) while annotations or glossaries for borrowed items are in consonance with Appiah's (1993) concept of 'thick' translation.

The insertion of magical spells or incantations in novels is not a common feature in modern English novels, and may not therefore be understood fully by English-speaking readers. Although magic is a universal human phenomenon which has been practised at one time or the other in different parts of the world, it does not seem to be a very common feature of modern English novel.[3] In the West, the significance of magical art – and its verbal accompaniment, incantations – seems to have diminished in the light of science and technology, and has largely been relegated to the world of fantasy. Although science regards magic as superstitious, not all phenomena can be scientifically explained or observed. However, the effectiveness or relevance of incantations in the context of scientific warfare may not be readily accepted or appreciated by the European because it would seem that no magic could suppress the lethal and devastating effects of atomic or nuclear bombs, or even machine guns. This is another instance of culture gap between traditional Africa and modern Europe which also entails a difference in the literary conventions of the two worlds. This point has implications for the principle of dynamic equivalence.

Furthermore, the content of incantations may be unintelligible to the reader (African or non-African) who is not familiar with the mystical or metaphysical essence of the genre. In other words, a proper grasp of the Yorùbá religious culture is important for the correct interpretation of ògèdè or ofò. For instance, all the incantatory lines are assertions or invocations, except SL7 and 21, which are prayerful requests or appeals. The underlying belief is that the assertions are so potent as to invoke supernatural forces that can protect Àlàbí during the war; and that the prayerful requests or supplications will be answered. The question then is: how does the reader who is unfamiliar with the Yorùbá world view make meaning out of the translation?[4] SL3 implies that Àlàbí will go to war and return home safely just as the hand goes from food to mouth, unhindered in the process of eating. It is a wish or prayer for safety. Alternative translations for SL 3 are: TL3a) To and fro the hand goes to the mouth; and 3b) Safely does the hand ply the mouth; or even 3c) The hand plies the mouth (and food) safely. Each option requires some modulation and compensatory amplification for the reader to make sense of the translation. Even if the ideational meaning is conveyed, there is still the problem of finding a stylistically or textually appropriate structure for the ritual language of the original (for details, see Surakat, 1987: 142ff.).

SL4 poses a problem related to the cultural untranslatability of *àgègé* which lacks an equivalent expression in English. *Àgègé* is a small, axe-shaped tool for plucking or chopping kernel from the palm tree (an item of material culture). As a result, the translator may have to resort to Catford's (1965) 'partial translation' in which case the SL item is transferred into the TL text with an annotation to explain the contextual meaning and significance of the tool. The other option is to use a paraphrase or amplification so that the meaning emerges from the context, as in, for example: TL4c) 'If the axe ascends the palm tree to pluck fruits, it will eventually descend'. Although there is an attempt to make the meaning of *àgègé* emerge from the context, the resulting text is not as succinct as the original. Moreover, SL4 contains a negative proposition, but the paraphrase TL4c) is a conditional proposition.

References to animals which have culture-specific connotations can also pose problems. *Àfèrèmòjò* (SL5) does not have an English equivalent. This is an ecological gap which can be filled through partial translation/annotation or compensatory amplification, but this does not resolve the problem of interpreting the cultural allusion and significance. *Àfèrèmòjò* is a fierce, dreadful beast similar to the bear in physical appearance, known for its ability to dig holes for refuge. It is amphibious, a good diver and a fast runner. Like the lion or elephant, *àfèrèmòjò* is not a common game or animal which the hunter can kill in large numbers. The exorcising sentence (SL5) therefore implies that Àlàbí shall not become a victim of war just as *àfèrèmòjò* is not easy prey for the hunter. Another option is the use of cultural translation or adaptation such as: TL5c) 'The lion does not suffer a collective death'. Although interpersonal and textual meanings of the original are reflected, there is a 'topical shift' in ideational meaning from *àfèrèmòjò* to lion (Surakat, 1987: 144–145), and, indeed, represents a clear example of domestication.

SL6 implies that Àlàbí shall survive the impending war, the way the fowl (adìę) escapes the danger posed by *burr* or *bur-reed* (*èèmọ́*). The burr is a prickly or spiny plant which can cling to or harm animals that pass through it. The belief is that the fowl will always pass through the burr unharmed perhaps because it can fly. SL6 can be rendered as TL6a: 'The fowl passes through a farm of burr unharmed' an alternative which has an 'unmarked theme' as opposed to the original which has a marked Manner-Adjunct theme (*gologínní*). This means that if the translator is able to give the ideational or cultural meaning, something may still be lacking, as in the case of SL6, where the difference between TL6a) and 6b) is a matter of texture or thematization.

The antelope (*àgbọ̀nrín*, SL8 and 9) is also believed to have some supernatural powers. The same belief extends to other animals such as the vulture (*igún* or *gúnnungún*, SL10 and 18), hornbill (*àkàlàmàgbò*, SL19), and cat (*ológbò*, SL 20). For instance, the traditional Yorùbá belief is that when a hunter encounters an antelope during a hunt, he must chant certain incantations before shooting; otherwise the animal will disappear miraculously. Even for the hunter who knows the necessary spells, if the antelope sneezes or bays while the incantation is being chanted, the animal may escape. In other words, the baying of an antelope portends safety. This is the significance of SL8 and 9 as incantations to protect Àlàbí against accidents in war.

Another belief is that the vulture, hornbill and cat (SL18, 19, and 20 respectively) do not die young. Therefore medicinal preparations (as well as the accompanying incantations) for longevity must include at least one of these birds in order to be effective. SL18–20, therefore, imply that Àlàbí will grow old before he dies, which means that he will survive the war and return home to his people. All these traditional beliefs may not make sense to a reader who is not familiar with the Yorùbá cosmology or religious culture. Even the translator may have to consult initiated members of 'the cult of elders', traditional healers or herbalists to be able to interpret meaningfully the incantatory lines. The translator may have to provide annotation for some lines of incantation, thereby sacrificing dynamic equivalence and transparency. This implies some form of exoticization or foreignization (see also Appiah, 1993 and Venuti, 1995).

At the micro level, there are a number of lexico-semantic problems. The Yorùbá word '*ọmọ*' is repeated nine times (see SL1, 2, 12–14, and 18–20). *Ọmọ* is a polyseme which has a wider semantic range than its closest TL equivalent 'child' as discussed below.

Both items can refer to the newly-born or young, old/adult, male or female human beings such as 'baby', 'son' and 'daughter'. But in addition, *ọmọ* applies to non-human, and non-living things as in: *ọmọ ajá* which literally translates

	OMO	CHILD
Age:	young/old	young/old
Gender:	masculine/feminine/neuter	masculine/feminine
Human:	human/non-human	human
Generation:	one or more generation	only one generation

Figure 1. Componential analysis showing the semantic features of ọmọ and 'child'.

as 'child or baby of dog' (i.e. puppy), omo odó that is 'child or baby of mortar' (pestle), and so on. Moreover, child normally applies where there is only one generation gap between the parent and the baby. In its connotative sense, ọmọ covers more than one generation as reflected in the following English words – grandchild, great-grandchild, progeny, offspring, and descendant. The possible English equivalents for ọmọ include: baby, child, son, boy, daughter, offspring, girl, progeny, and descendant. In the context of the oríkì/orílẹ̀ for Àlàbí (adult, male) the options must exclude baby, boy, girl or daughter, and since the reference to Àlàbí is not in connection with his immediate biological parents, either son or child would be a 'false approximate'. In the poem, he is linked to his ancestors, the legendary fathers or founders of Ìséyìn, and the most appropriate TL equivalents for ọmọ will be 'offspring', 'descendant' or 'progeny'. Essentially, the context, co-text or collocation should enable a competent translator to disambiguate ọmọ.

Ìlú is another polysemous word which can only be meaningfully interpreted within context, co-text or collocation. In isolation, ìlú can mean 'town', 'city', 'province', 'clan', 'nation', 'country', 'kingdom', 'council of state' or 'council of elders' (see also Abraham, 1981). In the SL text, ìlú occurs in several contexts including: 'Ìlú Arómirẹ́' (p. 1), 'Ìlú Eyọ' (p. 3), 'Ìlú-Ọba' (p. 4), and so on, although only the second falls within the text for analysis. In 'ìlú Arómirẹ́', 'city' is selected based on the fact that Aromire is the author's pseudo name for Lagos, the commercial nerve centre of Nigeria. In the context of the praise poem, it is more appropriate to choose 'town' rather than 'city' as the TL equivalent for ìlú, since it collocates with Eyọ which is an epithet for Ìséyìn, an ancient Yorùbá town. Ìlú-Ọba literally means 'the land of the king/queen' but it is used by the Yorùbá people to refer to England – where the Queen reigns. In this case, ìlú refers to a country (Surakat, 1987: 206).

The Yorùbá verb gbọ́ also has more than one English equivalent but collocational context can be relied upon for the appropriate word. It can mean 'to hear or listen', 'to smell or perceive', and so on. In the context of the incantations, *gbọ́* in SL18 and 20 collocates with 'news about something' which involves the sense of hearing. As a result, 'hear' is the appropriate word. But in line 19, *gbọ́* collocates with 'odour' involving the sense of smell. That makes either 'smell' or 'perceive' more appropriate in this context, but the translator can still rely on linguistics/stylistics to decide the more appropriate of the two words. *Ojú* is another Yorùbá word which (in isolation) can be rendered as 'eye', 'face', or 'surface'. For SL16, either 'eye' or 'face' are possible equivalents; although there is a hyponymic relation between the two words. However, since the idea of facial expression (or gesture) is implied in the figurative use of *ojú*, either 'face' or 'gaze' may be appropriate.

Conclusion

Of the two sub-genres of Yorùbá verbal art treated in this paper, it would appear that praise poems are 'easier' to translate than incantations. There are linguistic problems involved in rendering the Yorùbá oral art forms in literary English, but there are also cultural gaps between Yorùbá and English which compound the problems, particularly in achieving dynamic equivalence. Whereas issues of 'social culture' (legend, epithet, etc.) dominate praise poems, incantations carry with them certain aspects of Yorùbá 'religious culture' which are not readily intelligible or accessible to the English audience, or even the uninitiated, uninformed African audience. In other words, apart from the practical or pragmatic use of language in both *oríkì* and *ògèdè*, the latter carry ritual or magical functions which are more difficult to translate into English while retaining their cultural or religious significance. In translating complex texts, aesthetic or textual functions may have to be sacrificed in order to retain ideational meaning.

Intercultural communication cannot always be perfect. This is the case with translating aspects of Yorùbá orature into a predominantly written, rather than oral, culture.[5] The best a competent translator can do is to strive for minimal loss of meaning (cf. Makkai, 2003). Whether from the perspective of communication theory, linguistics or cultural studies, a translator could justify his approach to a particular translation. Critics as well as readers might acknowledge certain factors when assessing translations. These include: i) the purpose of translating (e.g. for economic motives, or as a purely academic, theoretical exercise); ii) the ideological orientation or philosophical background of the translator (e.g. a linguist, communication theorist, philosopher, cultural studies scholar, etc.); iii) the intended audience (a general or lay readership, or a specialized audience, etc.); iv) the genre type (literary, religious or scriptural, scientific/technical, legal texts, etc.); and, v) the nature or degree of complexity of the SL text (e.g. simple, complex, etc.).

It is necessary for scholars, researchers and practitioners to continue the search for ways of surmounting the numerous problems involved in translation. They should harness the resources from the various disciplines to methodically address the complex webs in which translation studies has been entangled. Some of the ideas that are currently being paraded as antagonistic approaches may, with time, become harmonized. Even then, disputation or argumentation is not peculiar to translation discourse alone. It is found virtually in all the social sciences and is a necessary impetus for further developments in scholarship. In spite of the numerous methodological and practical challenges in translation studies; despite the fear of economic, cultural, and linguistic imperialism in the translation business; and in spite of the problem associated with having a coherent universally acceptable theory of translation, the inevitability of translation as a major weapon for promoting cross-cultural discourse remains indisputable.

Notes

1. For a detailed discussion of the Yoruba royal bards, see Akinyemi 2001.
2. For a comparison of oral poetics in Southern and West Africa, and particularly a comparison of the West African *griot* and the Southern African *imbongi* see Kaschula (1999).
3. An obvious modern example is the Harry Potter series, replete with numerous magic spells and incantations, but they are not generally part of everyday reality.
4. There are numerous books about Yoruba beliefs and customs. See, for example, *Yoruba Culture: a Philosophical Account* by Kola Abimbola (2005).
5. Similar issues, albeit in a different context, are discussed by Basil Hatim with reference to Arabic and 'orate languages' (Hatim, 2007).

References

Abimbola, Kola. (2005), *Yorùbá Culture: a Philosophical Account*. Birmingham: Ìrókò Academic Publishers.

Abraham, R. C. (1981 [1962]), *Dictionary of Modern Yorùbá*. Seventh impression. London: Hodder and Stoughton.

Achebe, Chinua. (1963 [1958]), *Things Fall Apart*. London: Heinemann

— (1964), *Arrow of God*. London: Heinemann.

Akinyemi, Akintunde. (2001), 'The Yorùbá Royal Bards: their work and relevance in society', *Nordic Journal of African Studies*, 10, (1), 90–106.

Alkali, Zainab. (1984), *The Stillborn*. Ikeja. Nigeria: Longman.

— (1997), *Cobwebs and Other Stories*. Lagos: Malthouse Press.

Appiah, K. A. (2000 [1993]), 'Thick Translation' in *The Translation Studies Reader*, L.Venuti (ed.), London and New York: Routledge, pp.417–429.

Baker, Mona. (ed.) (1998), *Routledge Encyclopedia of Translation Studies*. London: Routledge.

Bámgbósé, Ayò (1974), *The Novels of D. O. Fágúnwa*. Benin-city, Nigeria: Ethiope.

Bassnett, Susan. (1980), *Translation Studies*. London: Methuen.

Beier, U. (1970), *Yorùbá Poetry: An Anthology of Traditional Poems*. Cambridge: CUP.

Catford, J. C. (1965), *A Linguistic Theory of Translation*. London: OUP.

Fagunwa, D. O. (1982 [1968]), *The Forest of a Thousand Daemons – A Hunter's Saga*, trans. Wole Soyinka. London: Nelson.

Fawcett, Peter. (1997), *Translation and Language: Linguistic Theories Explained*. Manchester: St. Jerome Publishing.

Finnegan, Ruth. (1977), *Oral Literature in Africa*. London: OUP.

Gutt, E. (2000 [1991]), *Translation and Relevance: Cognition and Context*. Manchester: St. Jerome Publishing.

Hatim, B. (2007) 'Intervention at text and discourse levels in the translation of 'orate' languages', in J. Munday (ed.) *Translation as Intervention*. London: Continuum.

Innes, G. (2003 [1990]), 'Formulae in Mandinka Epic: the problem of translation', in Okpewho I. (ed.) *The Oral Performance in Africa*. Ibadan: Spectrum, pp. 101–110.

Kaschula, R. H. (1999), 'Imbongi and griot: towards a comparative analysis of oral poetics in Southern and West Africa', *Journal of African Cultural Studies*, 12, (1), 55–76.

Kelly, Louis G. (1979), *The True Interpreter. A History of Translation Theory and Practice in the West*. Oxford: Blackwell.

Lindfors B. and Owomoyela O. (1973), *Yorùbá Proverbs! Translation and Annotation*. Ohio: Ohio University Center for International Studies.

Malone, Joseph L. (1988), *The Science of Linguistics in the Art of Translation: Some Tools from Linguistics for the Analysis and Practice of Translation*. Albany: State University of New York Press.

Makkai, A. (2003), 'The mystery of translation', in D. W. Coleman, W. J. Sullivan, and A. R. Lommel (eds), *LACUS FORUM XXIX – Linguistics and the Real World*. Houston, TX: Linguistic Association of Canada and the United States, pp. 5–21.

Matthiessen, C. M. I. M. (2001), 'The Environments of Translation' in E. Steiner & C. Yallop (eds), pp. 41–126.

Newmark, Peter. (1981), *Approaches to Translation*. Oxford: Pergamon.

Nida, E. A. (1975a), 'Linguistics and Ethnology in Translation Problems' in *Exploring Semantic Structures*. München: Wilhelm Fink Verlag.

— (1975b), *Language Structure and Translation: Essays by Eugene Nida*, introduced and selected by S. D. Anwar. Stanford, CA: Stanford University Press.

Nida and Taber, C. R. (1974), *The Theory and Practice of Translation*. Leiden: E. J. Brill.

Ògúnbòwálé, P. O. (1981 [1970]), *The Essentials of the Yorùbá Language*. Sixth impression. London: Hodder and Stoughton.

Oittinen, R. (2001), *Translating for Children*. New York: Garland.

Okpewho, I. (ed.), (1990), '*Towards a faithful record: On transcribing and translating the oral narrative performance*', in *The Oral Performance in Africa*. Ibadan: Spectrum, pp. 111–135.

— (2003 [1990]), *The Oral Performance in Africa*. Ibadan: Spectrum.

Olatunji, O. (1984), *Features of Yorùbá Oral Poetry*. Ibadan: University Press Ltd.

Onwurmene, M. C. (1981), 'Transliteration in Nigerian literature: The imaginary beauty of a nonentity', *Nigeria*, 137, 74–79.

Owólabí, O. (1980), *Eni Olorun O Pa*. Ibadan: Evans Brothers.

Robinson, Douglas. (1997), *Translation and Empire*. Manchester, UK: St Jerome

Rollason, Christopher. (2006), 'Beyond the Domestic and the Foreign: Translation as . . . Dialogue'. Available at: www.seikilos.com.ar/TranslationDialogue.pdf (accessed 31 May 2008).

Sa'Adeddin, Mohammed A. A. M. (1990), 'Towards a viable applied linguistic theory of translation: an ethnolinguistic point of view', *Bradford Occasional Papers*, 10, 14–45.

Senft, Gunter. (2007), 'Bronislaw Malinowski and linguistic pragmatics', *Lodz Papers in Pragmatics*, 3, 79–96.

Sheba, Laide. (2006), *Yorùbá Proverbs with Feminine Lexis*. Ibadan: Spectrum Books.

Soyinka, Wole. (1963), *The Lion and the Jewel*. Oxford: OUP.

— (1965), *The Interpreters*. London: Heinemann.

Steiner, Erich. (2001), 'Intralingual and Interlingual Versions of a Text: How Specific is the Notion of Translation', in E. Steiner & C. Yallop (eds), *Exploring Translation and Multilingual Text Production: Beyond Content*. Berlin: Walter de Gruyter, pp. 161–190.

— (2004), *Translated Texts: Properties, Variants, Evaluations*. Frankfurt: Peter Lang Verlag.

— (2005), 'Halliday and Translation Theory – Enhancing the Options, Broadening the Range and Keeping the Ground', in R. Hasan, C. Matthiessen and J. Webster (eds) *Continuing Discourse on Language – A Functional Perspective*. London: Equinox, pp. 481–500.

Steiner, George. (1992 [1975]), *After Babel: Aspects of Language and Translation*. (2nd edn). London: Oxford University Press.

Steiner, E. and Yallop, C. (2001), *Exploring Translation and Multilingual Text Production: Beyond Content*. Berlin: Walter de Gruyter.

Surakat, T. Y. (1985), 'Understanding translation problems: An ethnolinguistic perspective'. Paper presented at the 4th Annual Conference of the Nigeria Association of Translators and Interpreters held at the University of Benin, Benin-City, Nigeria (April 1985).

— (1987), 'Problems and prospects of translating aspects of Yorùbá orature into English: Olú Owólabí's *Eni Olórun Ò Pa* as case study', an unpublished M. A. dissertation, Ahmadu Bello University (A. B. U.), Zaria – Nigeria.

— (1988), 'Some comments on translation in relation to nation-building in Nigeria', in *Work-in-Progress – A Journal of the English Department, A. B. U. Zaria*, 6, 107–113.

— (1990), 'A translation of three Yorùbá poems into English', *Saiwa - A Journal of Communication*, 6, 23–24.

— (2007), 'Translating Yorùbá proverbs into English: A meta-functional perspective'. Paper presented at the 21st Annual Conference of the Linguistic Association of Nigeria, held at the University of Uyo, Uyo - Nigeria (November 19–23).

Tutuola, Amos. (1952), *The Palm-wine Drinkard*. London: Faber & Faber.

Venuti, Lawrence. (ed.) (1992), *Rethinking Translation: Discourse, Subjectivity, Ideology*. London: Routledge.

— (1995), *The Translator's Invisibility: A History of Translation*. London: Routledge.

— (ed.) (2004), *The Translation Studies Reader*. (2nd edn). London: Routledge

Translating the Third Culture: The Translation of Aspects of Senegalese Culture in Selected Literary Works by Ousmane Sembène

6

Charmaine Young

Introduction

Translating text is always a manner of transfer – a conveying of a system of norms, conventions and values – a cultural transfer within which the reader is confronted with a scenario which is not inherently familiar. This point is particularly relevant for the translation of text written within the postcolonial context, as the language used as a vehicle to convey the tale is often not the native language of the writer and thus does not necessarily denote the tale's cultural content. As a native Wolof and Bambara speaker, Ousmane Sembène writes in French but depicts a culture and era quite apart – that of the Senegalese people in a postcolonial age. He writes according to the linguistic and literary norms 'imposed' upon him by the French colonial authority, but he also appropriates this by representing the symbols, practices, idiosyncrasies and cultural uniqueness of his own society through particular stylistic and linguistic choices. What emerges is a third culture, so named as it does not actually reflect the peculiarities, norms or conventions associated with the source language, but rather depicts a foreign culture – in this instance that of Ousmane Sembène. The aim of this chapter is to illustrate how this world of imagery and diversity, as depicted in various cultural aspects[1] presented within the selected works by Sembène, is translated into a relatable concrete product – the third culture evident within the English translated text. It is my view that by compromising between domesticating and foreignizing strategies,[2] the translation of postcolonial literature and the inherent otherness evident within literature of this category can serve to resist the conventions of the colonial encounter, recognizing the 'crucial importance, for subordinated peoples, of asserting their indigenous cultural traditions and retrieving their repressed histories' (Bhabha, 1994: 13). The cultural singularity evident in the source text can be encountered within the target product through the introduction of the norms and conventions of the 'exotic', or unfamiliar, presented within a unique perspective. The translation will however need to gain acceptance in the target culture and thus, to a degree, will be domesticated to ensure its survival and acceptance into the receiving culture.

Contextualization of the corpus

Sembène, a celebrated novelist and cinematographer, clearly demonstrates this issue of cultural transfer in his novels and films.[3] Three of Sembène's novels (spanning 1956–1974) and translations of these novels (published between 1970–1987) have been selected to demonstrate the validity of the hypothesis that this third culture evident in text written within the postcolonial context can be effectively conveyed in translation through a process of cultural compromise and a balanced focus on both source and target audience-orientation. The texts were selected because of their particular significance within the development of Sembène as both a political activist and a writer and because they emphasize his urgent awareness of the need for political and social change in Africa.

Source Texts	Target Texts
Le docker noir (1956)	*Black Docker* trans. Schwartz (1987/1986)
Les bouts de bois de Dieu (1960)	*God's Bits of Wood* trans. Price (1970/1962)
Xala (1974)	*Xala* trans. Wake (1976)

Briefly, *Le docker noir* (1956) is the story of a young man who, as a result of a black diaspora, is forced to settle in isolation and disillusionment on the docks of Marseilles and is violently stripped of his self-respect through a systematic process of subjugation and discrimination. This work represents Sembène's début as a novelist and is broadly based on his own experiences. It emphasizes the desperation of the Senegalese to escape the uncertain political climate, poverty and misery in their homeland. Due to the policies of assimilation, the influence of colonialism and the empty promises made by the French system, many had immigrated to France in search of a better life. Both in Senegal and among the immigrants, a new group of African intellectuals emerged who responded to the general sense of disillusionment by establishing various influential movements against France's domination of its African colonies.

The second novel, *Les bouts de bois de Dieu* (1960), one of the most celebrated of Sembène's literary creations, deals with the world Sembène portrays as a world in flux and constant turmoil due to economic, political and social changes and recounts the events of the railway strike in French West Africa between 1947–1948. This novel constitutes a message to the people of Senegal to resist colonialism and reclaim their own freedom through the struggle depicted from an Afrocentric perspective. It is set in the period after WW II when the colonized were more exposed internationally and began to understand the Western concepts of equality and freedom. A hybrid of their own culture was evolving, crossed with that of the colonialists and resistance, and a desire for independence gradually developed (Bandia, 2003). The writing, which is vivid and vital, adopts the style of a script written for film or a play and, through its visual appeal, highlights the preoccupation of the writer to make the book not just a historical account of the strike, but a look into the culture, traditions and beliefs of the people. It serves as a record for Sembène's community, although with the contradiction that it is not written in the language of that community and was therefore generally inaccessible to them.

Lastly, the novel *Xala* (1974) is particularly important as a work of political resistance and social activism, stressing Sembène's satirical view of Senegalese bourgeois society of the time and the general sense of disillusionment experienced in response to the corrupt postcolonial rulers who had vowed to free the masses from the shackles of oppression and poverty. It also served as a warning to the people of Senegal that the time for blaming colonialism was over and that the only means of recovering from this domination was once again to exert control over their own destiny. The novel, set in the 1970s in

Senegal, reflects a recently independent country in a state of metamorphosis. The people are disillusioned with the idealistic government under the rule of Leopold Sédar Senghor, corruption is rife, and the ruling white elitists have simply been replaced with a new 'bourgeoisie'. Against this political and social backdrop, the story of *Xala*[4] (1974) is the story of a middle-aged Dakar businessman who has reached the pinnacle of the economic elite by participating in a native revolt against colonialist authorities and seizing control of the chamber of commerce. Despite the new board's 'altruistic' declarations for establishing compassionate socialism, corruption and abuse of power has become immediately apparent (Acquarello, 2002) and the widening gap between the self-absorbed wealthy elite and the general masses living in abject poverty has intensified. El Hadji's (the protagonist of the novel) social standing begins to slip when, after taking a third wife, he is unable to perform and prove his virility due to a *xala* which he believes has been placed upon him.

In order to establish how cultural transfer takes place in the translation process, and how the third culture is brought into existence, as well as to explore the influence of the English narrative system on the translation products, I examine the translations of these three novels. *Black Docker* (translated by Schwartz, 1987) was published by Heinemann as part of their 'African Writers' Series' in a political climate in which the voice of the West was overarching. It is presented to an anti-socialist and inwardly-centred Britain, a society which viewed colonialism as a thing of the past. However, this specific translation was not necessarily politically motivated or even directed towards social reform. *God's Bits of Wood* (translated by Price, 1970) is highlighted as an encounter with the 'other' (the foreign) during the era of colonialism, specifically centring the debate on the issue and meaning of 'Third World' and the identification of an interlanguage[5] and afrocentrism in the domain of translation. The translation was undertaken in 1962 and published in England, mainly for educational purposes, by Heinemann as part of their 'African Writers' Series' in 1970, ten years after the publication of *Les bouts de bois de Dieu* (1960), and therefore in the wake of the general trend towards independence of most previously colonized regions. Because of the educational affiliation of the publishing house, it is doubtful that there was any real political motivation for translating the work. The time of the translation would however have been considerably responsive or susceptible to text written in the postcolonial context. Thus, the social function of the text and awareness of the social and cultural situation would have been far more influential factors. Finally, *Xala* (translated by Wake, 1976) was received by an audience at a time when colonialism was beginning to be regarded as a historical phenomenon. This work is emphasized as a social awakening, both for Sembène and for the West, stressing the role of literature as an agent of social change. Only two years after the publication of *Xala* (1974),[6] the translation by Wake (1976) was also released in the United States. Considerable changes were underway in relation to increased legal equality and affirmative action and, given this climate of progress and reform, it is relatively easy to see why a novel by a controversial and even revolutionary character such as Sembène might be considered desirable.

This brief contextualization illustrates the importance of the colonial or postcolonial background for the source texts and establishes the settings and possible motivations behind the translations. It now remains to be determined which strategies the various translators adopted in order to release the third culture arising from the context in which these works were written and translated.

The cultural compromise

The literary translator's purpose is never merely to translate language as this nullifies the existence and importance of the heritage, culture, practices and peculiarities of a given people. It is acknowledged that translating text with a strong postcolonial influence, such as that by Sembène, is not therefore only translating from one language to another or from one audience to another, but rather translating a culture, despite the language in which the text is written. As the works of Sembène are written in a dominant language (French), but represent a foreign culture (that of the Wolof/Bambara of Senegal), the risk of losing the unique character and portrayal evident in the cultural aspects of the text is potentially quite considerable. This necessitates a careful transformation of the primary conveyors of culture in the narrative.

This issue is further intensified when exploring the space 'in between' within a translation, specifically in relation to how the aspects of culture are transferred from the source text into the target text through the strategies employed by the translator. As discussed by Bhabha (1994: 10):

> The borderline work of culture demands an encounter with 'newness' that is not part of the continuum of past or present. It creates a sense of the new as an insurgent act of cultural translation. Such an act does not merely recall the past as a social cause or aesthetic precedent; it renews the past, refiguring it as a contingent 'in-between' space, that innovates and interrupts the performance of the present.

In order to gain access to the culture depicted in the source text, two main concepts or orientations are highlighted. Strategies of foreignization and domestication respectively either permit us a view, or obstruct the encounter with the other, in the translation process. This does not however imply that only one or the other strategy has to be adopted. In fact, I demonstrate here that, through a process of compromise between these two models, an encounter with the otherness evident in text written in the postcolonial context, which demonstrates a culture not belonging to the language of the source text, is possible and will not alienate the reader, but rather allow him/her to sense that otherness.

Domestication, in brief, refers to the bringing over of a foreign text to the target culture and making it easily digestible to the target audience, whereas foreignization relates to the immersion of the target reader in the culture of the other, exposing the reader to beliefs, practices and norms not their own (Venuti, 1995, 2004). A brief categorization of the most prominent foreignizing and domesticating strategies identified in the translation of cultural aspects in Sembène's works and their translations is identified and briefly defined below.

Foreignizing strategies

Transference or loanword: This is the process of directly transferring a source language word to a target language text unchanged. This becomes a loan word transferring the nuances or local aspect of the novel and is also referred to as borrowing (Suh, 2005).

> [ST] [7]Dakarois (Docker noir, Sembène, 1956: 4)
> [TT] Le Dakarois (Black docker, Schwartz,[8] 1987: 16)
> [ST] Un sou (lit. a cent/penny) (Les bouts de bois de Dieu, Sembène, 1960: 98)
> [TT] A sou (God's bits of wood, Price, 1970: 82)

Literal translation: This refers to direct translation of some or all of the formal features of the item. Source text material is substituted with a direct equivalent and is referred to by Newmark (1988), Suh (2005) and Williams (1990) as transference. Although this facilitates the understanding of the target community, the quality or wording of the direct translation is often 'estranging', giving the impression that, although translated into a Western language (English), the item is foreign in its derivation.

> [ST] Petit père (Sembène, 1960: 18)
> [TT] Little father (Price, 1970: 15)

[ST] Mystique ermite (Sembène 1974: 82)
[TT] Hermit mystic (Wake 1976: 53)

Phonetic adaptation: This strategy is quite similar to transference or borrowing, but is used when an item is adopted from the source language with slight modification to remove *some* of the 'foreignness' (Suh, 2005: 117). In the examples which follow, the pronunciation of the items has, for example, been slightly adjusted to assist the target reader. The asterisk indicates that the item is footnoted.

[ST] Gri-gri (Sembène 1956: 15)
[TT] *Gree-gree** (amulet) (Schwartz 1987: 3)
[ST] Oulofou (Sembène 1960: 15)
[TT] Oulof (Price 1970: 13)

Translation couplet: Williams (1990) uses this term to refer to a combination of any two strategies, and is used here to refer to the combination of two specific strategies – paraphrase and loanword. It serves to retain the cultural tone of the item, but in such a way that the target text reader does not become irrevocably 'lost' in the dimension of the foreign.

[ST] Lémé, Lémé (Sembène 1960)
[TT] Lémé, Lémé. My child my child (Price 1970)
[ST] Facc-kaat (Sembène 1974: 66)
[TT] Facc-katt healers (Wake 1976: 42)

Domesticating strategies

Cultural substitution: This involves replacing a culture-specific item with a target language item which does not have the same propositional meaning but is likely to have a similar impact on the target reader. In discussing the concept of cultural substitution both Baker (1992) and Suh (2005) reiterate its function in ensuring that the text does not become 'estranging' for the target reader. This strategy is also referred to as cultural equivalence by Williams (1990) and Newmark (1988).

[ST] Frères (Sembène 1960: 110)
[LIT][9] Brothers
[TT] Comrades (Price 1970: 93)
[ST] Tu es bête mon vieux. (Sembène 1956: 18)
[LIT] You are an idiot/animal, my old.
[TT] You're a fool, my friend. (Schwartz 1987: 5)

Paraphrase/functional equivalence: Baker (1996) and Williams (1990) use the terms paraphrase or functional equivalence to refer to the use of a culturally neutral term, a less expressive or even a more general word to define the source language culture-specific term. Newmark (1988) refers to this process as neutralization in that the concept expressed by the source text item is not lexicalized in the target language.

> [ST] Les baobabs semblaient *avoir été oubliés*. (Sembène, 1956: 11)
> [LIT] The baobabs seemed to have been forgotten.
> [TT] The baobabs looked *neglected*. (Schwartz, 1987: 1)

This suggested process of negotiation in translation in order to release the third culture has however not simply evolved overnight. The cultural orientation in translation studies has been a gradual evolution during which the social, ethnic and cultural issues have become more central, making a study of works by, and translations of, an author such as Sembène particularly relevant. The gradual move toward a more social and even political orientation is described below, focusing on the influence of postcolonialism and the abusive (Lewis in Venuti, 2004) or resistive approach to translation.

Theoretical orientation

The influence of postcolonialism

The term postcolonial is generally used quite loosely to define the period prior to and after the departure of the imperial powers and, even more generically, to signify a position against imperialism and Eurocentrism (Bahri, 1996). As a result of the postcolonial context, this concept and the struggle for liberation is engrained in the works of the writers of that period (Tuma, 2003), and Sembène is an excellent example of this class of revolutionary nationalist.

The writer is tasked with recovering his/her society's lost identity by striking at the colonial system and its support – religion, education and the language itself. It is exactly this aspect which is highlighted and evaluated here – if the translation is to retain the intentional resistive, rebellious or revolutionary character of the source text, the norms, beliefs and values apparent in the source text (and not specifically in the language used) must be taken into consideration. Conveying the culture indicative of this genre of text should however not estrange the target audience. Thus, the translator is acknowledged as an 'intervenient being' who is simultaneously involved in, and separate from, the text and who is credited with the ability to 'alter the emotions and radically affect the thinking . . . ' (Maier, 2007: 10).

The loss of sovereignty and cultural confidence of the previously subverted colonies, according to Barber (Bandia, 1998: 358), is demonstrated through the use of European languages and the ensuing displacement of indigenous languages and literatures. As the lingua franca (French) ceases to convey the cultural undercurrent evident in the relevant society (Wolof and Bambara of Senegal), the author is forced to use various creative means to convey his culture although using a colonial or non-native language. This is achieved through the creation of the third culture – the symbols, imagery and particularities of the people represented – within the African context as conveyed in French. Although the influence of this linguistic dominance is subtle, far-reaching and enduring, a revolutionary, militant and combative literature has nonetheless emerged in postcolonial writing, and potentially in the translations of such texts, which, like the writings of Sembène, often serve a resistive, educational and transformative role. These works, although written by Sembène in the language of the oppressor (French), have been re-appropriated in translation through the estranging or exotic quality of the culture presented by this *griot*. His works serve to depict 'the very rich African culture and sharply satirize the European violation of the customs, traditions, values and . . . cultural heritage' (Suh, 2005: 112). The idiosyncratic manner in which these aspects of culture are portrayed should be conveyed in the translated text to ensure that the purpose of this genre of literature is fulfilled.

Due to the complex nature of postcolonial literature, a careful and purposeful translation is required which not only integrates with the target text culture, but also acknowledges the existence of differences and celebrates the 'other'. As a result, as Tymoczko suggests:

> The translator must decide how to handle features of the source culture (e.g. objects, customs, historical and literary allusions) that are unfamiliar to the receiving audience. (Tymoczko, 1999: 23)

The examples discussed below demonstrate that, although the translation strategies and orientations of each of the selected translators may vary considerably,[10] where cultural compromise is employed, a middle ground is conveyed. This expression of aspects of culture in the source text is vital in the postcolonial context and should be unfamiliar but not estranging to the receiving audience.

An abusive translation – encountering the other

In a given historical moment, abuse or 'violence' in translation is necessary in order for transformation to take place. It however does not corrupt or pretend to be what it is not – that is, the original – as the purpose of translation is not to erase differences, but rather to intensify the interaction between the reader and the foreign (Nornes, 2004: 464).[11]

As discussed by Bassnett (Stolze, 2002: 20), it is common for translators to present foreign cultures as distant, strange places incomprehensible to the target audience, instead of illustrating and emphasizing an empathy with the original message in their translation. This empathy is highlighted in the example below in that the reader of the translation is able to encounter the 'other' but, by the use of paraphrase, the 'strange' concept does not become 'estranging':

> [ST] Le *m'bague gathié* (Les bouts de bois de Dieu, Sembène, 1960: 90)
> [TT] The *m'bague gathie*, or 'protection from dishonour' (God's bits of wood, Price, 1970: 78)

Examining the Anglo-American tradition, Venuti highlights the prevalence of fluent strategies which make for easy readability, perpetuating the illusion of transparency, rendering the translator invisible (Venuti, 2004: 334). This results in the neutralization of the third culture present in the source text with the aim of ensuring that the target reader is able to digest the target text without experiencing its 'foreignness'. British and American publishing has reaped the financial benefit of successfully imposing Anglo-American cultural values on a vast foreign readership, producing monolingual cultures which are unreceptive to the foreign and accustomed to fluent translations that invisibly 'inscribe foreign texts with English language values and provide readers with the narcissistic experience of recognizing their own culture in a cultural other' (Venuti, 1995: 16). If we have learnt one thing from colonialism, it is that subversion will always lead to rebellion and ultimately to inevitable change. It is my view that, if translation is to perform a transformative purpose, it should be subversive in order to expose and revel in the existence of the third culture as illustrated within the source text.

Resistance aims to free the translator and the reader of the translation from the cultural constraints which threaten to overpower and domesticate the foreign text by utilizing techniques which make the text 'strange' and 'estranging' in the target language culture (Venuti, 1995: 305). It should however be noted that a text which proves to be too foreignizing may not appeal to the audience which it is intended to 'convert' or 'transform'. For this reason, a cultural compromise needs to be established.

Aspects of culture

In order to resist the conventions of the colonial encounter and introduce his own norms and conventions, Sembène often used the foreign language as a vehicle, inscribing the foreign into the text in an attempt to produce a type of liberation in the source text, an atmosphere which in itself is both 'strange' and 'estranging'.

In order to highlight the manner in which the third culture purposefully created within Sembène's writing is released into the translation, the relevant aspects or carriers of culture within his works are highlighted below. This relates to designations and names, figurative language and idiomatic expressions which are used by Sembène in order to convey the unique cultural dimension – the landscape, people and heritage of Senegal, an aspect not derived from or associated with the European language in which he writes.

Designations and names

Names are important in literary expression as they are given to the characters that cause or experience the events forming the plot (Ndlovu, 1997: 88). Proper names contain 'information load ... [and] semantic, semiotic, sociolinguistic significances indicate tribal and family affiliations, and give information about class and gender as well as racial, ethnic, national and religious identity' (Von Flotow, 2001: 7). In translation, the names chosen, whether Bambara/Wolof or French, and any specific additional implication which the name may have, are vital to the determination and transference of culture. Whether the names are domesticated, explained or merely retained will depend on the translator's interpretation of their importance and his or her concern with retaining or conveying their meaning.

This issue is a complicated one as, through a desire to preserve meaning, the translator may inadvertently lose certain other aspects of a name, such as added connotations. Place names are also vital in establishing culture, setting, plot and character; place names are also vital. Setting is obviously influenced by the occurrence of events in specific places and at specific times in the history of a society. This is of particular relevance in the work of Sembène, as the exact historical moment and societal and political situation (colonial period, independence or postcolonial disillusionment) play a pivotal role in the themes and images portrayed in the text and the characters' responses. The nationality, ideology, principles and norms of each role-player also exert an influence. This information is provided vicariously through names, designations and interjections, locations and items and the transmission of subconscious information.

Also of relevance are the names given to objects, situations, superstitions, religious practices and even interjections and terms of address (Ndlovu, 1997: 92). These contribute towards thematic development and assist in the conveyance of culture and character throughout the text. Furthermore, the names of food, animals, clothing, and cultural practices also provide a local quality, establishing these materials as belonging to a culture other than one's own. Although foreignizing, this also assists the reader in encountering and relating to the 'other' in the text. In the following example, the name given to the first wife of a polygamist husband carries certain cultural information: the reader encounters the traditional practices (polygamy), the language of religion (Islamic) and the social relevance (the status of the first wife in a polygamist structure) of the item. The translator must therefore decide whether to retain the foreign item provided or substitute it with an English 'equivalent'.

[ST] *AWA* (Awa: première épouse, nom de la première femme sur terre (mot arabe)) (Sembène, 1974: 29)
[TT] *Awa* * (Awa is the Arabic name for the first woman on earth and the title given to the first wife) (Wake, 1976: 14)

The following examples from the texts demonstrate the divergent strategies employed by the different translators:

Example 1

[ST] Son fichu glissa, laissant apparaître ses cheveux, où étaient fixés un gri-gri et un cauri. Elle se tordait comme si ses entrailles se consumaient. Son pagne se défit . . . (Sembène, 1956: 15)

[LIT] Her scarf slipped off, letting her hair show, where she had attached an amulet and a cowry. She writhed as though her entrails were consuming her. Her grass skirt came undone.

[TT] Her kerchief slid off, uncovering her hair in which she had fastened a *greegee* * (amulet) and a cowry shell. She writhed as if her insides were on fire. Her pagne came loose. (Schwartz, 1987: 3)

In example 1, it becomes apparent that Schwartz's (1987) focus is on the understanding and interpretation of the target language reader. The cultural substitute 'kerchief' (a relatively outdated and perhaps specifically English term) for the item 'fichu' has been selected. This choice is certainly not neutral. Perhaps a more standard term, for example 'scarf' or 'head cloth', would have provided a clearer image of an African women wearing a traditional scarf covering her hair as commonly worn by Muslim women. The choice of translation affects the setting on the macro-level because of the English associations of this item and the cultural elements associated with traditional attire.

In the translation of the word *gri-gri*, the translator has opted to use phonetic adaptation. In this instance, this word, not belonging to either the French or English system, conveys a strangeness. The pronunciation of the item is slightly adjusted to *gree-gree*, but the meaning is not clarified in the body of the text, but rather explained in a footnote which may create a barrier between 'our culture' and 'their culture' by isolating the meaning of a foreign item from the literary text itself.

Lastly, in this example, the suggestion that the focus is on domesticating the item may seem to be contradicted by the direct use of the item 'pagne' as a loanword. In fact, this item is explained in an earlier footnote and should therefore be familiar to the target audience.

Example 2

[ST] -Dieu merci, nous avons … une boîte de lait pour "Grève" et du *rakal**(tourteau d'arachides)¹² , et tout grâce à notre mad'miselle N'Deye Touti. (Sembène, 1960: 88)

[LIT] "Thank God, we have . . . a box of milk for Strike and rakal (nut cake), and all thanks to mad'miselle N'Deye Touti".

[TT] "God be praised, we have   a can of milk for Strike, and some earthnut cakes – all thanks to mad'mizelle N'Deye Touti." (Price, 1970: 73)

This example of the translation by Price (1970) demonstrates a compromise between source and target text orientation. In this instance, the translator has chosen to translate the name of the baby *Grève* (French) directly using the English equivalent 'Strike'. As the story under discussion deals with the railway strike, the name of this child honours the participants and symbolizes the future for which these men and woman are fighting. This name is therefore a metaphor for their dreams and hopes. To convey this, a loanword is not selected as the target text reader would not be aware of the significance of the name. Thus, in order to ensure coherence at the macro-textual level of theme and character, this item has been literally translated.

For the cultural item *rakal*, the translator has opted for a cultural substitute in the target text. The effect of this choice remains foreignizing, but not estranging. 'Earthnut cakes' are not something with which the target readership would be overly familiar, but this is an English term thus rendering it less alienating than the foreign item *rakal*.

The title given to the young lady, 'mad'miselle N'Deye Touti' has been transferred as a loanword with one minor adaptation in spelling to facilitate pronunciation. The transference of a French nickname for this young woman is specifically conveyed by Sembène to link her to the French system. Early in the novel she experiences a great sense of shame with regard to the customs, beliefs and language of her people. At this point, however, N'Deye Touti has realized her short-sightedness and joins forces with the community. Her nickname previously expressed contempt for her preoccupation with the French 'oppressors', but now conveys respect and affection and is used light-heartedly. The broken pronunciation of the name and fragmented presentation reinforce the idea that the speaker is not francophone.

Example 3

[ST] On le oignit de *safara* *(breuvage qui le guérisseur obtient par lavage des versets du Coran inscrits sur les *alluba* *(planchettes en bois)) (Sembène, 1974: 66)

[LIT] He had been anointed with *safara* (a liquid which the healers obtains by washing verses of the Coran written on *alluba* (little wooden planks)).

[TT] He had been anointed with *safara* – a liquid which the healer obtains by washing off verses of the Koran written on small planks of wood called *alluba* (Wake, 1976: 42–43)

In the extract above, Wake (1976) in the translation of the term *safara*, a concept which is completely foreign to the target reader, uses a translation couplet, transferring the local term unchanged into the target text and, thereafter, paraphrasing its meaning to ensure the understanding of the target reader. This same translation strategy is repeated as demonstrated below:

- 'facc-katt – 'facc-katt healers',
- 'alluba' – 'wood called alluba', and
- 'xatim' – 'xatim, esoteric writings'.

These items are explained in the source text either by using bracketed explanations or in footnotes as their meaning is not as vital as their appearance in the text. As Sembène's primary audience is Senegalese, these references are accessible to it. Wake generally prefers to incorporate these explanations into the text via paraphrase, making the understanding of the foreign term an integrated part of the narrative as opposed to separate from it. He has also on occasion used footnotes, but this strategy is infrequently employed.

Figurative language

As observed by Doke (Ndlovu, 1997: 202), figures of speech refer to 'a deviation from the plain and ordinary use of words with a view to increasing or specializing the effect'. As figurative language is uniquely poetic and conveys cultural content, considerable difficulties exist in its translation. Such language usually contains non-standard/non-formalized expressions and conveys insights into the culture and language in which they originate. They often provide a visual representation of the people, places and practices associated with a particular society. Because of their particular pertinence with regard to cultural transfer, only simile and metaphor have been selected as examples of figurative language.

Simile can be defined as 'a figure of speech which makes a direct comparison between two elements and which is usually introduced by like or as' (Ndlovu, 1997: 110). In the example below, an image of a 'legless cripple' dragging his filthy body along the floor and, in turn, leaving a snail-like trail behind him is used to highlight the dire state of the poverty-stricken masses and the repulsion and disgust experienced by the 'elite' of the desperate common folk of their land.

> [ST] Un cul de jatte . . . imprimait sa traînée noirâtre comme une limace géante. (Sembène, 1974: 161)
> [TT] A legless cripple . . . printed a black trail on the floor like a giant snail. (Wake, 1976: 108)

Metaphor however differs from simile in that the comparison is direct, employing a tenor (the primary image) and a vehicle (the secondary subject). This relationship through association (Kruger, 1991) is demonstrated in the example below which highlights the exhaustion experienced by the overworked dockers who had emigrated from Senegal to France with the promise of a better future. The effect of this fatigue can be interpreted both literally (the hunger and thirst of the poor, destitute workers) or figuratively (the current circumstances are gradually starving or 'killing them', but this same condition makes them thirst for change).

> [ST] Cette abattement amassé pendant de longs mois, durant des années, enlevait l'appétit, donnait soif. (Sembène, 1956: 131)
>
> [TT] This exhaustion, accumulated over long months and years, killed their appetite and made them thirsty. (Schwartz, 1987: 71)

In addition, figurative language provides insight into the setting, characters and themes and impacts upon the macro-textual level. Tampering too much with these representations may affect the macro-textual level of interpretation in the target text. The following examples illustrate the predominant focus of each translator with regard to figures of speech:

Example 4

[ST] À l'aube le levant comme le couchant était assombri… Par cette purée depuis, les nègres s'étaient évadés dans la nuit . . . (Sembène, 1956: 59)

[LIT] At dawn, as at dusk, it was dark. . . . Within this puree, the Negroes escaped into the night . . .

[TT] At dawn, the sky was dark, at it had been at dusk . . . In this pea-soup fog, the slaves melted into the night. (Schwartz, 1987: 28)

Example 4, referring to the 'pea-soup fog', is another attempt by Schwartz (1987) to substitute an image into the target language in order to replace source language elements with a target language equivalent. The image 'purée', referring to either a purée (liquidized fruit or porridge) or quite simply, a fog, is replaced with the informal British equivalent, a 'pea-soup fog' (purée de pois). In this instance, a metaphor is used in the target language to replace an equivalent metaphor in the source language; the target-text metaphor is not French or African, but rather English. Thus, again, the setting is disturbed, creating the illusion that this scene plays out in England instead of in France.

A second metaphor is present in this extract in the following phrase: 'les nègres s'étaient évadés dans la nuit' – 'the slaves melted into the night'. In order to soften the impact of directly translating the word nègres, the translator selected a functional equivalent, opting for the word 'slaves'. The imperial link and tone of servility is not lost in this translation, but through the choice of this cultural substitute, the negative or offensive connotation of the item *nègres* (negroes/niggers) is lost, although it is a term which evokes the themes of degradation, prejudice and subjugation, important themes in Sembène's writing.

The idea of enforced submission is however captured in the translation of the expression *être évadé* (escaped) which is substituted by the metaphor 'melted'. Escaped, in English, would connote freedom and would have contradicted the choice of the word 'slaves'. The choice of the substitute 'melted' highlights the virtual invisibility associated with slavery. Although this substitution demonstrates cultural sensitivity, it does not illustrate the dehumanizing aspect of the word *nègre*. This extract is taken from the novel written by Falla (the protagonist), and therefore expresses **his** impressions of the feelings of the white masters towards the natives. It is his 'first hand account' and although the cultural substitute 'slave' would effectively denote lack of freedom or bondage, it does not convey the hateful quality of the item *nègre*.

Example 5

[ST] Niakoro se tut un instant pour reprendre son souffle. Ses joues remuaient comme une pâte molle que se gonfle. (Sembène, 1960: 18)

[LIT] Niakoro kept quiet for a moment to get her breath back. Her cheeks moved [rose] like soft dough which swells.

[TT] Niakoro stopped for a moment to catch her breath, and her cheeks puffed out like rising dough. (Price 1970: 16)

In this example, Price (1970) has attempted to accommodate the target reader by minor adjustments, but has conveyed the image as created in the source text in order to ensure consistency in relation to theme, setting and characterization. Here, although the structure of the simile is altered considerably, a like image is conveyed in the target text. The visual representation created as a result of this expression is quite effective and, furthermore, the association with the rural and rustic atmosphere reinforced through the image of fresh, home-baked bread rising emphasizes the contrast with the natives' extreme state of hunger and poverty. The preoccupation with food due to the shortages experienced as a result of the strike serves as a cohesive thread in the source text. This image is reinforced by transferring it on a macro-textual level. Furthermore, the specific expression, 'cheeks puffed out like rising dough', provides the reader with information relating to the character of Niakoro. She is of the 'old school' – strong, resilient and stubborn. This particular scene takes place when Niakoro is discussing the potential strike and its implications with her granddaughter, Ad'jibid'ji. The retention of this simile clearly illustrates her frustration at her granddaughter's ideals and beliefs creating a physical image of the old woman huffing and puffing. Price (1970), in translating this simile, has opted for literal translation, but has also adapted the term, replacing the item 'moved' for 'puffed out'. The image and the insights into characterization are thereby replicated.

Example 6

[ST] Les prunelles avaient le jaune ancien de l'ivoire africain. (Sembène, 1974: 96)

[LIT] The pupils had the old yellow colour of African ivory.

[TT] They had the yellow colour of old African ivory. (Wake, 1976: 62)

The image presented in example 6, although standard, conveys cultural information with regard to the setting and characterization in the source text. This metaphor is paraphrased slightly, but more or less directly translated to create a similar effect as within the source text. The African setting, in the reference to 'old African ivory', is highlighted as is its connection with colonialism and colonial wealth derived from the African colonies through the use, until virtual depletion, of their natural resources. The associations of 'ivory' are furthermore quite similar in both cultures, establishing a distinctly African feel. A representation of El Hadji's exhaustion and poor mental and physical state is evident in likening his eyes to ivory. This dirty yellow colour vividly indicates the extent to which this *xala* (curse of impotency) has been weighing upon him. Also, reference to this opulent material creates an impression that his eyes are 'unseeing', inert or inanimate decorations and could relate to the fact that his wealth and greed (symbolized by ivory) have consumed him and have actually led to his spiritual demise.

Idiomatic expression

Idiomatic expressions are usually standard expressions which have been developed and formalized in a particular culture. Doke (in Ndlovu, 1997: 106) defines an idiom as 'a form of expression peculiar to a particular language, and one which reflects the genius of the language and the psychological workings of the speakers of such language.' They provide considerable information regarding mores, traditions and the national identity of a people and are almost always unique to a language as demonstrated through their unique meaning and construction.

Most importantly, idiomatic expressions refer to expressions which are natural to the mother tongue user, but which are often virtually illogical in their composition. They are groups of words established by usage as having a meaning not deducible from the individual words – for example, 'over the moon.' In translating or replacing a culture-specific item with an item of dissimilar propositional meaning but which is likely to have a similar impact on the target reader, the cultural dimension may become distorted or lost.

Suh (2005: 127) has emphasized that communicative translation (using cultural substitutes) is common in the translation of proverbs, idioms and clichés to convey the stylistic effect of the source text. This however, does not acknowledge a unique category of idiomatic expression identified in the writings of Sembène, which is aptly labelled 'original idiom'. Frequently, the idiomatic expressions used by Sembène are Wolof or Bambara expressions and are not derived from French, or even standard in the French language. They rather denote the Senegalese element evident at the cultural level of the text. Through the foreign cultural material presented, the reader immediately perceives that the idiom presented is Wolof or Bambara in its origin, but has been 'presented' in French or translated into English. In this instance, once again, the translator must intervene in order to ensure that the otherness evident in the original idiom is not lost in the translation process. Examples of the manner in which the various translators have dealt with the issue of the translation of idiomatic expressions are provided below.

Example 7

[ST] -A la soupe les gars, dit Pipo après avoir consulté sa montre. (Sembène, 1956: 149)

[LIT] 'Come and get it guys!' said Pipo after having consulted his watch.

[TT] 'Grub's up, lads,' said Pipo looking at his watch. (Schwartz, 1987: 81)

Schwartz (1987) frequently uses domestication as a strategy when translating idioms. In this example, a standard idiomatic expression in the source text – *à la soupe* – is replaced by a relatively standard (but not neutral) target language expression – 'Grub's up'. Although the effect on the target culture would be similar, it should be noted that instead of establishing a foreign quality in the writing, the impression that this novel is set in England rather than in France is created once again. This false context is reinforced through the translation of the expression *gars* (men/guys) by the cultural equivalent 'lads' which creates the perception that the characters depicted are British. Although the cultural content to which I refer in this instance is French and not specifically Senegalese, this nonetheless will have an implication on the cultural cohesion on a macro textual level, specifically in relation to the setting, characters and thematic interpretation.

Example 8

[ST] Tout ce que sait un enfant, une grande personne le sait mieux que lui. (Sembène, 1960: 29)

[LIT] All that a child knows, a big person knows better than him.

[TT] Whatever a child knows, a grown person knows better. (Price, 1970: 25)

In this instance, although the expression is uttered in French, it is not typical of this system, but rather reflects the languages of Senegal. It is therefore non-standard in both French and in English. More than likely, for this reason, and in order to retain the foreign aspect purposefully created within the source language, Price (1970) has opted to use direct translation. Had a more standard idiomatic expression, for example 'wisdom comes with age' been selected for the target text, the uniqueness of this expression and its association with the African rather than the French cultural system may have been lost. To reinforce the idiomatic quality of the item, Price (1970) has opted to retain the structure of the source text utterance. This creates the effect that, structurally, the item, even though presented in French, seems local as it is not a standard French idiom. This quality is transferred within the target text.

Example 9

[ST] Ici, nous ne sommes que des crabes dans un panier. (Sembène, 1974: 139)

[LIT] Here, we are only crabs in a basket.

[TT] We are nothing better than crabs in a basket. (Wake, 1976: 93)

The idiomatic expression presented in example 9 is also not standard in either the source or the target systems. In this case, Wake (1976) has also opted to transfer the idiom, reflecting the culture of the Senegalese characters and injecting a local flavour into the target text. Thus, *crabes dans un panier* has been translated as 'crabs in a basket'. The image created by this distinctive expression is one of being trapped, illustrating the idea that the members of the Senegalese Chamber of Commerce (the crabs) no longer control their own fate, but are merely pawns at the mercy of the previous colonial authorities. Like the ensnared crabs, they will figuratively be used to feed or fatten their rich 'overlords'. The irony is that these words are spoken by El Hadji (the protagonist) himself in retaliation to the accusation that he is corrupt and should be forced to leave the chamber. It is ironic that only now that he is truly bound is he able to see that he has merely served as a puppet to the imperialistic ideals. Furthermore, it is only because he will now have nothing, like the majority of the Senegalese population, that he is able to see the reality of the situation with genuine candour. His colleagues, still corrupted and blinded by the riches and power of which they are assured as long as they serve the French ideals, are portrayed as even worse than the imperialist authorities of the former empire, as they have betrayed the very people and principles which they had vowed to protect.

Through this process of negotiation, the unique social element evident in text written in the language of the colonizer in a postcolonial context, and which does not depict the associated oppressor's culture, can be effectively transferred in the translation process rendering this third culture in the target text:

> the only question which preoccupies us [is] how best to make the borrowed tongues carry the weight of our African experience by, for instance, making them 'prey' on African proverbs and other peculiarities of African speech and folklore. (Ngugi, 1989: 7)

If meaning is not distorted, foreignizing strategies are used to reinforce the cultural uniqueness of the source text and to enable the target reader to sense the otherness evident in the original. In order to maintain the balance, domesticating strategies are employed to explain concepts, characters and events and to tame elements which might have left the target reader feeling isolated.

Conclusion

In translation studies, a distinction is often made between 'bringing the text to the audience' and 'bringing the audience to the text' (Schleiermacher in Venuti,

1991: 129). Some works make more severe demands on the audience, requiring the audience to conform to the beliefs, customs, language and literary
formalism of the source culture, while other works conform more to the
dominant audience's cultural, linguistic and literary expectations (Tymoczko,
1999: 30). As demonstrated in the examples discussed above, in encountering
and conveying the third culture, the translator can consolidate two methodol-
ogies in exposing the reader of the translation to the 'strangeness' of the original, but in terms which he/she is able to grasp. The limitations in comprehension
and interpretation of the audience in accessing the cultural space of the source
text must however be considered as the source text should not be 'integrated'
into the systems of the target audience as a 'resident' piece. Rather, differences
should be highlighted and even celebrated due to the abstract and cultural
rather than linguistic aspect of the 'third culture'.

In relation to the strategies employed[13] by Price (1970), it was found that
the main approaches adopted in order to release the third culture evident
in the source text were as follows: literal translation in order to render the
Senegalese culture, cultural substitution to enable the target audience to
encounter the cultural aspects in the ST in a meaningful manner; loanwords to
ensure that the reader is immersed in a world of foreign symbols and practices,
and translation couplets (loanword plus paraphrase) in order to transfer
foreign elements in a manner accessible to the target audience. Wake (1976),
in utilizing similar strategies, also achieves this cultural compromise, thereby
releasing the third culture purposefully created within the postcolonial
context of Sembène. Foreignizing strategies (literal translation and loanword)
are used where meaning does not become distorted. This creates an alien
or exotic quality within the target text resulting in an experience of the otherness. In order to maintain the balance, paraphrase and cultural substitution
are however employed to explain concepts, characters and events and to
domesticate elements which may be too foreignizing, resulting in a sense of
isolation.

The strategies employed by Schwartz (1987) however, are generally in contrast to the balanced strategies utilized by Price (1970) and Wake (1976), as the
focus is considerably more target-oriented. The text does not truly express the
cultural distinctiveness of the source text, highlight its 'Africanness' or convey
Sembène's message and intention. Schwartz (1987) often opts for loanword
plus footnotes, domestication or functional equivalents in the translation of
cultural items and the substitution of the French and Senegalese culture by a
British one through the use of typically British expressions, settings and ideas.
The cultural undercurrent of the original becomes lost in the process and, in

this case, the text does not truly serve a resistive function and can only reinforce the status quo.

It can be seen, therefore, that translation, as an act of cultural transference, can serve as a means of making culture accessible to a wider audience, and, through the identification of a framework for analysing this genre of translation, a structure or 'scaffold' is erected upon which a theory for this specific genre of translation may be developed. This guideline should highlight a balance between foreignizing and domesticating strategies as integral to the transfer of the third culture between source and target systems. Foreignization and domestication however remain contextual phenomena and can never be labelled as creating an exclusive effect. Other aspects such as dominant norms, setting, characterization and general themes, to mention only a few, will also exert an influence on the resultant product.

Notes

1. Names and designations, figurative language and idiomatic expressions have been identified as the aspects of culture highlighted and selected in determining the manner in which the translators have chosen to translate the third culture presented within the works of Sembène.
2. These concepts are discussed in greater detail in the following section.
3. For the purposes of this discussion, and because of the vastness and scope of Sembène's work, only narrative writings of Sembène have been selected. This does not undermine the importance of Sembène as a filmmaker, an aspect which is covered at some length in my dissertation (Young, 2006).
4. The term *xala* is the Wolof word for the infliction or 'curse' of impotency.
5. This refers to the potential for the imported language to carry the indigenous culture and whether the interlanguage or third code can successfully explore the 'space between, the hyphen between mother tongue and other tongue' (Zabus, 1991: 4).
6. In addition, the film *Xala,* which received much acclaim, was released in 1974 which, along with cinema of the Third World in general, had grown considerably in popularity in the United States and abroad. This could also have proven to be a strong motivator for the translation of the novel.
7. The abbreviation ST refers to 'source text' and the abbreviation TT to 'target text'.
8. For purposes of clarity, the translator's name is given as a reference.
9. LIT has been used as an abbreviation for literal translation.
10. Full details on the initial and operational norms of the three relevant translators can be found in my dissertation (Young, 2006).
11. Although Nornes' comments relate specifically to the study of subtitles, subtitling in itself is a form of transference or translation and therefore the applicability of this comment is broader than just the realm of film.

12. The asterisk indicates that a footnote was inserted in the target text.

13. This section is a brief summation of the findings relating to the translation strategies utilized by each translator. Further detail and examples to validate these statements can be found in my dissertation (Young, 2006).

References

Sembène's works

Sembène, O. (1956), *Le docker noir*. Paris: Éditions Présence Africaine.

—(1960), *Les bouts de bois de Dieu*. Paris: Le Livre Contemporain.

—(1974), *Xala*. Paris: Le livre Contemporain.

Translations

Price, F. (1970). *God's Bits of Wood*. Translation of Les bouts de bois de Dieu by O. Sembène. London: Heinemann.

Schwartz, R. (1987), *Black Docker*. Translation of *Le docker noir* by O. Sembène. London: Heinemann.

Wake, C. (1976), *Xala*. Translation of *Xala* by O. Sembène. Connecticut: Lawrence Hill and Co.

Secondary sources

Acquarello, (2002), *Xala, 1975* [The Curse]. Available at: www.filmref.com/directors/dirpages/sembene.html (accessed 26 May 2008).

Bhabha, H. K. (1994), *The Location of Culture*. London: Routledge.

Bahri, D. (1996), *Introduction to Postcolonial Studies*. Available at: www.english.emory.edu/Bhari/Intro.html (accessed 26 May 2008).

Baker, M. (1992), *In Other Words: A Coursebook on Translation*. London: Routledge.

Bandia, P. (1998), 'Towards a history of translation in a (post)-colonial context: an African perspective' in A. Chesterman, N. G. San Salvador, and Y. Gambier (eds), *Translation in Context*, Amsterdam/Philadelphia: John Benjamins.

Bandia, P. (2003), 'Postcolonialism and translation: The dialectic between theory and practice', *Linguistica Antverpensia*, 2, 129–142.

Bassnett, S. (1998), 'The translation turn in cultural studies', in S. Bassnett, and A. Lefevere (eds), *Constructing Cultures: Essays on Literary Translation*. Clevedon: Multilingual Matters, pp. 123–143.

Dimitriu, I. (2002), 'Translation, diversity and power: An introduction', *Current writing: Text and Reception in Southern Africa*, October 2002, 12, (2), i–xiv.

Hermans, T. (ed.) (1999), *Translations in Systems. Descriptive and system-oriented approaches explained.* London: T. J. International Ltd.

Kruger, A. (1991), 'Translating metaphors that function as characterisation technique in narrative fiction', *Journal of Literary Studies*, 7, (3/4), 289–298.

Kruger, A. & Wallmach, K. (1997), 'Research methodology for the description of a source text and its translation(s) – a South African perspective', *South African Journal of African languages*, 17, (4), 119–126.

Lambert, J & Van Gorp, H. (1985), 'On Describing Translation', in T. Hermans (ed.), *The Manipulation of Literature: Studies in Literary Translation*. London: Croom Helm.

Lewis, P. (2004/1985), 'The Measure of Translation Effects', in L. Venuti (ed.) *The Translation Studies Reader* (2nd edn). London: Routledge.

Maier, C. (2007), 'The translator as an intervenient being', in J. Munday (ed.), *Translation as Intervention*. London: Continuum, pp. 1–16.

Mehrez, S. (1992), 'Translation and postcolonial experience: the francophone North African text' in L. Venuti (ed.), *Rethinking Translation. Discourse, Subjectivity, Ideology*. London & New York: Routledge, pp. 120–138.

Ndlovu, V. (1997), *Transferring culture: Alan Paton's Cry, the Beloved Country in Zulu*. Unpublished MA dissertation, Pretoria: University of South Africa.

— (2000), 'Translating aspects of culture in *Cry, the Beloved Country* into Zulu', *Language Matters*, 31, 72–102.

Ngugi, W. T. (1989), *Decolonising the Mind*. London: James Curry.

Newmark, P. (1988), *A Textbook on Translation*. London: Prentice Hall.

Nornes, A. M. (2004), 'For an abusive subtitling', in L. Venuti, (ed.), *The Translation Studies Reader* (2nd edn). London: Routledge.

Pfaff, F. (1984), *The Cinema of Ousmane Sembène: A Pioneer of African Film*. Westport, CT: Greenwood Press.

Stolze, R. (2002), 'Empathy with the message in translation', *Current Writing: Text and Reception in Southern Africa*, October 2002, 12, (2), 19 –31.

Suh, J. C. (2005), *A Study of Translation Strategies in Guillaume Oyono Mbia's Plays*. Unpublished doctoral dissertation. Pretoria, University of South Africa.

Tuma, H. (2003), *The African Writer and the Politics of Liberation*. New York. Available at: www.ethiomedia.com/commentary/African_writer_hama_tuma.htm (accessed 7 October 2005).

Tymoczko, M. (1999), 'Postcolonial writing and literary translation', in S. Bassnett and H Trivedi (eds), *Postcolonial Translation: Theory and Practice*. London: Routledge, 19 –40.

Venuti, L. (1991), 'Genealogies of Translation Theory: Schleiermacher', *TTR*, 4, (2), 125 –150.

— (1995), *The Translator's Invisibility: A History of Translation*. London & New York: Routledge.

— (ed.) (2004), *The Translation Studies Reader* (2nd edn). London: Routledge.

Von Flotow, L. (2001), 'The systemic approach: Postcolonial studies and translation studies. A review article of new work by Hermans and Tymoczko'. *CLCWeb: Comparative literature and culture*, 3, 1. Available at: docs.lib.purdue.edu/clcweb/vol3/iss1/9/ (accessed 6 June 2008).

Wallmach, K. (2000), '"Get them lost just as in the narrow streets of the casbah": Metaphors of resistance and subversion in translation', *Hermeneus: Revista de traducción e interpretación*. Universidad de Valladolid, 2/2000, 235–255.

Williams, J. (1990), 'The translation of culture-specific terms", *Lebende Sprachen*, 35, (2), 55–59.

Young, C. (2006), *Cultural transfer in film and narrative: The 'griot' translated.* Unpublished MA dissertation. Pretoria, University of South Africa.

Zabus, C. (1991), *The African Palimpsest: Indigenization of Languages in the West African Europhone novel.* Amsterdam & Atlanta: Rodopi.

Translating, Rewriting and Retelling Traditional South African Folktales: Mediation, Imposition or Appropriation?

7

Judith Inggs

A Bogeyman who lives up a chimney and is friends with Father Christmas, lions, tigers and snow on Table Mountain, pixies and fairies on the veld, a story about an African herdboy, an Afrikander ox and a 'garden ornament' gnome – all of these feature in collections published as 'South African Tales' from the beginning of the last century until the end of the 1940s (Jenkins, 2006: 64, 88).[1] The stories were often modelled on English and American books but set in a distinctly South African landscape (ibid.: 62). Apart from these rather whimsical stories, many of the collections also included tales which originated in South African folklore and had originally been told in one of the indigenous languages.[2] These tales include mythological and aetiological tales, animal tales, tales about human beings involving magic or taboo, and tales about supernatural beings, often featuring ogres, cannibals or the underworld (Mofokeng, 1951: 2).

Initially collected, transcribed and translated by missionaries, early publications were intended for scholars and students of the indigenous languages and cultures, and as material for teaching literacy in the indigenous languages (Bleek, 1864, Callaway, 1868).[3] The first collections aimed specifically at children included both European-influenced fairy tales and local folk tales, such as E. J. Bourhill and J. B. Drake's *Fairy Tales from South Africa* (1908), *Outa Karel's Stories: South African Folklore Tales*, by Sanni Metelerkamp (1914) and Annette Joelson's *How the Ostrich Got His Name and Other South African Stories for Children* (1926). As the century progressed the number of publications increased substantially, first in English and then also in Afrikaans, until today they represent the earliest, and largest, genre of of local South African children's literature.[4] The tales included retellings of traditional tales, as well as new tales, broadly based on traditional models (Jenkins, 1993: 9). Today, contemporary collections constitute a considerable proportion of the relatively small number of books published for children in South Africa each year.[5] Modern publishing technology has resulted in an increase in collections with lavish glossy illustrations such as *African Myths and Legends* (Heale and Stewart, 2001), *Stories of Africa* (Mhlophe, 2003), *Famous South African Folk Tales* (Grobbelaar and Verster, 2003), *The Zebra's Stripes and Other African Animal Tales* (Stewart, 2004), and *Folktales from Africa* (Stewart, 2006).

This chapter discusses stories from both older and contemporary collections, and seeks to identify the different processes at work within a context of translation and retelling as mediation, imposition or appropriation. These terms are used in this context in specific ways. Whereas Basil Hatim and Ian Mason define *mediation* as 'the extent to which translators intervene in the translation process, feeding their own knowlege and beliefs into their processing of a text' (1997: 147), the term is used here to refer to building bridges and increasing understanding between different cultures and peoples. Such an activity certainly represents intervention, but with a more positive motive which is discussed further below. *Appropriation*[6] is used in terms of taking over texts and using them as a basis for the creation of new stories within the target cultural and literary system.[7] Finally, *imposition* is used to describe the remoulding of texts, and the imposition of new world-views[8] and cultural assumptions onto those texts. The way in which texts are 'framed'[9] by writers, illustrators and publishers is also discussed with reference to illustrations, forewords, introductions, and other peritexts.[10] A range of texts has been selected for illustrative purposes, but the stories which are examined in greater depth are taken from Joelson (1926), P. Savory (1961), J. Heale and D. Stewart (2001), Godwin (n.d.), K.V. Sigenu (2003) and Gcina Mhlophe (2003).

The early collections are described overtly either in the title or the foreword as translations from transcribed source texts. H. Callaway's 1868 collection is entitled *Nursery Tales, Traditions and Histories of the Zulus, in their own Words, with a Translation into English and Notes* and appears in the form of parallel texts. In the collections by W. H. I. Bleek and Callaway and in later collections by ethnographers such as Harold Scheub (1975) and James Honey (1969) translation issues and methods are discussed or at least touched upon in the introductions or forewords. For example, in the first collections translators were careful not to offend their nineteenth century readers:

> It may be as well to remark that among the natives, as among all uncultivated people, there is great freedom of speech used in allusion to the relations between the sexes. Whenever I could soften down such expressions to suit our more refined taste, I have done so. (Callaway, 1868: ii)

At the same time he assures his readers that the method of collection involved requesting a 'native' to 'tell [a tale] exactly as he would tell it to children or a friend' and that 'we have thus placed before us the language as nearly as possible such as it is spoken by the natives in their intercourse with one another' (ibid.: i). Bleek writes that 'a few slight omissions and alterations of what would otherwise have been too naked for the English eye were necessary' although he also assures the reader that these did not 'in any essential way affect the spirit of the Fables' (Bleek, 1864: xxii). S. D. Ngcongwane also comments on the removal by the early missionaries of words such as *mokota* (shit) (1988: 186). Subsequent versions collected by Scheub in the 1970s, however, retain the word in translation – '"I'm a bird that shits amasi!" He said, "Please shit, that we may see!"' (Scheub, 1977: 47).[11]

Contemporary collections are more likely to be packaged as 'retellings' of 'authentic' African stories and comments on the translation process are less frequent, even if the writers had access to the source language of the tales.[12] There is therefore an ambivalent relationship between source texts, translations, retranslations, retellings and even new creations. Translation is here viewed in the broader sense of translation and rewriting, including translations from a specific source language text, and rewritings and retellings in the target language culture. It is commonly accepted that texts are manipulated during the process of translating and retelling, so that they can 'fit in with the dominant, or one of the dominant, ideological and poetical currents of [the] time' (Lefevere, 1992: 8). Examining the Anglo-American tradition, Lawrence Venuti (1992, 1995) shows how the predominant translation strategy is often one of domestication, with publishers and audiences insisting that a text be 'rewritten in the transparent discourse dominating the target-language culture' and which is therefore 'coded with other target-language values, beliefs, and social representations' (Venuti, 1992: 5). Folktales provide a rich source for the study of such rewritings given the processes of intervention and appropriation by and between differing cultural and linguistic groups, and given the majority of the stories constituting 'South African folktales' originated in a language other than English.[13]

The motives for translating and retelling folktales have been widely discussed (Jenkins, 1988: 191–202; Jenkins 1993: 8–26; Mutahi 1994: 26–35). Suggested motives include scientific curiosity, cultural superiority, nostalgia for a pre-European African paradise, post-colonial guilt and a desire to build bridges between cultures (Jenkins 1993: 25). It is appropriate to consider examples of such rewriting and retelling against a background of postcolonial translation studies. Tejaswini Niranjana, an Indian translation scholar, has proposed a project of retranslation that she terms 'reinterpellation', with the objective of reconstructing the subjectivity of colonized peoples, adopting the term 'interpellate' from L. Althusser, who used it to describe the constitution of subjects in language through ideology (Althusser, 1971: 82). Translations of indigenous texts generally construct a particular character, psyche, and world-view of the narrated people, who are powerless to narrate themselves. Niranjana (1992: 173) believes that such a project would result in a new practice of translation, which would be both speculative and interventionist, revealing a more nuanced understanding of the 'original texts' in their complexity and heterogeneity. In this way translation could be used to disrupt existing colonial stereotypes and to lead to 'a more densely textured understanding of who "we" are'. (ibid.: 186).

Writing in South Africa in 2001, after seven years of democracy, Samantha Naidu echoes this call and highlights the need to historicize the folktale genre and points out the lack of 'theoretical studies of folktale texts from a postcolonial perspective'. She proposes that South African indigenous folklore needs to be claimed back in a 'new nationalist discourse' which would acknowledge and embrace heterogeneity rather than identifying with a 'mythic memory of a unique collective identity' (Bhaba quoted in Naidu, 2001: 18). She shares Niranjana's distrust of the 'myths of nationalism' which 'are invoked to suppress heterogeneity in a decolonizing country' (Niranjana, 1992: 167). Elwyn Jenkins (2006: 92) comments that to critics such as Naidu, 'the motives of white writers who write about indigenous beliefs can never be innocent, but are always intended to impose Euro-centred subordination and control', but both he and Naidu acknowledge the difficulties inherent in striving to 'reconcile the tension between the cultural specificity of folktales and the project of national unity, a new shared identity for all the people of the country' (Jenkins, 2002: 272). As D. Robinson asks, 'How do we reinterpellate ourselves so as to transform our subjectivity in productive ways?' (Robinson, 1997: 24).

Niranjana's work refers to precolonial Indian literature in general, across a number of genres. The present chapter has a more specific focus – South African folktales in English – and it is therefore useful to refer to previous studies of retellings of traditional narratives in the Western world. One such study, by J. Stephens and R. McCallum (1998), analyses retellings of stories from various sources, ranging from biblical literature, classical mythology, medieval romance and stories about Robin Hood. They view the ideological effect of a retold text in terms of a 'three-way relationship between the existing, known, story, the metanarrative constituting its top-down framing, and its bottom-up discoursal processes' (Stephens and McCallum, 1998: 4). Metanarrative here refers to 'a global or totalizing narrative schema which orders and explains knowledge and experience' and which often frames the expression of social values, morals and attitudes (ibid.: 6). Retellings presuppose the existence of some kind of source text, which is called a 'pre-text', although this is rarely a single text by a specific author. Such retellings may be antagonistic or subversive, and Stephens and McCallum here propose the term 're-version', which is a 'narrative which has taken apart its pre-texts and reassembled them as a version which is a new textual and ideological configuration' (ibid.).[14] Stephens and McCallum do not discuss translation in detail, although they acknowledge translations as the source for many retellings in English (e.g. The Arabian Nights). They also acknowledge the need for a study of those retold texts and narratives which appropriate the 'beliefs and stories of indigenous peoples' in post-colonial societies such as Australia and North America (ibid.: 7), but they exclude indigenous stories retold by descendants of the colonizers from their study specifically because in such retellings the meta-ethic (a more abstract meta-metanarrative rooted in a specific culture) is often imposed from outside. Thus, whatever the cultural knowledge of the reteller, a Western audience will often contextualize the stories within the 'Western metaethic' (ibid.).[15]

Such contextualization by both readers and retellers is, I believe, an inevitable feature of the translations and rewritings examined here, which is why this framework, integrated with the processes of mediation, imposition and appropriation, is useful in examining how collections have developed and changed over the years. Not all the collections produced in South Africa consist of retellings and reversions by white writers (descendants of the colonizers) with a dominant 'European' world-view. Black South African writers, with direct access to oral performance in indigenous languages, have also produced collections of folktales in recent years (e.g. Makhupula, 1988; Leshoai, 1989; Mutwa, 1996; Mhlophe, 2003; Sigenu, 2003). Indeed, it is a significant and distinguishing feature of the South African context that the English translations and retellings exist alongside retellings in the languages of the original stories, as well as in live storytellings.[16] In fact, the focus of much previous research has been on the transformation of oral performance into the written medium, highlighting the need to compensate for the inevitable loss of tone, gesture, facial expression and song (Finnegan, 1970; Scheub, 1971; Soko, 1986; Jenkins, 1988).

One of the earliest examples of the imposition of an external metaethic and metanarrative on a story presented as a South African folktale, is found in Joelson's *How the Ostrich Got His Name and Other South African Stories for Children* (1926).[17] Joelson uses a 'kaffir-maid' as her narrator, who tells the stories to a little girl called Little Lady Blue Sun-Bonnet – a common ploy by

Figure 1. How the Ostrich Got Its Name (Joelson, 1926).

writers of the time, intended to add authenticity to the stories. Each night, Ayah Sarah would tell stories about 'fairies, elves, animals and strange beings that lived thousands of years ago' (Joelson, 1926: Prologue). The illustration in Figure 1 gives an idea of this, complete with a stereotypical European witch in the top frame.

The reader is told that the story took place thousands of years ago 'before ever a white man had set his foot in this large and mysterious continent' with no explanation for how the handsome white prince came there. The prince sets off on several unsuccessful quests to find his lost love, *Princess Silvery*, kidnapped on the eve of their wedding. These quests include the slaying of the 'fierce veld Dragon', rather inappropriately named Mamba, which is the Nguni name (imamba), also used in English, for two venomous African snakes, the green mamba and the black mamba. Finally the prince challenges 'Gimlet Eyes', the mountain witch, and forces her to release the princess, who looks so ill and pale that he rushes at the witch with his sword upon which she turns them both into two large birds, with long necks, and long legs. Hence Prince Austin the Rich and his descendants come to be known as 'Ostrich . . . es'. This collection by Joelson is just one of roughly 70 – mainly written by 'housewives, teachers, Guide and Brownie commissioners and a few semi-professional writers' (Jenkins, 2006: 63) – that were published from the beginning of the twentieth century until the end of the 1940s, featuring fairies, goblins, and pixies against a South African landscape.

The title 'How the Ostrich Got His Name' parallels indigenous aetiological folktales such as *How Giraffe acquired his long neck* (Stewart, 2004) or *Why the Hippo has a stumpy tail* (Jordan, 1973). For example, the story of *The Jackal, the Dove and the Heron* (Joelson, 1926: 14–17) is found in a collection by Honey, first published for an adult audience in 1910. Honey acknowledges the multiple sources or pre-texts for this story but tells the reader that 'in all cases they are as nearly like the original as a translation from one tongue to another will allow' (Honey, 1969: 1).[18] In Honey's verion Jackal asks Dove for one of her 'little ones'. When she refuses he threatens to fly up to fetch one. Twice she is persuaded to throw a bird down to him, and both times Jackal eats them. Heron then intervenes, telling Dove that Jackal cannot fly. When Jackal's ruse does not work the next day, he seeks to take revenge and tricks Heron into bending down upon which he breaks Heron's neck.

Joelson's retelling is extended and embellished. The dove and her young ones are called the little Mother and her babies, who are nesting in a mimosa tree. To trick the dove into giving him one of her young ones Jackal tells her that he has found an excellent school for her eldest child 'so that he might be well fitted for the life of a gentleman Namaqua-Dove' (Joelson, 1926: 14). He then tricks her into giving him the second bird by telling her the first is lonely without his brothers. Heron, here named Hercules, again intervenes, but this time escapes by scolding Jackal: 'Don't you ever say grace before meals, you wicked creature?' (ibid.: 17). Jackal is shamed into closing his eyes to do so, giving Heron the opportunity to fly away. In this way Joelson personalizes the characters and highlights the importance of good manners and a good education, imposing a metanarrative which in this case reflects British (colonial?) values and attitudes.

In many cases, at least until the 1980s, folktales were packaged and presented as representative of an alien, and often inferior, culture, with an intended white, often colonial, South African audience, or an audience in other parts of the English-speaking world. The idea that indigenous peoples and beliefs were primitive, inferior or childlike dates back to early comments by missionaries and ethnographers of indigenous peoples, and to nineteenth century books by travellers and novelists.[19] Niranjana (1992: 64–69) points out, with reference to Derrida, that ethnography and anthropology originated in a discovery of cultural difference which challenged European ethnocentricity, and yet this very ethnocentricity persisted in that it presumed 'a European self that sought to incorporate a non-European other' (Robinson, 1997: 40). Only through translation into European speech could 'savage' speech be heard, making the relationship between source-cultural discourses and target texts 'far more complex than between traditional source text and target text in translation studies' (Robinson, 1997: 43). Niranjana quotes from the anthropologist Godfrey Lienhart:

> The problem of describing to others how members of a remote tribe think . . . begins to appear largely as one of *translation*, of making the coherence primitive thought has in the language it really lives in, as clear as possible in our own. (Niranjana, 1992: 69)

The 'native' has a voice only through the translator and ethnographer, emphasizing the passivity of the author and the activity of the translator or ethnographer and thus projecting an image of the 'native' subject as backward, unaware, silent, and unable to create or influence the translated product (Robinson, 1997: 43–45).

The forewords and introductions to early collections confirm this image. Callaway (an English medical missionary and the first Bishop for Kaffraria) refers to an 'uncultivated people' (1868: ii), and Metelerkamp (who was born in 1866 and translated Khoi stories from Afrikaans) states that the tales in her collection 'embody the superstitions, the crude conceptions, the childish ideas of a primitive and rapidly disappearing people' (1914: Foreword). These attitudes became less extreme during the course of the century, but the stories were still presented as belonging to an alien culture, distant in time and place from the implied reader.[20] For example, the foreword to Phyllis Savory's *Zulu Fireside Tales* (1961) tells readers that the book is 'a little collection of Zulu tales, which tell of the adventures of Zulu children' (Savory, 1961: 5) and her introduction informs the reader that Zululand was 'a nation of strong men and brave warriors, some of whose customs were both strange and barbaric' (1961: 8). Hugh Tracey, enthusiastic about the songs which form an important part of the stories, and one of very few writers who accompanies his stories with musical scores, comments that the tales are 'fragments of the oral literature of simple folk who think only in terms of sound and invent wonderfully vivid exclamations to describe natural phenomena where no words exist adequate to match the event' (Tracey, 1967: xi).

In Savory's collections this distance between the characters and the readers is also evident in the narrative. A story about the origins of the Xhosa 'tribe' (written in 1963) concludes: 'The tribe fought many fierce battles against the British before they put down their arms to become the civilized and peaceful people they are today' (Savory, 1982: 96), an attitude not so far removed from Bourhill and Drake's collection written some 50 years earlier, the introduction to which states that 'The Kafir people . . . no longer make war on one another for the white people oblige them to live in peace' (1908: xi). Identification between the reader and the British is assumed, while identification with the Xhosa people is precluded. In early colonial collections the intended audience was white British colonial children, or children living in Britain.[21] Both of these groups could be expected to have experience of European folk and fairy tales and Joelson no doubt sought to make her stories accessible to her readers, despite presenting them as 'authentic' African stories. In the 1960s, Savory was writing for a white English-speaking South African audience living under *apartheid*, and as unfamiliar with the cultures of the stories as an international audience would be. History, ethnography and geography lessons were therefore often included, along with glossaries of words and pronunciations, maps and sketches. For example, Savory's 1963 introduction to her collection of Xhosa tales reads:

> The land inhabited by the Ama-Xhosa clans occupied the area of roughly 27 to 29 degrees East latitude, but 32 degrees to 34 degrees South latitude . . . Coming as they did from the North East of Central Africa, many of the characteristics of the Xhosa people are shared with the East African people. (Savory, 1982: 11)

More recent writers and retellers, and new translations of indigenous tales (such as Sigenu, 2003; Mhlophe, 2003) are more aware and politically conscious of the content of their works. However, the issue of who is best placed to retranslate and rewrite the tales remains a thorny one. Some scholars are convinced that a melting pot of cultures and stories is needed in order to create a common cultural base, expressed as a wish that 'African mythology . . . should become fused with western and other values enabling all children from Africa to internalize it as part of their common culture' (Tötemeyer, 1989: 397). However, there are dangers of dilution and distortion inherent in such an ideal, as stories are then inevitably remoulded to fit in with existing European metanarratives and a Western interpretation of the folktales.

Some modern rewriters state openly that their stories are not retellings of original tales. The back cover of M. Poland's 1987 collection tells the reader that '[T]hey are not folktales retold . . . but original stories inspired by African world-views', indicating a process of appropriation. Inspiration and writing entails interpreting those world-views, which are then reshaped and remoulded in reversions of the tales. In fact, this particular collection does include a fairly close retelling of a Zulu tale, here entitled *Child of the Doves* (Poland, 1987: 51–63).[22] Such appropriation has been widely criticised by scholars of African oral literature who are suspicious of the claim that rewriting protects and preserves the folktale tradition, and who suggest that the resulting translated texts 'may not be authentic at all' (Soko, 1986: 113–114). Indeed, the very use of the word 'authentic' is problematic given the numerous versions that continue to be retranslated and retold in both oral and written form. S. M. Guma goes further, and states that if a tale is African, it 'must be genuine, and not a poor imitation' and 'must come from African loins and presented as such to the world, without any internal or external trimmings' (Guma, 1967: 185). This is an ideal that is difficult to achieve in practice as any tales retold in

English for a contemporary audience, whether European or African, cannot avoid a degree of adaptation.

This process of rewriting and adaptation influences both the content and the selection of stories. As indicated above, early collectors tended to sanitise tales for their audience, a tendency that is also apparent in the selection of tales, with the omission of gory or scary, tales, or stories with tragic endings, echoing a similar kind of bowdlerization as found in contemporary retellings of Perrault or the Brothers Grimm and in the more general phenomenon of the 'disneyfication' of European folktales (Darcy, 2004). This desire to avoid unpleasant tales is often influenced by whether or not a work conforms to the dominant culture's expectations and image of the dominated culture (cf. Jaquemond in Robinson, 1997: 35). Many traditional South African tales involve ogres, monsters, and cannibals, but these are largely absent in recent English collections, reflecting a perpetuation of an attitude expressed by Jenkins that such stories 'are likely to repel young white readers' (1993:13) and reinforced by Tracey (1967: xi) in his foreword to *The Lion on the Path*:

> Many African stories have such brutal and tragic endings that they can only properly be featured in the case books of psychiatrists, where they should be noted by those students whose idealism for Africa outruns their capacity for realism.

One story featuring cannibals that does appear in several collections is a story about a magic cow or bull, which has to give permission before it can be slaughtered or eaten, which it can only be persuaded to do by the child hero, usually a boy, who by the end of the story brings it back to life. The tale reflects the importance of cattle in Southern African culture, as well as the significance of the particular relationship between a boy and his father's cattle (Knappert, 1977: 77). Individuals often had special relationships with a particular bull or cow, for whom names were assigned and songs composed to encourage them to walk in the right direction, or to follow the herd boy. One Nguni/Zulu version, *Mshayandlela – the Striker of the Road* (Du Toit, 1976: 35–38) is published in an academic work with Zulu and English parallel texts, implying, at least, a close similarity between the two texts. In keeping with oral performance, the language is simple and repetitive and the sentences short. The story begins:

> Once upon a time, a boy was herding. He was herding a big herd. When he was herding, he would sit on top of a big rock. One day cannibals came. (Du Toit, 1976: 35)

The cannibals threaten to kill and eat the herd boy who is forced to command the animal to allow the cannibals to slaughter it. In this version the boy brings the bull back to life before it is eaten, wrapping the meat in the hide before commanding the animal to wake up. When the cannibals chase him and the bull, the boy tricks them and the cannibals drown in the river – outwitting the cannibals is a common feature in such tales. At the end of the story the boy is given the bull as a reward for his bravery.

The other two retellings of this story are intended for children, one in Savory's *Zulu Fireside Tales* (1961: 43–46), the introduction to which was discussed above, and the second in a recent collection with a description of the tales on the back cover as 'lessons for good conduct and conduits of morality' (Godwin n.d.: 35–39) Both follow a similar storyline, but differ in style and register. Savory includes cannibals in her story, but this time the animal is a cow named Kenelinda. This story begins very differently from the previous one:

> In a golden valley in the heart of Zululand there lived a man called Thulwane, who had many cows. Next to his only son, Fana, they were nearest to his heart of all his possessions. Among them was one more precious than the rest. Her name was Kenelinda. Her sleek coat shone like gold in the sunshine. Her horns, as long as a man's arm, rose in graceful curves from her pretty head, and two great soft eyes looked out with love upon the world. (Savory, 1961: 42)

The most striking characteristic of this retelling is the romanticization of the narrative, the personalization of the characters, and the inclusion of extensive descriptive detail, indicated in the use of adjectives to describe both characters and the landscape, with references to 'rich grasses', 'grazing lands', and 'awakening countryside' in the 'early morning stillness'. The narrative follows a clear sequence with fluid links between the episodes. The text is accompanied by black and white illustrations which are rather stereotypical, but also highly romanticized, an example of which is seen in Figure 2.

In the undated, but post-1994 retelling,[23] *Dulube the Wonder Ox*, which we are told was collected and translated into English from *isiXhosa* by S. J. Neethling (Godwin n.d.: 35–39), there is no mention of cannibals, but the story is combined with another common element – twins – often considered unlucky and frequently abandoned at birth. The boy and girl survive by eating soil in the anthill where their mother leaves them and when they are old enough they set out to find their home, taking an ox from a homestead along the way. The ox is subsequently stolen in an event similar to those described

Figure 2. 'Kenelinda' (Savory, 1961: 46).

above. This time the girl commands the ox, representing a departure from the traditional male herd boy. The ox is again eventually brought back to life and the children return home to their village in time to stop their uncle from killing their mother in anger at her having abandoned them. An important feature of this version is the retention of the traditional isiXhosa (plus English translation) opening and closing formulae, beginning with *Kwathi ke kaloku ngantsomi* (It is time for a story, here it is) and ending with '*Phela phela ngantsomi*' (Thus my story ends) and the extensive use of the oral features of rhyme and repetition, such as:

> Dulube Dulube Dulube Dulube
> You should be roasted now Dulube
> You should be roasted now Dulube (ibid.: 38)

This version bears a more striking similarity to the academic version than Savory's version. The language is simple, the sentences are short, and there is no real characterization of either the ox or the children. Savory's, in contrast, may be described as a reversion framed by a European metanarrative. The main theme of the story becomes that of love – love for a favourite cow and a cow's love for her master. Although cattle remain an important indicator of wealth in South African indigenous cultures, Kenelinda is constructed in terms of Western culture and ideology – the cow is a nurturer, a symbol of domesticity, providing milk for calves and for humans (cf. Horsburgh, 1991: 49). Indeed, we are told 'her milk gushed forth at milking time so that all around her had their fill' (Savory, 1961: 42).

The stories discussed above are all translated or retold by white South African writers. In the 1980s several collections appeared in English written by black South African writers, such as *Isong le nkhono: African Folktales for Children* (Leshoai, 1989), and *Xhosa Fireside Tales* (Makhuphula, 1988). A feature of these collections is that both authors claim authenticity by telling the reader that they heard the stories from their grandmothers or elders. Naidu views such attempts to claim authenticity with suspicion, referring to a 'rhetoric of authenticity' established by colonial authors to 'imbue their texts with authority and epistemological status' (Naidu, 2001: 20). She considers that such a compulsion presupposes a belief that the reader needs to be convinced of the authenticity, and, by extension, the quality of the tales. Such a rhetoric today operates to affirm African culture, which is 'preserved' by the retelling of traditional tales in a continuation of attempts to 'reinvent a cultural identity for black people by romanticizing pre-colonial Africa (ibid.: 21) In any event, the tradition of storytelling continues today, traditionally taking place after dark, when the children would gather around a fire to listen to tales usually told by an older female member of the community. B. L. Leshoai tells the reader that the stories served as 'conscience-prickers and also to educate and entertain children and adults alike' (Leshoai, 1989: Foreword). The back cover of N. Makhuphula's collection tells us to imagine the author 'as a grandmother encircled by her children and grandchildren as they listen careful to every gem that pours from her mouth'. In a similar fashion, a recent collection of stories by a black African writer and storyteller, Geina Mhlophe, also acknowledges her grandmother as her source, telling the reader: [My grandmother] encouraged my imagination to run wild, and I really believed in those laughing crocodiles and flying tortoises that she told me about' (Mhlophe, 2003: Author's Note). But, although she also tells the reader that she loved the tales about the 'scary *amaZimzim*' , she does not include any of these tales in her collection, which may reflect her wish to attract as wide an audience as possible.[24]

Another collection by a black African writer, Kholeka Sigenu, was published in 2003, and provides a possible example of reinterpellation. It is a collection of five Xhosa tales published as part of a community project[25] intended to enable writers to publish independently.[26] The primary objective of the publication was to educate and stimulate discussion among South African readers

Figure 3. Illustration inside the front cover of *Ezakowethu – Folktales from Home* (Sigenu, 2003).

on aspects of modern society based on traditional tales (Sigenu, 2003: 4). It was first published in *isiXhosa* based on folktales narrated by her paternal grandmother and then translated by Sigenu into English (ibid.: 3). Each of the five tales involves ogres or cannibals, who are usually, but not always, outwitted by the human characters. The stories are accompanied by graphic black and white drawings by Siphiwe Ratsibe, such as in Figure 3, providing readers with a clear image of the cannibals and talking beasts in the stories.

The writing style is simple and straightforward, again in keeping with the oral tradition. Sigenu also retains the rhymes, repetitions and the opening and closing formulae typical of Bantu folktales. Each story begins with the expression 'long, long ago' (in English) and ends with the traditional ending in isiXhosa (with no translation): *Phela phela ngantsomi* ('here ends the tale'). The characters all have Xhosa names, sometimes extremely difficult for an English speaker to pronounce, with no simplification or pronunciation guide. Other Xhosa words used in the stories are footnoted, uncommon in children's literature but included here for educational purposes, given that local English-speaking readers would most probably be learning at least some Xhosa at school.

In the first tale, *The Story of Ntonganayentsimbi*, a young girl is kidnapped by a clan of ogres and made the wife of the chief. Many years later, her brother, Bhuzalusiba, comes to rescue her. In one bizarre scene the reader is told that when the ogres go hunting, it is customary for them each to take off one leg and leave it at home, piling them in a 'carefree manner' (ibid.: 12). By means of a variety of complex and lengthy ruses Bhuzalusiba and his sister eventually escape while the ogres are hunting, taking all the cattle and other domestic animals with them. In this story, the rather dull-witted ogres are tricked by Bhuzalusiba and all drown in the river.

Humans do not always outwit the cannibals in these stories however, and may come to a gruesome end, usually as a result of their own stupidity or failure to follow good advice. *The Story of Nonqana* tells of a man who disobeys strict instructions from the only survivor in his wife's village not to kill a goat, despite his hunger, as the smell will attract the cannibals who ate all the other inhabitants. He ignores the warning and both he and his wife are devoured in a scene that is described in gory detail:

> They had almost finished eating her *before* she died. Each one of them took a piece of the poor woman. One took an arm, one took the other. At the same time one took a leg and another the other. While some tore the body into pieces the others were feasting at her head. They finished her off by licking even the smallest speck of blood from the floor. (ibid.: 29)

Despite the gruesome nature of the tales, in the second section of the work, which is a critical analysis by Yoliso Madolo of the themes and the behaviour of the characters, aimed at teachers and others who work with children, Madolo remarks that the 'scary characters . . . do not have any impact on the child', because the tales are set clearly in a magical world, distant in time and space, and when the narrator announces that the tale has ended the child is brought back to reality (Sigenu: 59). This may sound unconvincing to those unfamiliar with the storytelling tradition in South Africa. In discussions with a number of people who remember hearing these stories as children they confirmed that they did not feel in any way afraid. The opening and closing formulae play an important role in this process, demarcating the fictional from the real world. At the same time, however, the critical analysis acknowledges the very real dangers present in children's lives, focusing on attitudes towards women, the abuse of women and children and especially the so-called 'idiocy and selfishness' of the male characters (ibid.: 58). Indeed, the reader is told that the ogres are symbolic of male behaviour – 'especially of some South African men in the twenty-first century', and that the cannibalistic eating is symbolic of abuse, domination and even rape (ibid.: 62). This collection is unique among English language collections, and may be seen as the beginning of a new trend in which African storytellers are rewriting their own stories within an African metanarrative and metaethic. It is particularly interesting that this collection has appeared in both isiXhosa and English and is being read in schools by speakers of both languages.

Information on the intended audiences of the recent collections is provided not only by the content and language of the stories, but also by the illustrations, packaging and peritexts. D. Godwin's publication is a small format, low cost publication, with one or two black and white illustrations (with no named artist) for each story. The blurb tells us that the compilation 'reflects the multicultural diversity of South Africa', and that all the stories 'have their origin in the oral tradition and are rendered in typical narrative form using dialogue, rhythmical repetition and onomatopoeia'. The introduction also explains that the stories serve as lessons for good behaviour, warnings or explanations of mysteries. The Sigenu collection is also a small format, cheaply produced book with distinctive black and white illustrations (see Figure 3 above). The work is addressed to a young South African audience, as Sigenu refers to 'our indigenous traditional literature' (implying 'our' = South African, and because the work originally appeared in Xhosa) (Sigenu: 4) and the lengthy analysis of each tale at the end indicates the primarily educational intention of the authors in producing a work intended for use in schools. Although it may appear unlikely to appeal to an overseas audience, the author reports that 30 or 40 copies of the English version have been sold in the United Kingdom.

Heale and Stewart's glossy colour collection (2001) is clearly aimed at both a South African and international[27] audience. The back cover describes it as 'a fascinating collection of myths, legends and folktales to enliven the imagination of young readers'. There is a brief introduction in which the authors make inclusive reference to 'our country' and 'our shadowy history', indicating the dual audience of South Africans and international readers. The introduction also frames the stories against a Western background, stating that the myths are 'a bit like the fairy stories of old Africa'. The illustrations are rather Europeanized, with the children portrayed with European or Asian features rather than African, as shown in Figure 4.

Its international appeal does not however detract from the fact that this collection along with others such as *Madiba Magic* (Rode, 2002) were published in a real attempt to forge unity and national identity between the

Figure 4. Illustration from 'The cattle herder's song' (Heale and Stewart, 2001: 24).

formerly disparate cultures of South Africa, and to efface the divisions inherent in a formerly divided country. They contain tales from different Southern African cultures, San, Khoi, Nama, Swazi, Zulu, Xhosa, Sotho together with Cape Malay stories and South African Dutch/Afrikaans stories and legends. Indeed, Jenkins describes Heale and Stewart's collection as 'a creation of a transformed South Africa' (2006: 106). It can certainly be regarded as an attempt to mediate between these different cultures, especially given the historical and ethnographical notes accompanying each story. P. W. Grobbelaar and S. Verster attempt the same in *Famous South African Folktales* (2003), which includes 'stories borrowed from Western Europe, Eastern cultures and the rest of Africa' (2003: back cover).

The inclusion of the explanatory notes may appear to perpetuate the exotic nature of the tales, 'presenting them as curiosities from 'other' and different cultures' (Naidu, 2001: 20), although the inclusion of tales from several different cultures counteracts any such perception. Another glossy, colour collection by D. Stewart, *Folktales from Africa* (2006) also includes stories from other African countries, which all end with a 'fact file' on the country of origin, and is aimed at familiarising both contemporary South African and international readers with places such as Togo, Ghana and Ethiopia. In her introduction Stewart states that

> this collection of folktales drawn from the African landscape is intended for enjoyment and entertainment, but it is hoped you will gain more insight into the countries from which the tales have been sourced. (Stewart, 2006: 4)

The collections discussed above provide evidence of all three processes of mediation, imposition and appropriation. Retellings within the framework of a Western metanarrative and reversions of virtual source texts are present in the majority of collections by white writers. Early collections such as Joelson's (1926) provide evidence of both appropriation and imposition, in that elements of traditional stories are taken and rewritten within an external meta-ethic. More recent collections are indicative of a process of genuine attempts at mediation, in keeping with a project of national unity in translation and rewriting, despite the conflict between acknowledging and claiming the stories as South African and the need to provide extensive background knowledge for both local and international readers.

Retellings within the framework of an African metanarrative are apparent in collections by black African writers. These have a more direct relationship with a source text – often acknowledged as the author's grandmother – which affects the narrative style and language used. This reflects attempts by A. C. Jordan (1973) to create a hybrid text in which difference is synthesised into 'something new and progressive' Naidu (2001: 23). In Scheub's introduction to Jordan's collection he writes that Jordan 'used techniques of the short story to bring life to the skeletal outlines, and he thereby moved away from the original *ntsomi*[28] performances into the hybrid art form that exists on the pages of this book' (Scheub in Jordan, 1973: 13). As in the collections by Godwin and Mhlophe, these stories include repetition and rhymes in isiXhosa or other languages, but the narrative is reworked in accordance with Western tradition and the norms of English style, representing a combination of strategies of domestication and foreignization.

The fact that Mhlophe's work is published in a glossy hardback format places it at the crossroads of the two trends and as such it is also an example of hybridisation and mediation – the stories have been passed down, and Mhlophe produces reversions which incorporate her own mixture of language and culture as she tells the stories as if to her own child, who is half German, half Zulu, drawing on both Western and African traditions. She includes closing formulae and Zulu words in her narrative, and her characters have names that an English-speaking child or parent would struggle with, such as 'Gongqongqo' and 'Dabulamanzi' but it is clear that her intended audience is both local and international when she writes: 'Because of the flexibility of this medium, one story can be interpreted in a variety of ways, making it possible for audiences of different ages and cultures to find what they need in it' (Mhlophe, 2003: Author's Note). In addition she travels extensively, taking her stories all over the world. In negotiating between different cultures her work may be regarded as part reinterpellation and part mediation.

There is a balance to be drawn in order to present cross-cultural translations and reversions in a way that benefits both the traditional tales and contemporary readers. Mhlophe and Sigenu are storytellers who tell their stories in both English and their mother tongues, with inevitable modifications and changes directly related to the nature of the two languages involved. Mhlophe comments: 'when I have to express myself in English . . . I find that some things are not possible to say'. But, she goes on: 'that never stops me from continuing to tell the wonderful stories of my [African/Zulu] people and share their imaginative richness with others' (2003: Author's Note). In pursuing a project of national unity and identity, writers, translators and storytellers need to be acutely aware of the issues raised by such a project, and avoid falling into the trap of continuing to represent a 'pre-colonial African paradise'. The collections by Sigenu and Mhlophe indicate that a process of retranslation and reinterpellation has begun.

Notes

1. For a more detailed discussion see Jenkins (2006: 61-86).
2. Today there are eleven official South African languages, nine of which are indigenous languages with the official names: isiZulu, isiXhosa, isiNdebele, siSwati, Sesotho, Sepedi, Setswana, Xitsonga and Tshivenda (salanguages.com). The earliest transcriptions of indigenous tales were the stories told in /Xam, one of the group of San languages (Bleek and Lloyd, 1864) and Zulu tales (Callaway, 1868).
3. Without these early recordings, the large number of subsequent retellings could not have been produced (cf. Jenkins, 2006: 89). The Bleeks, for example, made the recording of the stories of the San people a life's work, transcribing some 12 000 pages of their folklore.
4. Up until the 1970s South Africa produced approximately 12 to 15 times more collections of folktales than published in Canada or Australia (Jenkins, 2002: 269).
5. In 2001 the total number of new children's book titles, excluding readers, published in South Africa in all eleven official languages was only 371 (Arnold, 2004). Unfortunately there is no available breakdown of these figures according to type, genre or age group.

6. This term is widely used in Translation Studies, but in varying ways. See Bassnett and Lefevere 1990, Baker 2006.

7. Concern surrounding cultural appropriation is reflected in a recent San Media and Research Contract which was drawn up by the Working Group of Indigenous Minorities in Southern Africa (WIMSA) 'to ensure that all San intellectual property (including images, traditional knowledge, music and other heritage components as recorded in any medium) is controlled and protected' (WIMSA, 2001).

8. 'World-view' is used here rather than 'ideology', which is a more complex and problematic term. 'World-view' can, however, be defined as Hatim and Mason define ideology, following P. Simpson (1993), as 'the tacit assumptions, beliefs and value systems which are shared collectively by social groups' (Hatim and Mason, 1997: 144).

9. See Mona Baker on the framing of narratives in *Translation and Conflict* (Baker, 2006).

10. 'Peritext' is defined by G. Genette as 'those liminal devices and conventions, both within and outside the book, that form part of the complex mediation between book, author, publisher and reader' (1997: i). See Jenkins 2001 for an analysis of peritexts in South African children's literature.

11. Amasi is a thick, sour form of buttermilk.

12. For example, Marguerite Poland, a prolific South African writer for both children and adults, grew up in the Eastern Cape and speaks fluent isiXhosa, but describes her stories, such as those published in *The Wood-Ash Stars* (1983) as "not folk tales retold . . . but original stories inspired by African world-views (Poland, 1987 [1983]: back cover).

13. This chapter is confined to a discussion of collections in English. A comparative study of collections in the other languages of South Africa would be a useful area of further research.

14. Reversions generally have numerous pre-texts, with no identifiable 'first telling', and intermediary versions are often used. An extreme example of a reversion is Terry Pratchett's retellings of Shakespeare's plays – *Lords and Ladies* (1992) (Stephens and McCallum, 1998: 4, 255).

15. It is however problematic to assume a universal 'Western metaethic' in that 'the West' is by no means homogenous, an issue taken up by Michael Cronin (see Munday, 2001: 137–138).

16. A study of live story-telling might well link up with Hatim's discussion of the translation of 'orate' languages, which rely more than other languages on repetition, alliteration, rhythm and formulary expressions (Hatim, 2007: 92). Morula Pictures has recently pioneered a television series of 'shorts' consisting of folktales for South African children, *Magic Cellar*, which they describe as 'designed to give African children an understanding of their own culture' and which are 'based on African folktales, collected in part from interviews conducted with elders in villages across South Africa'. (www.morula.co.za/productions.htm)

17. This work was published by Juta, in Cape Town, a prominent educational publishing house, but earlier works for children had been published by Juta in London, such as Mary Carey-Hobson's *The Farm in the Karoo* (1883). Publishing in South Africa was well-established by the early years of the twentieth century, concentrated in the major towns: Cape Town, Johannesburg, Durban, Bloemfontein and Pretoria (Jenkins, 2006: xii).

18. Charles Briggs describes this sometimes dubious conviction of similarity between original tales and their translations as the 'image of intertextual transparency' or the belief that 'texts created

through transcription, translation and editing bear an intrinsic connection to their source such that the former are extensions or synecdoches of the latter' (quoted in Naidu, 2001: 19).

19. Just one example comes from George Mannville Fenn who wrote in his novel *Off to the Wilds* (1882): 'These people seem to me more like children than men'. Darwinism also governed perceptions at the time of indigenous people 'representing earlier stages in the evolution of human society' (Jenkins, 2006: 100).

20. This term was first developed by Wolfgang Iser (1974). It is now widely used in literary theory, and particularly in relation to children's literature as it refers to a hypothetical reader who is guided by the text itself to a particular interpretation; it is also closely linked to notions of subjectivity and point of view.

21. The early books were published in England, or by publishers such as Juta and MacMillan, which had offices in both South Africa and England.

22. This text is discussed in more detail, comparing a translation by Callaway (1868), a retelling by Savory (1974) and a retelling in Zulu (Msimang, 1987) in Inggs (2004).

23. The collection begins with a reference to Archbishop Desmond Tutu's use of the term 'Rainbow Nation' in 1994.

24. Her books are marketed overseas, for example, and are readily available via websites such as amazon.com.

25. The Community Publishing Project was launched in August 2001 by the Centre for the Book and NB Publishers in Cape Town, funded by Nasboek. Subsequent funding was also received from other sources (see Community Publishing, National Library of South Africa).

26. Two print runs in isiXhosa of 500–600 have sold out, and are being used in some schools for Grades 4 and 5. The English print run of 600 copies has not done so well but copies are also being used in schools (Personal conversation with author, April 2008).

27. I deduce this from the fact that the books are commercial ventures and publishers need to sell them as widely as possible. All of the recent colour publications (and the older works by Savory) are readily available on amazon.com.

28. *Ntsomi* is a Xhosa word meaning the fictitious, mythological and fantastic.

References

Althusser, L. (1971), *Lenin and Philosophy, and Other Essays*, trans. Ben Brewster. New York: Monthly Review Press.

Arnold, A. M. (2004), 'Review of the State of the Publishing Industry in South Africa and National Influences'. Available at www.liasa.org.za/interest_groups/lacig/LACIG_Conference_May2004_Arnold.pdf (accessed 17 January 2008).

Baker, M. (2006), *Translation and Conflict*. London and New York: Routledge.

Bleek, W. H. I. (1864), *Reynard the Fox in South Africa, or, Hottentot Fables and Tales*. London: Trubner.

Bourhill, E. J. and Drake, J. B. (1908), *Fairy Tales from South Africa Collected from Original Native Sources*. London: Macmillan. Available at: www.archive.org/details/fairytalesfromso00bourrich (accessed 21 May 2008).

Callaway, H. (1868), *Nursery Tales, Traditions and Histories of the Zulus, in Their Own Words, with a Translation into English and Notes*. Vol. 1. Springvale, Natal: J. A. Blair.

'Community Publishing' National Library of South Africa. Available at www.nlsa.ac.za/NLSA/centreforthebook/projects/publishing (accessed 4 June 2008).

Darcy, J. (2004), 'The disneyfication of the European Fairy Tale' in N. Campbell, J. Davies and G. McKay (eds), *Issues in Americanisation and Culture*. Edinburgh: Edinburgh University Press, pp. 181–196.

Du Toit, A. (1976), *Content and Context of Zulu Folk-narratives*. Florida : University of Florida.

Finnegan, R. (1970), *Oral Literature in Africa*. Oxford: Clarendon.

Genette, G. (1997 [French text 1987]), *Paratexts: Thresholds of Interpretation*, trans. Jane E. Lewin. Cambridge: CUP.

Godwin, D. (n.d.), *Folktales from the Rainbow Nation*. Pretoria: Van Schaik.

Grobbelaar, P. W. and Verster, S. (2003), *Famous South African Folk Tales*. Cape Town: Human & Rousseau.

Guma, S. M. (1967), *The Form, Content and Technique of Traditional Literature in Southern Sotho*. Pretoria: Van Schaik.

Hatim, B. (2007), 'Intervention at text and discourse levels in the translation of "orate" languages', in J. Munday (ed.) *Translation as Intervention*. London: Continuum, pp. 84–96.

Hatim, B. and Mason, I. (1997), *The Translator as Communicator*. London and New York: Routledge.

Heale, J. and Stewart, D. (2001), *African Myths and Legends*. Cape Town: Struik Publishers.

Honey, J. A. (1969), *South African Folktales*. New York: Negro Universities Press.

Horsburgh, S. (1991), *The translation of Zulu folktales for English speaking children in South Africa*. Unpublished MA Research Project. University of the Witwatersrand, Johannesburg.

Inggs, J. A. (2004), 'What is a South African folktale? Reshaping traditional tales through translation and adaptation'. *Papers: explorations into children's literature*, 14, (1), 15–23.

Jenkins, E. (1988), 'The presentation of African folktales in some South African English versions', in E. R. Sienart and A. N. Bell (eds), *Catching Winged Words: Oral Tradition and Education*. Durban: Natal University Press, pp. 191–202.

— (1993), *Children of the Sun*. Ravan Press: Johannesburg.

— (2001), 'Reading outside the lines: peritexts and authenticity in South African children's books', *The Lion and the Unicorn*, (25), 1, 115–127.

— (2002), 'Adult agendas in publishing South African folktales for children', in *Children's Literature in Education*, 33, (4), 269–284.

— (2006), *National Character in South African English Children's Literature*. New York and London: Routledge.

Joelson, A. 1926. *How the Ostrich Got His Name and Other South African Stories for Children*. Cape Town: Juta.

Jordan, A. C. (1973), *Tales from Southern Africa*. Berkeley, Los Angeles and London: University of California Press.

Knappert, J. (1977), *Bantu Myths and Other tales*. Leiden: E. J. Brill.

Leshoai, B. L. (1989), *Iso le Nkhono: African Folktales for Children*. Braamfontein: Skotaville.

Lefevere, A. (1992), *Translation, Rewriting and the Manipulation of Literary Fame*. London: Routledge.

Makhuphula, N. (1988), *Xhosa Fireside Tales*. Johannesburg: Seriti sa Sechaba.

Metelerkamp, S. (1914), *Outa Karel's Stories: South African Folklore Tales*. London: Macmillan.

Mhlophe, G. (2003), *Stories of Africa*. Pietermaritzburg: University of Natal Press.

Mofokeng, S. M. (1951), *A Study of Folktales in Sotho*. Unpublished MA dissertation. Johannesburg: University of the Witwatersrand.

Msimang, C. T. (1987), *Kwesukasukela*. Pretoria: Sigma Press.

Munday, J. (2001), *Introducing Translation Studies*. London: Routledge.

Mutahi, K. (1994), 'Translation problems in oral literature', in A. Bukenya, W. Kabiri and O.Okombo (eds), *Understanding Oral Literature*. Nairobi: Nairobi University Press, pp. 26–35.

Mutwa, C. (1996), *Isilwane: The Animal*. Cape Town: Struik.

Naidu, S. (2001), 'The myth of authenticity': folktales and nationalism in the "new South Africa"', in *Scrutiny2*, 6, (2), 17–26.

Ngcongwane, S. D. (1988), 'Some serious evaluation of the oral literature in the African languages', in *Catching Winged Words: Oral Tradition and Education*. Durban: Natal University Press, pp. 182–190.

Niranjana, T. (1992), *Siting Translation*. Berkeley: University of California Press.

Poland, M. (1987 [1983]), *The Wood-Ash Stars*. Cape Town: David Philip.

Robinson D. (1997), *Translation and Empire: Post-colonial Theories Explained*. Manchester: St Jerome.

Rode, L. (ed.) (2002), *Madiba Magic: Nelson Mandela's Favourite Stories*. Cape Town: Tafelberg.

Savory, P. (1961), *Zulu Fireside Tales*. Cape Town: Howard Timmins.

—(1974), *Bantu Folk Tales from Southern Africa*. Cape Town: Howard Timmins.

—(1982) *African Fireside Tales: Part 1: Xhosa, Matabele, Batswana*. Cape Town: Howard Timmins.

Scheub, H. (1971), 'Translation of African oral narrative-performance to the written word', in *Yearbook of Comparative and General Literature 20*, pp. 28–36.

—(1975), *The Xhosa Ntsomi*. Oxford: Clarendon Press.

—(1977), 'The technique of the expansible image in Xhosa Ntsomi-performances', in B. Lindfors (ed.) *Forms of Folklore in Africa*. Austin & London: University of Texas Press, pp. 37–63.

Sigenu K. V. (2003), *Ezakowethu – folktales from home*. Cape Town: Khol Publishers.

Simpson, P. (1993), *Language, Ideology and Point of View*. London: Routledge.

Soko, B. J. (1986), 'Translating oral literature into European languages', in R. A.Whitaker, E. R. Sienaert (eds), *Oral Tradition and Literacy: Changing Visions of the World*. Durban, Natal University Oral Documentation and Research Centre, pp.113–121.

Stephens J. and McCallum R. (1998), *Retelling Stories, Framing Culture*. New York: Garland.

Stewart D. (2004), *The Zebra's Stripes and Other African Animal Tales*, Cape Town: Struik.

—(2006), *Folktales from Africa*. (Cape Town: Struik).

Tötemeyer, A. (1989), 'Impact of African mythology on South African juvenile literature', *South African Journal of Library and Information Sciences*, 57, 4, 392–401.

Tracey, H. (1967), *The Lion on the Path and Other African Stories*. London: Routledge and Kegan Paul.

Venuti, L. (1992), *Rethinking Translation: Discourse, Subjectivity, Ideology.* London and New York: Routledge.

—(1995), *The Translator's Invisibility: A History of Translation.* London: Routledge.

WIMSA (2001), *San Media and Research Contract.* Available at: www.san.org.za/wimsa/ar2001_2/ar_02_p26.htm (accessed 5 June 2008).

The Concepts of Domestication and Foreignization in the Translation of Children's Literature in the South African Educational Context

Haidee Kruger

8

Chapter Outline

Introduction

In South Africa, linguistic diversity is protected by the Constitution, which awards official status to 11 languages which 'must enjoy parity of esteem and must be treated equitably' (South Africa, 1996: 6(4)). Translation is playing an increasingly important role within this multilingual context, in all areas of the social domain: administrative, legal, commercial, literary and educational. Against this background it is important to note that the functions of translation in South Africa (as elsewhere), extend beyond the traditional conception of translation as simply aimed at facilitating communication. As Venuti (1998: 3) points out: 'Translations are produced for many reasons, literary and commercial, pedagogical and technical, propagandistic and diplomatic'. While communication is undoubtedly one of the functions of language (and translation) it is never merely that.[1]

Children's literature is no exception in this regard. The Children's Literature Research Unit at the University of South Africa (UNISA) points out the role that translation plays in the children's literature market in South Africa:

> As a result of the small local market, few original books with full colour illustra-
> tions are published. Collaboration with overseas publishers and the simultaneous
> publication of a book in various indigenous languages is often the only way to
> make a publication viable. Also publishers of children's books concentrate on the
> publishing series, beginner and second language readers. (Children's Literature
> Research Unit, 2006)

This comment raises a number of issues that play a significant role in the translation of children's literature in South Africa. Firstly, it clearly indicates the defining and constraining role of commercial considerations. It also reflects the continuing emphasis on the interfaces between children's literature and education in South Africa (to some degree also, of course, linked to commercial considerations). Lastly, in an oblique way, it suggests some of the issues of ideology and power that shape and are shaped by book publishing in South Africa, though these factors are not given any prominence in this comment.[2] Moreover, this assessment of the current state of children's book publishing in South Africa does not reflect the complexity of the situation. Specifically, there are a number of different scenarios in which the translation of children's books takes place, involving different relationships of power. These different scenarios may be broadly organized into two categories, based on very generalized geographical and cultural relationships between source and target texts.

In the first instance, there is the translation of (mostly) English-language children's books produced in Northern and Western cultures, translated mostly into Afrikaans and occasionally into the other indigenous languages. Venuti (1998: 2) describes this type of situation as one which allows transnational corporations to dominate the print and electronic media in developing countries by entrenching established unequal cultural relations between the hegemonic Northern and Western countries and countries in Africa, Asia and

South America. This is also the situation outlined by Dankert (quoted in Hunt, 1992: 111–112), who points out that increasing literacy in Africa has attracted the interest of multinational publishing companies, which export European, Anglo-American and 'superficially Africanized' children's books to African countries, or have them produced by their African subsidiaries. This may lead to a situation which Dankert (quoted in Hunt, 1992: 112) describes as 'a kind of uncontrolled, which is to say strictly market economy governed, proliferation of originally English-language children's books'.

In the second instance, there is the translation of locally produced Afrikaans and English books from one to the other language, and into African languages. However, virtually no books produced in the African languages (and there are comparatively few)[3] are translated into Afrikaans and English. Unequal relationships of power are therefore also evident on this level.

These scenarios, though similar in some ways, involve different ideological, social, commercial, literary, textual and linguistic dynamics, thus calling for different translation approaches and strategies. In this, the tension between domesticating and foreignizing approaches is significant, but in this chapter I argue that the situation in South Africa problematizes distinctions between the domestic and the foreign, and calls for hybridized translation approaches as much as for hybridized concepts of translation. This chapter therefore considers the usage, relevance and application of the concepts of domestication and foreignization in the context of the translation of children's literature in South Africa, with particular emphasis on the educational function of children's literature.

Translation and the educational discourse in South Africa

Within the flux of local and global discourses, translation plays a crucial and complex role. Venuti (2000: 468) makes this complexity clear:

> Translation never communicates in an untroubled fashion because the translator negotiates the linguistic and cultural differences of the foreign text by reducing them and supplying another set of differences, basically domestic, drawn from the receiving language and culture to enable the foreign to be received there. The for-

eign text, then, is not so much communicated as inscribed with domestic intelligibilities and interests.

Venuti (2000: 486) then suggests some of the stages in the translation process during which this inscription takes place: the selection of a text for translation, the development of discursive strategies to translate it, and the processing of the text by readers.

These comments also apply to the translation of children's literature, and are particularly relevant to a study of the translation of children's literature in the South African educational context. Children's literature texts in South Africa form part of a system of discourses: literary and otherwise, global as well as local. The choice of texts to be translated, in the educational context and elsewhere, is profoundly affected by this network of discourses (or systems) and the positions and functions of children's literature within it (see also Oittinen, 2006: 40; Pascua-Febles, 2006: 111). Similarly, the choice of translation approaches and strategies used during the translation process, the establishment of the translated product, the dissemination of this product, and its reception by readers are all affected by this ever-changing network of discourses.

In the context of this paper, a particularly significant discourse is the educational discourse, itself a repository of the social, political and cultural values, norms and discourses prevalent in a society. Education, in the broader as well as the narrower sense, is one of the many uses of children's books. Stephens, for example, points out the broad educational function of children's literature, which, generally speaking, aims to instil in the child a positive apperception of particular sociocultural values, including morality, ethics, traditions and aspirations (1992: 3).

In Africa, the educational function of children's literature has received a great deal of emphasis. Dankert (quoted in Hunt, 1992: 111–112) points out that the expansion of educational systems has been an important goal in newly independent African states, with the result that school books and readers have formed a significant focus of publishing for children. In South Africa currently, the basis of the educational discourse is the *Revised National Curriculum Statement* (Department of Education, 2002). This policy document makes the interconnectedness of the various discourses that constitute society clear, focusing particularly on the interconnectedness of the social, political, economic and educational discourses. The document describes the educational system under apartheid as follows:

This education system prepared children in different ways for the positions they were expected to occupy in social, economic and political life under apartheid. In each department, the curriculum played a powerful role in reinforcing inequality. What, how and whether children were taught differed according to the roles they were expected to play in the wider society. (2002: 4)

In contrast, the *Revised National Curriculum Statement* bases itself on the aims of the Constitution of the Republic of South Africa (Act No. 108 of 1996), and wishes to aid the establishment of a society based on democratic values, social justice and human rights (Department of Education, 2002: 7). In this process, a great deal of emphasis is placed on nurturing values, such as democracy, social justice and equity, non-racism and non-sexism, human dignity, an open society, accountability, respect, the rule of law and reconciliation (Department of Education, 2001: 3). This educational discourse constructs the child (and the child-reader) and the function of learning (and reading) in a very particular way. In the critical and developmental outcomes, the backbone of the curriculum (Department of Education, 2002: 11), significant emphasis is placed on the pragmatic and social outcomes of learning. The seven critical outcomes, for example, centre on problem-solving, teamwork, personal responsibility, information skills, communication skills, technological and environmental skills, and the ability to develop macro-vision. The five developmental outcomes focus on learning skills, citizenship, cultural appreciation, job-seeking skills and entrepreneurial skills.

Just as the education system under apartheid 'prepared children in different ways for the positions they were expected to occupy in social, economic and political life', so does the current education system – though this society has changed dramatically, in both concept and reality. In part, these changes account for the focus of the current education system, which also has to function as a kind of corrective for the social, cultural and economic consequences of apartheid.[4]

Naturally, this educational discourse and the way that it constructs children and readers, and the function of learning and reading, will have a determining effect on literature produced for children, the literature selected for inclusion in the curriculum, as well as the way that literature is taught in schools. It will also impact on the types of texts selected for translation, and the way that they are translated. This is also true for children's books used outside the formal school environment, as these books interact with the same educational and larger social discourses.

Foreignizing and domesticating approaches to the translation of children's literature

Van Coillie and Verschueren (2006: v) make the following comment about the translation of children's literature:

> Translators do not simply stand 'in between' source text and target audience, from the beginning they are always an intrinsic part of the negotiating dialogue itself, holding a fragile, unstable middle between the social forces that act upon them (the imposed norms of the publishing industries and the expectations of the adults who act as buyers and often as co-readers), their own interpretation of the source text and their assessment of the target audience.

This comment raises many of the difficulties inherent in the translation of children's literature (difficulties to a large extent shared by all translated literature, but exacerbated in children's literature because of the problems surrounding the dual child/adult readership). In a postcolonial context, there are other difficulties too. Ray (1996: 653–654), for example, points out that developing countries have had to develop an established body of children's literature in a relatively short space of time (less than half a century), whereas children's literature in European countries has developed over centuries. In this accelerated process, translation can, and often does, play a key role, despite the fact that the common problems and challenges of post-colonial societies complicate the situation – particularly, power differentials between powerful colonial languages (like English) and the indigenous languages, as well as cultural differences and conflicts (Pellowski, 1996: 665). However, while the merits of translating children's literature, as opposed to writing original works in the indigenous language, may be argued (see Ghesquiere, 2006: 29–32), the fact remains that in many developing countries, including South Africa, the translation of children's literature plays a significant role, in the educational context and elsewhere.

As in general approaches to translation, the tension between source-text orientation (foreignization) and target-text orientation (acculturation or domestication) is a central concern in the study of translated children's literature. Bassnett (2005: 120–121) simplifies the issue in the following way:

> The issue hinges on whether a translator should seek to eradicate traces of other-ness in a text so as to reshape that text for home consumption in accordance with

the norms and expectations that prevail in the target system, or whether to opt for a strategy that adheres more closely to the norms of the source system . . . foreignization ensures that a text is self-consciously other, so that readers can be in no doubt that what they are encountering derives from a completely different system, in short that it contains traces of a foreignness that mark it as distinct from anything produced from within the target culture.

The tension between foreignization and domestication has been a staple of debates in translation studies for centuries (Bassnett, 2005: 120), but remains particularly topical, especially in a post-colonial context like South Africa. The work of Venuti (1995, 1998) is especially important in this regard. For Venuti (1995: 20) domesticating approaches are a type of 'ethnocentric violence', excluding or reducing cultural difference to sameness. In his opinion, foreignizing translation strategies, however, have the potential to be a means of resisting ethnocentrism, racism and imperialism.

In the case of children's literature it appears that most translators and scholars favour a target-text orientation,[5] as suggested by Tabbert (2002: 314), who points out the tendency to effect radical changes in translations of children's literature – ranging from the linguistic (spelling, vocabulary and idiom) to culturally specific allusions, settings and character names, all with the aim of making the text more accessible to and aligning it more closely with the experience of the child reader in the target culture. Oittinen (2006: 39–41) similarly refers to the manipulation of children's literature in translation, which may, in her view, have positive or negative consequences.

Scholars like Nikolajeva (1996), Oittinen (2000) and Shavit (1986) all favour a target-text oriented approach (exercised to various degrees) to the translation of children's literature – for well-motivated reasons, most saliently the emphasis that is placed on the reader in children's literature. Oittinen (2000: 3) clearly states that her attention is focused on the needs of the readers of a children's book in translation, including both the translator and the target-language readers. Shavit (1986: 112) points out that approaches to the translation of children's literature are largely target-text oriented, because of the emphasis that is placed on the 'prevailing society's perceptions of the child's ability to read and comprehend'. Nikolajeva (1996: 28) also makes her target-oriented preference clear: 'It is not only permitted but highly desirable to deviate from the source text if this is demanded by the reader's response.' Nikolajeva (1996: 30) argues her point from within a semiotic approach, stating that semiotic signs in a children's book are familiar to the reader, and help the child to relate details in the book to a social and cultural system existing outside the text and interacting with it. However, translation complicates this process, particularly when no cultural adaptation is done (Nikolajeva, 1996: 30).

The preferred option, therefore, seems to be a target-text oriented approach of domestication, localization and cultural adaptation (to varying degrees). However, this option also brings along with it various problems. If one of the functions of children's literature is to foster international cooperation, mutual respect, and intercultural understanding and tolerance (Biamonte, 2002: 27; IBBY, 2007; Joels, 1999: 66) one could argue that the foreignization of the translated text may well serve this purpose better than domestication or localization. Yamazaki (2002: 53) points out that the domestication of the children's book in translation 'deprives child readers of the chance to realize the wealth of cultural diversity that surrounds them'. Yamazaki (2002: 59) aligns her argument with that of Stolt (2006 [1978]: 72–73), who feels that the overuse of cultural context adaptation is a result of the preconceived opinion of adults about child readers, in particular the tendency of adults to underrate 'what can be expected of children, of their imagination, of their intuitive grasp of matters, of their willingness to concern themselves with what is new, strange, difficult' (Stolt, 2006[1978]: 73). Yamazaki (2002: 59) goes even further, and suggests that there is another, largely concealed, factor forming the basis of arguments in favour of cultural context adaptation – a lack of respect for other cultures, or ethnocentrism. She goes on to say that translated books that retain signs of their source cultures can provide children with opportunities to become aware of and familiar with the existence of other cultures (Yamazaki, 2002: 60). This argument may well have some relevance to the translation of children's books in the South African educational context, where a great deal of emphasis is placed on multiculturalism and intercultural understanding. However, as Oittinen (2006: 43) points out, domestication and foreignization remain 'delicate issues' as far as the translation of children's literature is concerned.

What is at issue here is the fact that language, culture, identity, ideology, economics, power and translation are densely interwoven. The choice of domestication, for example, may well be motivated as necessary to make the text accessible for the child reader in the target culture – but this motivation may discount, or even conceal, the web of ideological, cultural and commercial tensions involved in this decision, tensions that merge in the issue of identity. Venuti (1998: 68) makes this particularly clear, pointing out that the act of translation, inevitably involving a domestic representation of a foreign text and culture, always simultaneously involves the construction of a domestic subject. The domestic subject is an ideological position created by the intersection of various discourses, reflecting the interests and agendas of particular social groups in the domestic culture. He continues:

> Circulating in the church, the state, and the school, a translation can be powerful in maintaining or revising the hierarchy of values in the translating language . . . Whether the effects of a translation prove to be conservative or transgressive depends fundamentally on the discursive strategies developed by the translator, but also on the various factors in their reception, including the page design and cover art of the printed book, the advertising copy, the opinions of reviewers, and the uses made of the translation in cultural and social institutions, how it is read and taught. (Venuti, 1998: 68)

In the South African context, then, an investigation of the choice of children's texts for translation and how they are translated (and produced, disseminated and used) needs to take account of the discourses constructing 'the child' as a reader, an individual, and a member of a society. Who do the author, the translator, the publisher, the teacher, the parent, and all the other adults (both individually and collectively) involved in the production, dissemination and use of children's books think 'the child' is? Possibly more importantly, who do they (as part of the larger society) *want* or *need* 'the child' to be, and what should this 'child' gain from reading the book? Ultimately, most producers of children's books need to create texts (both original and translated) that are economically viable, and a basic precondition for this is that books conform to dominant discourses in order to be regarded as appropriate for use in or against the background of the general educational environment.

Clearly, this is a complex situation, and within it the tensions between domestication and foreignization are not easily resolved: Does the translation of a children's book in the South African educational context serve the interests of multiculturalism first, or the interests of identification? Does domestication denaturalize and pedagogize children's literature, excluding otherness and the foreign (Oittinen, 2006: 43)? Does foreignization produce a text that is too 'strange' and inaccessible for the child reader? Or even more extreme, could foreignization have a wholly alienating effect, possibly reinforcing stereotyping and skewed representation?[26]

What emerges very distinctly from the above discussion is that domestication and foreignization are almost invariably, and inevitably, conceptualized as a mutually exclusive dichotomy, particularly in discussions of the concepts as they relate to children's literature. Furthermore, 'domestication' and foreignization' (and related terms) are used with variable meanings and foci, and consequently a variety of linguistic, textual and/or cultural dimensions may be implicated in the processes of domestication and foreignization. This dichotomization and simultaneous terminological diffusion often has the effect of oversimplifying matters. In the following section I argue that in South Africa, specifically, linguistic and cultural situations are such that seemingly unproblematic oppositions such as domestic/foreign, and by extension, domestication/foreignization, are, in fact, deeply fraught with complexity and difficulty, to the degree that it is not possible to view domestication and foreignization as simple and unproblematized concepts or practices. Partly as a consequence of this, I also suggest that, rather than being viewed as mutually exclusive approaches, domestication and foreignization are more productively regarded as divergent, but complementary strategies that inevitably coexist, in various modulations, in every translation, and that both domesticating and foreignizing strategies may have value for opening up plural, open, and ethically responsible discourses by means of translation.

The domestic and the foreign in the South African context

The two broad scenarios for the translation of children's books in South Africa outlined at the start of this chapter raise questions about what exactly constitutes the 'foreign' and what the 'domestic'. In the first translation scenario outlined, where books produced internationally (mostly in English) are translated into Afrikaans or the indigenous languages for the South African market, the 'foreign' culture seems easy to designate as geographically and culturally distinct from South Africa. However, given that most of these texts are produced in the British or American cultural context, one might well argue that they are not, in actual fact 'foreign', given the globalizing dissemination of Anglophone and specifically American popular culture in South Africa by means of music, television and film, and to a lesser extent books and the Internet. In fact, the domestic culture in South Africa may be regarded as a hybrid of various local subcultures and languages (in themselves mixtures of traditional and modern elements) that are sometimes separate, sometimes strongly interwoven – and simultaneously strongly linked to the 'foreign', usually American, context through both language and cultural elements. Beinart (2001: 183), for example, points out that during the 1960s and 1970s

American consumer icons and lifestyles provided reference points to what white and black South Africans alike perceived as an international culture distinct from both colonial British and Afrikaner heritage. In 1993, an article in *The New York Times* (Keller, 1993) described South Africa as 'a country awash in American consumer goods, colonized by American pop culture, and obsessed with American celebrities'. With developments in communication and increasing globalization, the assimilation of American popular culture (and English) into South African culture(s) is becoming more prominent, and also more complex, hybridized and nuanced (see also Campbell, 2000; Nuttall, 2004: 738–739; Strelitz, 2004). In this context, the 'foreign' becomes increasingly difficult to designate.

In the second translation scenario, in which books produced in South Africa in English or Afrikaans are translated into Afrikaans, English or the African languages, similar questions of hybridity complicate an easy, essentialist distinction between the domestic and the foreign. Due to the multicultural and multilingual nature of South African society, the majority of readers in South Africa are, to some degree, caught up in cultural and linguistic multiplicity. For example, in a survey conducted in 2000, the Pan South African Language Board (PANSALB) comments on the 'considerable multilingualism' (PANSALB, 2000: 10) evident in South African society, providing statistics suggesting that multilingualism is prevalent, although its extent varies among different language groups. In some language groups (and for some language combinations), bi- and multilingualism is moderate to high. For example, 30 per cent of home-language speakers of Sesotho understand other African languages, while 24 per cent understand Afrikaans and 28 per cent understand English. A total of 54 per cent of English home-language speakers understand Afrikaans. Among Siswati-speakers, 42 per cent understand other African languages. In other groups, however, bi- and multilingualism is much lower. For instance, only 13 per cent of Tshivenda-speakers understand other African languages, while 4 per cent understand Afrikaans and 0 per cent English (PANSALB, 2000: 10).[7]

Despite this variance, it is clear that a degree of multilingualism is the rule in South African society. Even at home, an average of 36 per cent of South African families are at least bilingual, and make use of code-switching and code-mixing in their use of language in the home among family members including children (PANSALB, 2000: 2). In some language groups the degree of bi- and multilingualism in the home is very high. The PANSALB report cites Siswati-speakers as one such group, where 62 per cent of respondents mix Siswati with isiZulu, English and/or Xitsonga at home (PANSALB, 2000: 2).

In more general terms, the cultural plurality and hybridity of various dimensions of South African society (as a reality and also as a political ideal and discourse) are widely acknowledged (and also, of course, contested), and have been investigated by researchers in various disciplines, particularly in cultural studies (see, for example, Nuttall and Michael, 2000; Strelitz, 2004; Barnard, 2006; Martin, 2006).

The above comments on multilingualism and multiculturalism in South Africa are not intended to suggest that all South African readers(be they adults or children) are fully immersed in other languages or cultures: naturally cultural and linguistic divides do remain, in various configurations and to various extents. However, I would suggest that in the second translation scenario outlined above, the fact that both source and target text are produced in the same geographical and cultural space – and a space that is characterized by multiplicity, diversity and hybridity – destabilizes easy distinctions between the foreign and the domestic. The degree of linguistic and cultural permeability evident in the situation outlined above is much greater than is usually assumed in discussions of domestication and foreignization in translation, where cultures are often approached in essentialist terms as if they were distinct and definable entities. Viewing 'the domestic' as a singular entity does not take cognizance of the fact that the target culture in South Africa itself consists of a multiplicity of linguistic and cultural forms and expectations(often with one or more subculture and language dominating). And within this target culture, the various subcultures may be experienced as more or less familiar or foreign, depending on the position and background of the individual reader. In South Africa, multiple possible sets of 'domestics' and 'foreigns', experienced as familiar and strange to various degrees, therefore exist, depending on the subject position of the reader.

Simon (1999: 58) explains this type of situation in particularly useful terms. Following Pratt (1992) she speaks of the contact zone, a place where previously separated cultures come together and establish relations. These spaces are the result of colonialism, and have therefore been characterized by conflict and inequality. However, she also points out that Western society as a whole has grown into one large contact zone. She continues:

> The idea of culture as an envelope which securely binds all the members of a
> national community within the same coherence of meaning today belongs to the
> realm of myth. The great migrations of post-colonialism have produced

a new socio-demographic situation: all Western nations now have increasingly mixed populations. The ease and rapidity of global communication have created an international mass culture, which competes and interacts with local forms . . . Every culture speaks a language traversed by two kinds of codes, the complicit idioms of the vernacular and the vehicular codes of international communication. (Simon, 1999: 58)

I would argue that this conception of cultures as 'bonded spaces character-ized by a plurality of codes and languages' (Simon, 1999: 58) also holds true for the South African context, and that straightforward, essentialist distinctions between the domestic and the foreign (and therefore between domesticating and foreignizing translation approaches) are therefore not tenable.

This creation of a false polarity is one of the hazards of a theoretical frame-work based on pairs of oppositions, as Boyden (2006: 121) points out in his discussion of Venuti's concepts of domestication and foreignization.[8] Venuti's (1995, 1998) discussion of domestication and foreignization does hinge on the opposition between the two approaches, but domesticating and foreignizing approaches do not necessarily need to be mutually exclusive. Venuti clearly favours foreignization (or minoritizing translation), but he also suggests the impossibility of avoiding domestication (Venuti, 1998: 5). However, while accepting that domestication is inevitable, it is also crucial to acknowledge that such domestication cannot simply be uncritically accepted as an innocent act committed purely in aid of the pragmatic ideal of effective communication, or in the case of children's literature, effective identification of the child reader with the book. But if domestication needs to be accompanied by a critical awareness, so must foreignization. The point made by Boyden (2006: 122) in this regard is crucial: 'In general, there seems to be no self-evident link between domesticating strategies and a "transparent" view on translation, or vice versa, between foreignization and a more "resistant" attitude.' Neither domestication nor foreignization is intrinsically and naturally in the service of any 'ideal' of translation or is necessarily linked to any predefined outcome. Both domesti-cation and foreignization may be appropriated for various ends, and may serve various functions. For example, Rendall (1996: 362) points out that in post-colonial cultures 'bending the foreign text to domestic norms might itself be a form of resistance', while Tymoczko (2000: 35) reiterates that any translation procedure can be appropriated for the ends of cultural colonization, including foreignizing translation procedures.

In addition, a translated text cannot be regarded as a monolithic 'domesti-cated' or 'foreignized' entity. Such a reified view of the translated text denies the complex, multivalent, textured interplay of textual effects – some domesticating, some foreignizing; some familiar, some strange – that are created by the collaborative process of meaning-making in which the writer, translator and reader are involved.

Conclusion

Translations may therefore be regarded as hybrids, as complex, polyphonic blends of the domestic and the foreign, of the familiar and the strange, of other-ness and self-ness, created by the multiple writers and readers involved in the continual reshaping of the translation as discourse among other discourses. I believe that such a hybrid (rather than polarized) theoretical approach promises to be useful for a study of the translation of children's literature in the South African educational context, and am hypothesizing[9] that translators of children's books in South Africa tend to approach translation in this hybrid way, as a flexible and constantly mutating mixture of domesticating strategies (to ensure that the translation is accessible for the child reader and promote identification) and foreignizing strategies (to introduce the child reader to cultures that he/she may not be familiar with, to broaden horizons, to foster intercultural awareness and tolerance, to ensure that the otherness of the translated text is respected). I would suggest, therefore, that the tensions between domestication and foreignization remain salient and relevant, but possibly need to be re-approached with a different modulation: not as mutually exclusive approaches, but rather as strategies to be used in hybrid ways to reflect, contemplate and engage with cultural and linguistic diversity in various ways.

It is essential to continue interrogating the assumptions underpinning the use of concepts such as 'domestication' and 'foreignization', especially in post-colonial contexts such as South Africa. The development of theoretical constructs such as these (as set out, for example, in the work of Venuti) is rooted in a particular cultural and historical specificity, and the functional transfer or applicability of such concepts to other, very different contexts, cannot be assumed as a given (see also Tymoczko, 2000).

Furthermore, considering the myriad complex language and education-related difficulties that South Africa faces, philosophical and theoretical generalization cannot be sufficient. In terms of further research, therefore, it is of crucial importance that specific attention be given to delineating the particular strategies resulting in domesticating and foreignizing effects in particular texts and contexts (or possibly, to demonstrate how the same strategy may have domesticating or foreignizing effects, depending on the specific text and context as interactive site where author, reader and translator meet). It is also necessary to investigate more thoroughly the relationships between foreignization, domestication, accessibility and readability, particularly given the highly problematic levels of literacy and language proficiency among learners in South Africa.[10]

It is therefore essential to investigate in practical terms how translators' decisions and readers' responses interact in the process of creating domesticating or foreignizing textual effects and reader responses – and how these processes may be utilized best to facilitate and enhance the learning and developmental process for South African children from diverse backgrounds.

Notes

1. In the context of the translation of children's literature in South Africa, the ideological motivations for publishing translations of African folktales are pointed out by Jenkins (2002) and Tötemeyer (1989).

2. One might argue that the commercial considerations outlined in this comment function to conceal the ideological issues at work in the translation of children's literature in South Africa.

3. Jenkins (2002: 269) points out that school readers constitute virtually the only published children's literature in the African languages. While it is difficult to gauge the exact language distribution of books published for children in South Africa, statistics from the 2006 annual industry survey by the Publishers' Association of South Africa (PASA) (Galloway et al., 2007) suggest that the African languages, collectively, are losing out against English. While no separate statistics for children's books are provided, statistics for the overall net turnover of local books per language show that 71.92 per cent of all local book sales (across sub-sectors) were English books, 18.63 per cent were Afrikaans books, and 9.44 per cent were books in African languages (Galloway et al., 2007: 28). In the educational sub-sector (which includes school readers and textbooks) statistics for the net turnover of local book sales show that 75.01 per cent of books sold in this sub-sector were in English, 14.03 per cent were in African languages and 10.96 per cent were in Afrikaans (Galloway et al. 2007: 30). Given the fact that English is the mother tongue of only about 8.2 per cent of the South African population (Statistics South Africa, 2001), the overwhelming prevalence of English in publishing remains a cause for concern. However, there does seem to be a growing awareness of the importance of publishing literature for children in the African languages, as evidenced by the extensive Writing in Nine Tongues catalogue (PASA, 2007), which lists available readers and other literature in the nine African languages that are official languages in South Africa.

4. However, it seems to me that this focus on the social, on the functional, on cooperation, on community has the potential to relegate aspects such as individualism, creativity, and the imagination to a position of lesser importance. It may result in a preponderance of books dealing with

social and cultural issues in a realistic mode, with fewer books making use of fantasy, or focusing on wholly personal issues. However, this is a broad overgeneralization which requires further investigation.

5. Klingberg (1986) is the exception in favouring a more source-text oriented approach. While Klingberg (1986: 10) is evidently aware of the tension between source-text and target-text oriented approaches, and clearly states that there are no universally applicable rules for choosing the one over the other (it depends largely on the individual text and readership), he does seem to favour a source-text oriented position: 'In principle the source text must have the priority, and cultural context adaptation ought to be the exception rather than the rule. At all events it should always be borne in mind that the source text is to be manipulated as little as possible' (Klingberg, 1986: 17).

6. See Bassnett (2005: 127) for a discussion of this possibility in terms of news reporting.

7. These examples necessarily provide a very limited view of the situation. For complete statistics, see PANSALB (2000: 10). This document also suggests some of the reasons for the particular patterns of bi- and multilingualism among particular language groups, which have to do with geographical location, language relationships and contact with other languages.

8. Boyden (2006: 122) outlines other criticism that may be levelled against Venuti's argument, such as Venuti's tendency to draw broad, universalising conclusions based on narrow, contestable assumptions, and his failure to outline specific criteria to differentiate foreignizing and domesticating strategies. See also Tymoczko (2000), Pym (1996) and Robinson (1997: 97–112) for criticism of Venuti's theories, including his less-than-rigorous style of argumentation, his failure to define concepts in specific terms, the cultural specificity of his conceptual framework, and the implicit normativity of his theories, all of which make it 'difficult to use his concepts or to extend his arguments' (Tymoczko, 2000: 35).

9. Testing this hypothesis by means of textual analysis as well as surveys among translators of children's books forms a part of my current PhD research at the University of the Witwatersrand, Johannesburg, South Africa.

10. For example, in 2006, the Progress in International Reading Literacy Study (Pirls) showed that between 86 per cent and 96 per cent of South African children who speak and were tested in English, Afrikaans and African languages did not reach the lowest benchmark in an international test of children's reading skills (Blaine, 2006). The study was conducted for the Evaluation of Educational Achievement (IEA), and involved 215, 000 Grade 4 learners across 40 countries. In South Africa the study was conducted by the University of Pretoria, with about 30, 000 Grade 4 and 5 pupils from 400 schools being tested in all 11 official languages. In the international survey, South African learners came in last.

References

Barnard, Ian. (2006), 'The language of multiculturalism in South African soaps and sitcoms', *Journal of Multicultural Discourses*, 1, (1), 39–59.

Bassnett, Susan. (2005), 'Bringing the news back home: strategies of acculturation and foreignization', *Language and Intercultural Communication*, 5, (2), 120–130.

Beinart, William. (2001), *Twentieth-Century South Africa*. Oxford: University Press.

Biamonte, Christina. (2002), 'Crossing culture in children's book publishing', *Publishing Research Quarterly*, 18, (3), 26–42.

Blaine, Sue. (2007), 'Pandor acts on shock reading figures', *Business Day*, 3 December. Available at: http://allafrica.com/stories/200712031358.html (accessed 1 February 2008).

Boyden, Michael. (2006), 'Language politics, translation, and American literary history', *Target*, 18, (1), 121–137.

Campbell, James T. (2000), 'The Americanization of South Africa', in Elaine Tyler May and Reinhold Wagnleitner (eds), *Here, There and Everywhere: The Foreign Politics of American Popular Culture*. Hanover: University Press of New England, pp. 34–63.

Children's Literature Research Unit (UNISA) (2006), 'A short history of South African children's literature'. Available at: www.childlit.org.za/history.html (accessed 14 August 2006).

Department of Education, South Africa (2001), 'Manifesto on values, education and democracy'. Available at: www.education.gov.za (accessed 20 June 2006).

—(2002), *Revised National Curriculum Statement Grades R–9 (Schools)*. Pretoria: Department of Education.

Galloway, Francis, Venter, Rudi M. R. and Struik, Willem. (2007), 'PASA Annual Industry Survey 2006 Report', Available at: www.publishsa.co.za/docs/PASA_Survey_Report_2006_13Sept2007.pdf (accessed 14 February 2008).

Ghesquiere, Rita. (2006), 'Why does children's literature need translation?', in Jan Van Coillie and Walter P. Verschueren (eds), *Children's Literature in Translation: Challenges and Strategies*. Manchester: St Jerome, pp. 19–33.

Hunt, Peter. (1992), 'Internationalism', in Peter Hunt (ed.), *Literature for Children: Contemporary Criticism*. London: Routledge, pp. 110–114.

IBBY (International Board on Books for Young People) (2007), 'What is IBBY'. Available at: http://www.ibby.org/index.php?id=about&L=o.html (accessed 10 October 2007).

Jenkins, Elwyn. (2002), 'Adult agendas in publishing South African folktales for children', *Children's Literature in Education*, 33, (4), 269–284.

Joels, Rosie Webb. (1999), 'Weaving world understanding: the importance of translations in international children's literature', *Children's Literature in Education*, 30, (1), 65–83.

Keller, Bill. (1993), 'Transition in Africa: American culture (and goods) thrive in South Africa', *The New York Times*, 25 September. Available at: http://query.nytimes.com/gst/fullpage.html?res=9F0CE0DA1F38F936A1575AC0A965958260 (accessed 17 October 2007).

Klingberg, Göte. (1986), *Children's Fiction in the Hands of the Translators*. Lund: CWK Gleerup.

Martin, Denis-Constant (2006), A creolising South Africa? Mixing, hybridity, and creolisation: (Re)imagining the South African experience, International *Social Science Journal*, 58, (187) 165–176.

Nikolajeva, Maria. (1996), *Children's Literature Comes of Age: Toward a New Aesthetic*. New York: Garland.

Nuttall, Sarah. (2004), 'City forms and writing the "now" in South Africa', *Journal of Southern African Studies*, 30, (4), 731–748.

Nuttall, Sarah and Michael, Cheryl-Ann. (eds) (2000), *Senses of Culture: South African Culture Studies.* Cape Town: Oxford University Press.

Oittinen, Riitta. (2000), *Translating for Children.* New York: Garland.

—(2006), 'No innocent act: on the ethics of translating for children', in Jan Van Coillie and Walter P. Verschueren (eds), *Children's Literature in Translation: Challenges and Strategies.* Manchester: St Jerome, pp. 35–45.

PANSALB (Pan South African Language Board) (2000), *Language Use and Language Interaction in South Africa: A Sociolinguistic Survey.* Pretoria: PANSALB.

PASA (Publishers' Association of South Africa) (2007), *Writings in Nine Tongues: A Catalogue of Literature and Readers in Nine African Languages for South Africa.* Cape Town: PASA.

Pascua-Febles, Isabel. (2006), 'Translating cultural references: the language of young people in literary texts', in Jan Van Coillie and Walter P. Verschueren (eds), *Children's Literature in Translation: Challenges and Strategies.* Manchester: St Jerome, pp. 111–121.

Pellowski, Anne. (1996), 'Culture and developing countries', in Peter Hunt (ed.), *International Companion Encyclopaedia of Children's Literature.* London: Routledge, pp. 663–675.

Pratt, Mary Louise. (1992), *Imperial Eyes: Travel Writing and Transculturation.* New York: Routledge.

Pym, Anthony. (1996), 'Venuti's visibility', *Target,* 8, (1), 165–177.

Ray, Sheila. (1996), 'The world of children's literature: an introduction', in Peter Hunt (ed.), *International Companion Encyclopaedia of Children's Literature.* London: Routledge, pp. 653–662.

Rendall, Steven. (1996), 'Review: changing translation', *Comparative Literature,* 48, (4), 359–364.

Robinson, Douglas (1997), *What Is Translation? Centrifugal Theories, Critical Interventions.* Kent: Kent State University Press.

Shavit, Zohar. (1986), *Poetics of Children's Literature.* Athens: University of Georgia Press.

Simon, Sherry. (1999), 'Translating and interlingual creation in the contact zone: border writing in Quebec', in Susan Bassnett and Harish Trivedi (eds), *Post-colonial Translation: Theory and Practice.* London: Routledge, pp. 58–74.

South Africa. (1996), *The Constitution of the Republic of South Africa.* Pretoria: Government Printer.

Statistics South Africa (2001), 'Census 2001: key results'. Available at: www.statssa.gov.za/census01/html/Key%20results_files/Key%20results.pdf (accessed 14 February 2008).

Stephens, John. (1992), *Language and Ideology in Children's Fiction.* London: Longman.

Stolt, Birgit. (2006[1978]), 'How Emil becomes Michel: on the translation of children's books', in Gillian Lathey (ed.), *The Translation of Children's Literature: A Reader.* Clevedon: Multilingual Matters. pp. 67–83.

Strelitz, Larry. (2004), 'Against cultural essentialism: media reception among South African youth', *Media, Culture and Society,* 26, (5), 625–641.

Tabbert, Reinbert (2002), 'Approaches to the translation of children's literature: a review of critical studies since 1960', *Target,* 14 (2), 303–351.

Tötemeyer, Andreé-Jeanne. (1989), 'Impact of African mythology on South African juvenile literature', *South African Journal of Library and Information Science,* 57, (4), 393–401.

Tymoczko, Maria. (2000), 'Translation and political engagement: activism, social change and the role of translation in geopolitical shifts', *The Translator,* 6, (1), 23–47.

Van Coillie, Jan and Verschueren, Walter P. (eds) (2006), *Children's Literature in Translation: Challenges and Strategies*. Manchester: St Jerome.

Venuti, Lawrence. (1995), *The Translator's Invisibility: A History of Translation*. London: Routledge.

—(1998), *The Scandals of Translation: Towards an Ethics of Difference*. London: Routledge.

—(2000), 'Translation, community, utopia', in Lawrence Venuti (ed.), *The Translation Studies Reader*. London: Routledge, pp. 468–488.

Yamazaki, Akiko. (2002), 'Why change names? On the translation of children's books', *Children's Literature in Education*, 33, (1), 53–62.

Translation and Shifting Identities in Post-apartheid South Africa: Rethinking Teaching Paradigms in Times of Transition

9

Ileana Dimitriu

In times of transition, social identities are bound to undergo profound shifts, while identity practices can usefully be deciphered from the ways people position themselves through language. Although the case of South Africa offers a good illustration in this regard, not much has been written about the language/translation implications of its post-1994 transition to democracy. Commentators have tended to dwell on the socio-political aspects of transition – for example, Neville Alexander (2002) – and have focused less on how racial and class identities, which continue to be problematic, find expression in language practices. It goes without saying that such practices inform inter-language positions and transfer practices, as well as translation training. This is why I shall start by presenting the challenges of shifting language identities in South Africa and then I shall suggest a formula for translation training that takes into account some of the paradoxes of multiculturalism, South Africa style.

Language identities in South Africa: mono-cultural institutions in wider multi-cultural settings – the role of English

Two years after the first free elections in 1994, the country's celebrated Constitution declared all eleven official languages as equal before the law, thus honouring the country's multilingual character and officially attempting to destabilize the hegemony of English. Furthermore, in 1997, the Department of Education introduced the Language in Education Policy, which promoted the use of learners' mother-tongues as the language of teaching and learning. However,

> [f]rom the vantage point of 2007, we know that language policy has [had] disappointingly little impact in practice. Rather, as is the case elsewhere in post-colonial Africa, the power and status of English is growing, witnessed in its widespread use in high status domains of politics, the media and education. (McKinney and Soudien 2007: 3)

The poor implementation of the language policy has, over the last decade, become a new kind of truism: 'it has become passé to point out the huge gap between government policy that promotes additive bilingualism and . . . practice in schools where English has become increasingly hegemonic in the post-apartheid era' (McKinney, 2007: 10).

Numerous studies have been conducted to analyze the reasons why English has, ironically, strengthened – in spite of sustained governmental efforts to the contrary.

Vivien de Klerk (2000) shows that most parliamentarians' speeches are conducted in English rather than in African languages. Nkonko Kamwamga-malu (2003) points to the dominance of English in the South African public television broadcast, and indicates that the overwhelming spread of English in other areas of public life signals the fact that people perceive it as an economic resource. Kamwamgamalu (2003 and 2004) has also shown that mother-tongue education is not fully appreciated by most parents, especially African, as relevant and empowering in the post-ideological world; this is also a finding identified by De Klerk, who claims that African/ Xhosa parents are actively promoting English over mother tongue: 'For political, economical and educational reasons, they want their children to be assimilated into a single unified national culture' (2002: 11). Other researchers have also focused on English and its hegemonic position in education (Kapp, 2000 and Rudwick, 2004), and its changing ownership and shifting identity politics (De Klerk and Gough, 2002). Some of the latest research on the social role of English in a multicultural society has been commissioned by the English Academy of Southern Africa, which, in 2002, published a special journal issue of *English Academy Review* (*EAR*) on 'Language and Empowerment' (Klopper, 2002), and in 2007, a special issue of the same journal on 'Language, Identity and English Education in South Africa' (McKinney and Soudien, 2007). As the guest editors of the latter special issue have pointed out, 'new identities are taking place in the country, which can be read in young people's use of language,' as well as in the ways they are educationally integrated, for, 'it is in this new [educational] system that the country's experimentation with difference is now taking place' (McKinney and Soudien, 2007: 2).

Owing to the prestige position of English as symbolic and economic resource, the social integration taking place in both secondary and tertiary education in South Africa inescapably involves teaching and learning through the medium of English. The paradigms of the former 'Model C schools' – former white, mainly English medium, schools which, starting in the early 1990s, opened their doors to all races – have also been replicated at tertiary level, with English now dominating the scene. However, as Crain Soudien (2004), George Makubalo (2007) and Nomakhalipha Nongogo (2007) have shown, racial considerations have not completely disappeared but have been overshadowed by social class – for example, the emerging Black middle class – and a certain prestige attached to 'white' English, as compared with English varieties spoken by other racial groups. This valorizing process is inevitably responsible for 'multiple, and at times contradictory, identities [being] continually constructed and reconstructed' (Makubalo, 2007: 26) around one's English proficiency. The phenomenon is not surprising given that – as Pierre Bourdieu (1992: 105) has indicated – prestige language use is associated with forms of 'cultural capital' and of 'symbolic power', leading to acts of 'inclusion' into, and 'exclusion' from, various social groupings and classes.

To summarize my considerations regarding the mutating social identities in South Africa after 1994, I would like to point out that my current research into 'translation and shifting identities' is informed by broad post-structuralist, non-essentialist, views of identity as a multiple, mutating and flexible category, by what Jan Blommaert (2005) refers to as a semiotic construct that is influenced by its specific access to different identity-building resources.

Translation training and shifting identities: western expectations and/ in the South African context

Insights into the complexities of post-apartheid identity formation around language issues (and the role of English) should help shed more light on the multifaceted translation scene in multicultural South Africa, where established western assumptions about various pre-conditions for proper translation training need to be carefully weighed up against a diverse number of harsh realities. The South African translation scene is significantly different from its western counterpart, which has a relatively homogeneous and prosperous population, able to offer a satisfactory economic income for translators and interpreters; a financially accessible tertiary education for most translation trainees; and a small number of working languages. Differences also exist regarding the social and educational background of trainees: for example, the South African marketplace has many mature translators who require re-training. Furthermore, the number of languages is far greater here than in most other, say, west European countries, while African languages do not, as yet, feature in the (imported) textbooks used in the various translation programmes, which are still mainly based on western models. These differences prompt a closer look at the relationship between western models of, and assumptions about, translation training in the South African situation – given that countries which are relatively new to the field tend to take up foreign role models and readily apply them to their own circumstances, sometimes uncritically. It is important, therefore, to acknowledge this risk of imitation and make certain necessary adjustments to the assumptions and expectations of the West.

One of the most established expectations is that translation training builds on the students' solid knowledge and mastery of their future working languages. This assumption appears to point to the obvious reality that an advanced degree of language competence is indispensable for proper translation training; yet in some countries and some language combinations, there are simply not sufficient candidates for a type of training that assumes mastery in both languages. The question, as far as South Africa is concerned, therefore, is not whether it is advantageous to have a good grasp of two or more languages, but whether useful translation training may be given to those who fall short of this requirement. Linked to the above assumption is the further assumption that training top professionals needs to take place, preferably, at postgraduate level. There are certainly advantages involved in the rigorous screening procedures offered by postgraduate admissions policies, but the question arises as to what extent this type of training is the optimal solution in countries with urgent needs for translators, but where the numbers of suitable postgraduate candidates are limited. The purpose of this chapter is to seek a more immediate solution by focusing on the modular approach at *undergraduate*, rather than postgraduate, level.

The issue of translating, mainly or exclusively, into the mother tongue is certainly one of the most widespread assumptions we have all internalized. Again, it is to state the obvious to say that proficiency in one's mother tongue is always higher than in another language, which makes the mother tongue the desirable target language in translation. But the question remains of how to handle a situation where translators are needed for target languages that are not their mother tongue. Applied to the South African situation, it is English that complicates matters, since it is, more often than not, either source or target language in translation processes. Furthermore – as analysed in the previous sub-section – with the racial diversification of educational institutions and the increasing numbers of additional language learners (previously disadvantaged students) becoming educated in urban, English medium schools, the very concept of English-as-first-language becomes 'a misnomer . . . and there seems to be little opportunity for real meaning-making [around EL1 and EL2] to take place' (McKinney and Soudien, 2007: 4). One could ask rhetorically: 'What mother tongue? Whose mother tongue?' However, as the majority of African students have not benefited from ex-Model C schooling, the issue of remedial English teaching is still highly relevant today. This is why – as Stuart Campbell (1998) has noted – it is counterproductive, in English-speaking countries, to separate the need for English language enhancement from the practice of translation. I also believe in the possibility of what Allison Beeby (1996) terms 'inverse translation', that is, translating into one's non-native language usefully, if not optimally, a process that can be sped up by integrated teaching.

While this is an approach that has been gaining increasing support among translation scholars (e.g. Pokorn, 2005), it is in fact also a reflection of larger shifts in teaching and research models worldwide, away from dogmatic and prescriptivist orientations. In her recent, groundbreaking handbook for trainers, Dorothy Kelly, for example – starting from the premise that 'student groups are becoming *increasingly heterogeneous*, essentially due to internationalization and to the *inclusion of groups previously excluded from, or seriously underrepresented in, higher education*' (2005: 51; my emphases) – encourages trainers to adjust their curricular content and teaching methodology to the needs and expectations of diverse sociocultural contexts (2005: 62– 78). Kelly's approach is also supported by John Kearns, who similarly highlights the need for an increased awareness-cum-adjustment to a 'variety of *contexts* in which translator training takes place [especially] in certain cultures of Languages of Limited Diffusion' [as, for example, in multilingual South Africa] where the development of a translation training culture is . . . relatively young' (2006: 205–207). Both Kelly's and Kearns's recent comments suggest a refreshing departure from dogmatically de-contextualized approaches to training.

The advantages of modular approaches to translation training

Let me start by briefly circumscribing South African tertiary education in relation to translation training. Here we are also confronted with certain institutional problems, as universities are required to train increasing numbers of translators in a climate of uncertainty about future student growth. A new outcomes-based education policy has added the requirement that universities become more relevant to the practical needs of the community. In the humanities, this has led to a re-evaluation of historically established general formative disciplines in favour of more vocationally-based disciplines; although beneficial in terms of interdisciplinary co-operation and viability, this tendency continues to meet with resistance from more conservative academic departments. In the light of this, *I make a case for the integration – that is, not the marginalization or ghettoization – of vocationally-oriented courses into mainstream undergraduate academic commitments*. With interdisciplinarity increasingly replacing old disciplinary boundaries, it is now possible for Translation

Studies in South Africa to become more widespread and accessible to students, and more integrated. *I am arguing for a modular approach to transla-tion training, which – based on recent academic restructuring and merging processes – gives students more flexibility in packaging translation courses in their degrees.* Modularity makes possible the implementation of inter- and intra-language translation paradigms, both in tandem and separately.

A modular approach presupposes that a translation training programme is broken into autonomous learning units – as opposed to traditional majors, which are based on a fixed structure/ number of courses making up a coherent whole. Here, I shall refer to semester-length modules that are interwoven into degree courses, with each focusing on a particular subset of knowledge and skills. Modularity is not necessarily the best principle underlying all learning situations. Programmes offered against the background of considerable insti-tutional stability, or as part of established fields of study, may find more tradi-tional approaches attractive. Modularity is appealing within less established institutional frameworks, or when major educational restructuring exercises are afoot – as is the case in South African universities. Other conditions that make modularity an attractive option are the urgent needs for crash-courses for medium-level translation practitioners with less than optimal proficiency in the marketplace. When one also considers the exceedingly low number of potential applicants for top-level translation courses, it becomes clear that solutions other than the traditional degree courses must be considered.

It needs to be stressed that this approach presents many advantages. Semester-long (non-) degree courses can be cost-efficient in that they focus on a certain area of skills and knowledge and help practising translators (who may not have the means to enrol for full major degrees) to enhance their skills. It is evidently also easier for shorter courses to be integrated into various programmes and full degree courses, while they may, at the same time, remain fairly self-contained and flexible in their content; long degree courses, in contrast, are more dependent on formal constraints and are, therefore, more difficult to adapt to non-standard situations. The integration of translation modules into various cognate programmes has the added advantage of being promoted via those very institutional channels.

Structural flexibility is possibly the most important advantage of modular-ity; this approach makes it easier to implement changes to certain parts of the programme, should the need arise to accommodate a particular situation. In the traditional, highly integrated academic courses, in contrast, changes are more difficult to implement. Flexibility makes co-operation easier as well, particularly when it comes to recruiting experienced practising translators to augment the more theoretical components taught by academics. Owing to the lower investments and the potential for higher mobility, co-operation with professional institutions may be easier via self-sufficient modules.

The modular approach is gaining ground in South Africa, as for example, illustrated by Johan Blaauw (2006: 7–21), who analyses instances of interpreting with limited resources/training in a restructured post-apartheid university. Modularity is also changing traditional ways of teaching internationally, and especially so in Europe, where universities are shaping up for a new restructuring: 'modularisation and student choice are key to the practical application of the Bologna Declaration, as well as are the discussions about the simplification of education' (Declerq, 2006: 123).

Translation studies and cognate (inter-)disciplines

As indicated by Alet Kruger (2000 and 2004), translation research – mainly DTS and corpus-based paradigms – as well as research-driven training in South Africa, is experiencing an unprecedented development, having already made the shift from bilingual (English and Afrikaans) to multilingual teaching and research initiatives. As indicated earlier, it is important to remember that, in spite of the country's multilingual language policy, the one language that is being used in almost every combination is English. Paradoxically, this situation is not imposed from above, but arises as a result of pragmatic considerations; as Gillian Finchilescu and Gugu Nyawose have shown in a study on Zulu students' views: 'English is seen as the language of work and commerce [helping] prevent interethnic clashes between the indigenous language groups' (1998: 58, 56). People do not seem to be resentful towards English, which is generally accepted as a neutrally convenient vehicle of communication; for most translators with African languages, therefore, English is either source language (mostly for translations into African or languages) or target language (for translations out of African languages). An interesting fact related to the ideal direction for translations is an increasing number of translations are done by non-mother tongue speakers of English. This implies the need to improve English as a second language. Later in this chapter, I point to some ways of improving English through intra-language translation and pre-translation text analysis.

With English being considered the predominant official language in South Africa, I feel it makes sense to attempt a closer institutional link between the academic interests of English Studies and Translation Studies. The discipline of English has lately been variously described as a 'shifting site', one constantly reforming under the influence of the media and the global heterogeneity of cultures. The traditional aspects of Rhetoric and History (literary and linguistic) mingle with a wide range of interdisciplinary endeavours. As Rob Pope puts it, 'looking to the early twenty-first century, we see English both embracing and, to some extent, being replaced by Cultural, Communication, Composition and Media Studies, as well as by a wide range of other more or less interdisciplinary studies' (2002/1998: 8), including Translation Studies, which Pope also offers for consideration, together with a cautionary note regarding the need to approach translated texts based on a theoretical understanding of the discipline. He says that English 'courses which use translation extensively need to be informed by at least some work on the theory, practice and implications of translation' (2002/1998: 37). Briefly, English Studies today ranges across literature, language and culture and can no longer be neatly compartmentalized. This tendency has such far-reaching implications that it has been suggested one accept English itself as an 'interdiscipline' (Greenblatt and Gunn, 1992; Pope 2002/1998 and 2005).

Interdisciplinary dialogues are to be encouraged in countries where, paradoxically, English – in spite of the country's wider multilingual circumstances – is the main official language in institutions. It is my belief that Translation Studies should enter into a (mutually beneficial) dialogue with English Studies by finding meaningful points of entry into ongoing debates around the redefined role of English. When becoming actively involved in the rethinking of English Studies, translation scholars in South Africa are in fact arguing for the need to view translation as part of larger social and civic concerns regarding empowerment through language enhancement. Translation, in South Africa, acquires more than purely linguistic significance; it is meant to play a crucial role in civil living, which certainly implies a willingness to grant the act of linguistic transformation the status of textual and social intervention. Accordingly, interdisciplinary cooperation has started to take place between English and translation scholars. It is by engaging in debates around the critical and interpretive dimensions of text construction and reconstruction, with a special emphasis on the role of formative rewriting, that a meaningful link has been attempted between the two disciplines.

It has been amply proven by various initiatives into ways of making English Studies more meaningful today, in research on curricular transformation conducted over the last decade or so (e.g. by Pope 2000/1995, 2002/1998 and 2005), that a new attitude towards writing and communication can resuscitate students' interest in taking English as a university subject, that is, one that goes beyond literature. Pope's concept of 'textual intervention' (2000/1995) is an important contribution towards overcoming the current impasse that has seen English literature departments worldwide experience a dramatic drop in student numbers. He suggests that one regard texts (literary, as well as non-literary) not merely as products to be analyzed, but also as processes requiring creative intervention. The need for training imaginative readers/ interpreters of texts (catered for by the traditional approach) has to be linked with the newly redefined need for 'textual intervention' as active rewriting of the texts to be analysed. The new approach requires that, in order better to understand various text-types, students should intervene in their construction and recon-struction. Instead of viewing texts as fixed products, students should submit them to successive moments of re-narration as process. He also refers to this process as ' "re-centring", "re-genreing", the generation of various kinds of "parallel", "alternative" and "counter-text" (writing with, across and against the grain of the initial text), as well as exercises in paraphrase, imitation, parody, adaptation, hybridization and collage' (2000/1995: xiv). Pope's declared aim of engaging with re-narration is fundamentally hermeneutic: 'The best way to understand a text as product is to change it; to play around with it, to intervene in it in some way (large or small), and then to try to account for the exact effect of what you have done' (2000/1995: 1). Pope's main message here is that interpretation is (textual) intervention, which clearly brings to mind George Steiner's famous dictum that 'understanding is translation': 'inside or between languages, human communication equals translation' (1975: 47) – as well as Theo Hermans' recent call for translation to be approached from a hermeneu-tic perspective (2007).

The parallel between the new orientation in English Studies and the herme-neutic approach to Translation Studies is striking, and definitions of transla-tion as forms of 'textual intervention' (Pope) and 'rewriting' (Lefevere) are worth pursuing in the teaching of both disciplines. Translators, as well as liter-ary critics, historians and anthologizers, are constantly rewriting texts, for they are image-makers who have the power of subversion under the guise of objec-tivity (Lefevere, 1992: 7). Translators have always engaged in acts of textual intervention through which they can exert the power of introducing new concepts, new genres, new devices and various linguistic innovations – whether as image- or decision-makers, cultural mediators or negotiators. This phenomenon begs larger contextualizing questions related to who rewrites, for whom, what for, and under what circumstances. As André Lefevere aptly comments: 'Rewriting manipulates and is effective. [It is] a way to restore to a certain study of literature some of the more immediate social relevance the study of literature as a whole has lost' (1992: 9). I would add that to consider translation as a form of rewriting is to foreground its intrinsic social relevance, which inevitably applies well beyond the boundaries of literary studies. It is precisely the often ignored dimension of translation as both textual *and* social intervention that would help the discipline enter into dialogue with other cognate disciplines, such as English or Media Studies.

A few more considerations regarding the institutional position of English Studies are worth noting. It is important to regard this new 'interdiscipline' as a system bound together by certain principles of coherence, which is at the same time open-ended and never finally made. Major efforts at redefining English internationally are also reflected at the level of academic restructuring in various South African universities. I shall use the Faculty of Humanities at the University of KZN-Durban as a case study because this faculty has, so far, been involved in a number of pioneering educational initiatives – ranging from voluntary restructuring to enforced merging with another faculty or university. With old disciplinary boundaries collapsing, or under constant re-negotiation, new interdisciplinary modules have been integrated into mainstream academic research and teaching commitments. The English programme itself offers a good example of integration and restructuring, as it is involved in a process of expanding beyond its traditional literary focus. The two new study-streams on offer, one a language- and the other a culture-oriented stream, are closely linked to the cognate fields of Media and Translation Studies, both of which may enhance the communicational aspects of English. Members of staff from the three fields of study are closely co-operating across disciplines, with various courses in each programme being accepted as cognate modules in the other two. Although the process of restructuring is still in its incipient stages, it is already noticeable that the new institutional structures are able to accommodate the modular approach in its practical implementation. Needless to say, however, that – for all the benefits of the modular approach in terms of interdisciplinary cross-fertilization, cost efficiency, and course viability – there is still resistance from more conservative quarters regarding the mainstreaming of what used to be considered 'simply vocational' courses.

Practical implementation of modularity: a formula for undergraduate studies, UKZN-Durban

At the University of KZN-Durban, the translation-related modular approach has been on offer for over a decade now, and has so far materialized in four types of modules that may be either taken as self-contained units or as a meaningful whole.[1] Although students may choose to register for any of the modules independently (as they are also elective courses in the cognate programmes of English and Media Studies), students are encouraged to register for the whole package comprising the Translation track. The added advantage of the latter approach is that the modules inform and promote one another across disciplines.

I shall offer a brief outline of the four modules and their interconnectedness. Each of them focuses on one specific aspect of translation-related relevance, and – keeping in mind the logical sequence of skills-acquisition – have been strategically placed in either first or second semesters, respectively. The *first semester* focuses on Intercultural Communication and Intra-language Translation, and the *second semester* on Inter-language translation and Editing and Rewriting.

First semester modules

Module 1: 'Intercultural Communication'

The final aim of intercultural communication (as a field of study, as well as a module offered at this university) is the base line of translator/interpreter training; this is the reason this module is placed in the first semester. Although the module is training mono-cultural individuals to deal with intercultural situations, its implicit, deeper aim is eventually to prompt and promote an active engagement with translation as social practice, as well as an academic discipline.

The general aim of this module is to provide students with a conceptual framework within which to raise questions such as: How does communication contribute to a climate of respect for, not just tolerance of, cultural diversity? What kind of communication is needed in order to ensure cultural diversity, while seeking common goals? In South Africa, one of the most pluralist societies in the world, how can one best establish national consensus and global competitiveness, while at the same time protect the complex character of its many languages and cultures? How do the local media present diversity, in both the domestic and international arena? How do the English print media or advertising companies, for example, reflect multicultural issues in South Africa, and what can be done to increase the industry's intercultural awareness?

To answer such questions, students are exposed to recent debates (e.g. Samovar and Porter, 2001; Hall, 2002) about the influence of culture on communication, the emphasis lying on the impact of vast cultural systems on intercultural dynamics, in terms of, to borrow Charles Sanders Peirce's (1966) terminology, 'abduction' (projection into the foreign), 'induction' (immersion in the foreign/ other) and 'deduction' (intercultural awareness). At the end of the module, students should be able to classify diverse cultural patterns and apply established intercultural taxonomies to everyday situations; recognize patterns of thought and verbal processes in intercultural encounters; interpret and classify certain non-verbal communicational clues of action, space, time, silence; increase their intercultural competence by overcoming stereotyping and ethnocentrism; reduce intercultural misunderstanding and develop strategies of 'translating'/ negotiating communication difficulties.

Theoretical highlights include recent evaluations of well established taxonomies of cultural patterns – Geert Hofstede's (1984) individualism/ collectivism, uncertainty avoidance, power distance, masculinity/ femininity; Florence Kluckhohn and Fred Strodtbeck's (1961) value orientations: human nature, person/ nature, time, activity, social relationships; E. T. Hall's (1976) high/low context orientation and his (1983) monochronic/ polychronic time classifications. Once students have mastered these by now classical taxonomies, they are asked critically to reflect on them in everyday occurrences and text-types, for example, in the ways the print media construct news events of intercultural relevance and the manner in which they describe the 'fundamental attribution error' of stereotyping, prejudice and ethnocentrism (Hall, 2002: 199–231).

Insights into cultural patterns, as well as into the risks of intercultural misunderstandings due to stereotyping, culturally prepare and sensitize students, as they are now about to embark on the more language-oriented module, which is described below. This is the kind of preparation also advocated by David Katan, whose book, tellingly titled, *Translating Cultures* (2004/1999), brings the 'cultural turn' in TS from theory to pedagogy, and provides a model for teaching culture to translators and other mediators by raising our awareness of the role of culture in perceiving, constructing and translating reality. The tendency of making intercultural communication skills part of translation training has been gaining ground recently, a phenomenon also noted by Kelly, who lists 'cultural and intercultural competence' (2005: 32) among the core competences required for becoming a translator; it is an approach that goes beyond simply acquiring encyclopaedic knowledge (cf. the traditional 'Civilization' courses). As Kelly puts it: 'for translators, it is essential to acquire competence [including experiential competence] in their working cultures' perceptions, myths, values, stereotypes' (2005: 74).

Module 2: 'Intra-language Translation: Context, Structure and Content'

This is the second (first semester) module of the Translation track and may be taken by English and Media students as part of their majors in their second year of study. It builds on the previous module (which is, however, not a prerequisite). The aim of this course is, firstly, to alert students to the pitfalls of intercultural communication due to misunderstandings of both culture-specific contextual assumptions and language-specific structure-cum-content elements. Secondly, through text-intensive application, the course suggests ways of intra-language translation: rewriting, re-centring or dis-ambiguating unintentionally imprecise, incomprehensible or offensive formulations that have the potential of creating intercultural tensions, misunderstandings and even conflict.

This course is inspired by recent research around the discourse approach to intercultural communication, also referred to as 'inter-discourse communication' (Scollon and Scollon 2003: xii), which analyses verbal interactions across diverse cultural, professional, generational groups. The focus is on inter-discourse aspects of communications between speakers of English (as lingua franca) and another language – in the case of South Africa, an African language – with a view to de-mystifying the falsely perceived 'universal nature' of certain cultural patterns as embodied in English-language usage. Ron Scollon and Suzanne Wong Scollon draw attention to the fact that 'many aspects of western culture, especially western patterns of discourse, which ultimately lead to confusion or to misinterpretation in intercultural communication, are carried within English, and are also transmitted through the process of the teaching and learning of English' (2003: 4).

In order to help overcome the sense of entrapment in the cultural and communicational patterns of the second language/ lingua franca, the module also draws on Erving Goffman's influential 'frame analysis' (1974), a theory proclaiming that world-knowledge is informed by delimited contextual assumptions embodied in culture-specific frames/ types of action-exchanges, which are shared in the form of 'cultural expectations' by members of any given community. Students are exposed to three types of expectations that have been found to produce intercultural misunderstandings: 'frames and expected actions' (e.g. ways of introducing oneself); ' frames assuming informal rules' (e.g. politeness in help-giving or paying a visit); 'frames assuming identities' (e.g. greetings and social hierarchy). The gaps between 'frames' and 'expectations' in localized intercultural communication are explored, and ways are suggested on how to control/ define cultural differences that, if ignored, are easily missed and may escalate into conflict.

Once having understood the reasons behind the diversity of contextual assumptions (which has different cultures frame situations/contexts differently) students are exposed to a second area that has the potential of cultural miscommunication: differences at the level of verbal structure and content. Paul Grice's (1975) four conversational maxims are helpful in reviewing many important differences in this regard: the 'quality maxim' assuming that statements are true and accurate (which becomes problematic when applied to idiomatic language use); the 'quantity maxim' assuming that each culture has its own codes about what is a correct amount of speech/silence or action for a specific situation; the 'relevance maxim' referring to what is coherent or meaningful information for a given interaction; the 'manner maxim' referring to clarity/lucidity of expression given a multiplicity of semantic possibilities.

Apart from offering an introduction to professional writing skills, the module is also an introduction to translation – in its intra-language form – thus preparing the way for the second-semester course of inter-language translation. More specifically, students learn how to rewrite (English to English) the text's communicative function and cultural values; how to adjust changes in context and register; how to 'disambiguate' inaccurate formulations based on certain cultural expectations; how to re-encode missing information, etc. The module culminates in a report, in which students have the opportunity to demonstrate their rewriting skills by producing complex intra-language translations between various text-types at all three levels of pragmatic text analysis (situational, communicative, cultural). The report may require students to analyse a news event as constructed by different daily newspapers, and then to rewrite the same news event so as to make it publishable in, for example, a student newspaper. Rewriting headlines or captions is also a useful exercise for learning how to distinguish between who is speaking and who is silenced, whose opinions are omitted and why, and how to interpret the distinction between the literal and the metaphoric significance of words. Needless to say, such skills are invaluable for any future translator.

This module represents a pedagogical effort that is of particular relevance for South African students today, as translation (not only inter-, but also intra-language) in this country needs to teach people how to operate in a functionally multicultural world. I have found that rewriting texts for different audiences who are expected to use different language registers and to have different ideological points of view (from the original audience) is a most useful exercise. Intra-language translation may be profitably used to help enhance English-language skills; for second-language speakers, in particular, this becomes a linguistically and socially valuable exercise in itself. The module emphasizes the function of translation (in this instance, via its intra-language aspect) as a form of social, cultural and critical intervention that plays a crucial role in civil living. Students become increasingly aware that the exercise in intra-language transformation is also a form of intercultural intervention and mediation. The module also helps them refine their general writing skills, as well as their critical thinking and decision-making potential. Translation functions as process, and the translator functions as an imaginative reader and creative rewriter of texts.

I have found that offering students an exposure to the fundamental concepts and practical implications of, on the one hand, intercultural communication and, on the other, intra-language translation – via the self-contained modules described above – is a useful exercise in itself, while it also serves the purpose of offering a solid introduction to the inter-language translation course that is offered in the second semester. To reiterate, promoting cognate courses by teaching inter-related aspects of the discipline via (self-contained study units as part of) a modular approach makes both pedagogical and logistical sense.

Second semester modules

Module 3: 'Translation and Communication'

I shall now outline the aims of this second year, second semester course that focuses on *inter*-language translation; it is the third offering in the modular package and, clearly, the main contribution to the modular Translation track at UKZN. This course can be taken as a self-contained unit, but most students come via the two courses described above; most would, therefore, be already familiar with the main principles of intra-language translation practices. Grice's (1975) 'contextual assumptions', as well as his maxims – most frequently those of 'quality' (e.g. regarding idiomatic language use) and 'manner' (e.g. literal/ figurative language use) – are here usefully taught in conjunction with Charles Fillmore's (1977) prototype semantics, his 'scenes and frames' theory that is increasingly applied to translation studies. As Paul Kussmaul says: 'Fillmore's "frames" activate mental pictures ('scenes' in Fillmore's terminology) in the minds of the readers . . . . Fillmore uses his model for explaining word meaning, but it can also be used for explaining . . . situational and pragmatic meaning' (1995: 13).

Frame semantics, therefore, offers a useful introduction to the first part of this module, that of *pre-translation text analysis*. Students are initiated into what is also referred to as *translation-oriented text analysis* by being exposed to various points of entry (but mainly drawing on Christiane Nord (1991) and Kussmaul (1995)). I have found Kussmaul's interpretation of Juliane House's 'situational dimensions' (1995: 55–60) – referring to significant non-linguistic situational factors as reflected in linguistic forms – to be easily accessible to students and easily replicable when using African languages. His commentaries on, and illustrations of, the 'communicative functions' of texts (drawing on Ernst-August Gutt's and Steiner's insights into the interpretive uses of languages) are equally appreciated by students, helping them understand the 'far-reaching considerations of text-function within situation within culture' (1995: 72); such an understanding is a welcome 'warm-up' phase helping ease the way for the full integration of Nord's rigorous 'checklists for source-text analysis: extra- and intra-textual factors (1991: 85–93). I have found Nord's checklists extremely useful for focusing students' minds on the need for a methodical approach to the complexities of source-texts in relation to the exigencies of target receivers. Over the years, I have adjusted these checklists to make them more accessible, as well as more relevant, for South African translators, having thus produced a 'South African version' of the by-now famous 'Nord checklists'). In devising this section of the course I have kept abreast of international debates around the role of Discourse Analysis for translator training (e.g. the debate around Trosborg's model, in Schäffner, 2002), and concur with Christina Schäffner (2002), who – while pointing out that 'there is general agreement that understanding a text is a prerequisite for translating it' (2) – notes that 'the problem, however, is that such an analysis needs to be fully understood as a *translation-oriented* analysis, and not as a text analysis in its own right' (5) – that is, an analysis whose final scope it is, firstly, to identify potential translation pitfalls and, secondly, influence appropriate translation decisions.

As a complex whole, the 'pre-translation' stage occupies the first few weeks of the course, but the skills acquired in this intensive manner are, of course, replicated in an abbreviated form before the commencement of each single translation project. A few weeks into the course, therefore, students attempt their first practical translations; while the theoretical lectures are conducted in English (which is the only lingua franca shared by all), for the practical work, students are divided into language-specific groups led by translation trainers who are also practising translators between English and one of the following languages: isiZulu, isiXhosa, Afrikaans, French, German, Italian, Spanish.

This part of the course is informed by the tenets of the functional/ action-school, also referred to as Handlung/Skopos-school (especially as espoused by Nord 1991, 1997), which is well-known to South African trainers. This target-oriented approach is most suited to the local situation as it lays emphasis on concrete communicative situations and social functions, real agents and networks exploring their own inductive experiences of translating in the professional world, for example, what social forces 'initiate' and 'control' translation as textual intervention, and what 'really' happens when people translate. Based on my experience at UKZN, I believe that this approach is well-suited to the needs of South African students more generally, in that it emphasizes practical realism and awareness of translation as *social practice* (all this, in a country still struggling with the legacy of a racially and linguistically divisive past).

By teaching students the complexities of the social processes involved in inter-language transformations, translation trainers implicitly also teach them how to use translation as social intervention, and how to play a responsible role in society. Making active and informed choices about how – as a translator – to engage in 'intercultural cooperation' (Nord, 1991: 28–29) with the various factors/ agents of 'translation as process of intercultural communication' (Nord, 1991: 7) has certainly more than purely linguistic implications: translation students learning how to invest texts with social meaning are also learning how to engage as cultural mediators and negotiators, skills sorely needed in our developmental state. In tests or exams, for example, students are always given a translation brief that simulates real-life expectations regarding a specific communicative situation. An example of a brief might be:

a) The initiator of this translation is the head of the language services division of Metro City Council, and s/he requires the given text for a newsletter aimed at a Zulu-speaking target readership that is largely female, rural (living in Umlazi township) and over the age of 60.

b) Once you have adjusted the social function and effect of the target text to the needs of the target readership, briefly reflect on whether your intervention supports Nord's statement that 'The function of the target text is not arrived at automatically from an analysis of the source text, but is pragmatically defined by the purpose of the intercultural communication'. (1991: 9)

The functional, profession-based and learner-centred, approach advocated by Skopos theory continues to inspire translation trainers worldwide (from Europe to Latin America and beyond), as it 'admirably combin[es] professional realism with pedagogical progression' (Kelly and Way, 2007: 3). Emphasizing the action-based thrust of practical translation tasks is relevant for the modular and inter-disciplinary approach suggested throughout this paper and constitutes itself into a unifying concept for all the modules under discussion. Students of English Studies, for example, find useful the tools of critical intervention of pre-translation text analysis (in English), while an in-depth pragmatic analysis of text-typology strengthens the future media practitioner's competence in operating intra-language translations. Both emphases – on translation-oriented text analysis and on translation as textual-cum-social intervention, as espoused by the functional approach – help form core skills for translating, as well as for editing, revising and rewriting, as I will suggest in the next sub-section.

Module 4: 'Editing and Revising'

Again, much like the other modules in the Translation track, this second semester module – whose designation echoes the title of a book by Brian Mossop (2001), insights of which are usefully employed on this course – can be either taken as a stand-alone or as part of the modular track. If the latter, it actually forms the logical end-stage of the modular Translation track, a stage aiming to bring the finishing touches to the translation process, as well as to broaden the concept of rewriting into other professional writing areas, mainly editing and publishing.

In the more restricted, popular understanding of the term, editing refers to polishing up text and making stylistic, grammatical or technical adjustments to a rough draft. While these are indispensable skills translators should painstakingly acquire and tirelessly apply to their target text, I believe that a module on editing has a much wider scope that goes beyond the accuracy of 'finishing touches' to encompass 'revising and rewriting' as mind set. The latter understanding can, of course, be considered to be omnipresent throughout the translation process (one constantly re-positions oneself by re-adjusting text as one goes along; we should also keep in mind Lefevere's now famous definition of translation as a process of rewriting).

However, I found it useful to have a distinct *post-translation/ post-editing* stage built into the Translation track, a stage where students are encouraged to reflect on the translation/editing problems encountered and the choices made to overcome them, and to do so by using an adequate critical and terminological vocabulary. I have taught students how to use TAPs or 'think-aloud-protocols', that is, problem-solving opportunities based on 'introspection and conscious observation' (Kussmaul, 1995: 6) of internalized strategies and techniques, as advocated by Kussmaul in a tellingly dedicated chapter – 'What goes on in the translator's mind?' – of his course book (1995: 5–37). While I concur with the author that 'process-based' TAPs may be more beneficial for the on-going translation process (7), I also believe there is merit in 'product-based' TAPs, which naturally happen in the end-stage (editing/revising) of the translation process, where students critically contrast their translatorial-cum-editorial interventions (based on hindsight, of course) with the demands of the given brief. I found Nord's particular application of functionalism most useful at this stage; it is an approach that highlights 'function *plus* loyalty' (1997: 123), with the latter emphasizing the desired nature of relationships between the various agents not only on the translation, but also on the editing/publishing scenes. Just as translators are called upon to mediate equitably between two textual actions (source text-as-action in SC and target text-as-action in TC), so are editors and publishers called upon to bring their ethical considerations into play when they notice too great a discrepancy between two textual actions (the text as originally submitted for revision vs the edited end-product); and just as translators have to determine the 'function-in-culture' of the source text, while at the same time taking into account the initiator's requirements, so too must editors show loyalty to both horizons of expectation – by 'balancing the interests' (Mossop, 2001: 5) of clients, publishers, professional associations and other social gatekeepers.

In exams, students have to rewrite a given text (English/English) for an audience with a different profile. A typical exam task-sheet would simulate real-life expectations of an editing brief:

a) Rewrite the given article from the *Sunday Times* (a South African weekly), in a register that is appropriate to the imagined publication – Dorling Kindersley's series 'Eyewitness Guides' – a large-format, heavily illustrated publication using a style popular with 12/13 year olds. You will need to be extremely selective about the amount of information you present to the reader, as well as the register you choose. You may have to delete repetitive information and re-arrange the original's structure, as well as pay careful attention to achieving the appropriate balance between relevant content and adequate language use.

b) Critically reflect on the nature of your editorial intervention by justifying your decision to include/exclude information, and the manner in which it is presented, including references to visual aids.

Conclusion

As I hope this chapter has shown, in countries experiencing transition – where 'First World' and 'Third World' are learning to live together – at societal and educational level, trainers need to be open to experimenting with less established forms of teaching translation that go beyond the concept of a traditional disciplinary major. I have suggested some of the benefits of the modular approach – which is also an inter-disciplinary approach, based as it is on inter-dependent, yet self-contained, teaching units across cognate disciplines – and have shown possible ways of practical implementation that, for over a decade, have been tested and proven to be successful. To reiterate, translation in South Africa requires far more than linguistic proficiency, for it is meant to play a crucial role in civil living. By emphasizing the teaching and practice of translation as a form of social, cultural and critical text-intervention, we are playing a crucial role in the on-going effort of integrating diverse communities, culturally and linguistically. By adopting a modular approach we, at the same time, practise social flexibility regarding the need to adapt to the educational challenges and the shifting identities of a society in transition.

Notes

1. An earlier formula of the modular approach was first implemented at UKZN-Durban in 1997 – see Dimitriu (2001) for the earlier version, and abbreviated presentation, of the modular approach. In the last couple of years, this approach has been modified to accommodate new developments; while the main principles of modularity remain in place, the process of inter-disciplinary adjustment to, and implementation of, the modular approach is on-going and open-ended.

References

Alexander, N. (2002), *An Ordinary Country. Issues in the Transition from Apartheid to Democracy.* Scottville: University of Natal Press.

Beeby, A. (1996), *Teaching Translation from Spanish to English.* Ottawa: University of Ottawa.

Blaauw, J. (2006), 'Interpreting with limited training: experiences in the interpreting of academic lectures at the North-West University, South Africa', in J. Kearns (ed.), *New Vistas in Translator and Interpreter Training*. Special issue of *Translation Ireland*, 17 (1), 7–21.

Blommaert, J. (2005), *Discourse. A Critical Introduction*. Cambridge: Cambridge University Press.

Bourdieu, P. (1992), *Language and Symbolic Power*. Oxford: Blackwell.

Campbell, S. (1998), *Translation into Second Language*. New York: Longman.

Declerq, C. (2006), 'Tomorrow's translation studies today: some considerations', in J. Kearns (ed.), *New Vistas in Translator and Interpreter Training*. Special issue of *Translation Ireland*, 17, (1), 121–133.

de Klerk, V. (2000), 'Language shift in Grahamstown: a case study of selected Xhosa-speakers', in *International Journal of the Sociology of Language*, 146, 87–110.

—(2002), 'Language issues in our schools: whose voice counts? in *Perspectives in Education*, 20, (1), 1–14.

de Klerk, V. and D. Gough. (2002), 'Black South African English', in R. Mesthrie (ed.), Language in South Africa. Cambridge: Cambridge University Press, pp. 356–378.

Dimitriu, I. (2001), 'Academic restructuring and modularity in the Humanities: the role and meaning of translation training in the South African context', in M. Thelen (ed.), *Translation and Meaning*. Part 5. Maastricht: Universitaire Pers Maastricht, pp. 207–216.

Fillmore, C. J. (1977), 'Scenes-and-frames semantics', in A. Zampolli (ed.), *Linguistic Structures Processing*. Amsterdam/ New York/ Oxford: North-Holland Publishers, pp. 55–81.

Finchilescu, G. and Nyawose, G. (1998), 'Talking about language: Zulu students' views on language in the new South Africa', in *South African Journal of Psychology*, 28, (2), 53–61.

Goffman, E. (1974), *Frame Analysis. An Essay on the Organization of Experience*. New York and London: Harper & Row.

Greenblatt, S. and Gunn, G. (1992), *Redrawing the Boundaries: The Transformation of English and American Studies*. New York: Modern Language Association.

Grice, H. P. (1975), 'Logic and conversation', in P. Cole and J. Morgan (eds), *Syntax and Semantics: Speech Acts*. New York: Academic Press, pp. 41–58.

Gutt, Ernst-August. (2000), *Translation and Relevance: Cognition and Context*. Manchester: St Jerome.

Hall, B. (2002), *Among Cultures: The Challenge of Communication*. Orlando, FL: Harcourt College Publishers.

Hall, E. T. (1976), *Beyond Culture*. Garden City NY: Anchor Books/Doubleday.

—(1983), *The Dance of Life: The Other Dimension of Time*. Garden City NY: Anchor Books/ Doubleday.

Hermans, T. (2007), *The Conference of the Tongues*. Manchester: St Jerome.

Hofstede, G. (1984), *Culture's Consequences: International Differences in Work-related Values*. Beverly Hills: Sage.

—(1991), *Cultures and Organizations: Software of the Mind*. London: McGraw Hill.

House, J. (1997/ 1977), *Translation Quality Assurance: A Model Revisited*. Tübingen: Günter Narr.

Kamwamgamalu, N. (2003), 'Social change and language shift: South Africa', in *Review of Applied Linguistics*, 23, 225–242.

— (2004), 'The language policy/ language economics interface and mother-tongue education in post-apartheid South Africa', in *Language Problems and Language Planning*, 28, (2), 134–146.

Kapp, R. (2000), '"With English you can go everywhere": an analysis of the role and status of English at a former DET school', in *Journal of Education*, 25, 227– 259.

Katan, D. (2004/ 1999), *Translating Cultures: An Introduction for Translators, Interpreters and Mediators*. Manchester: St Jerome.

Kearns, J. (2006), 'In the broader context: reflections on curricular design principles for training translators', in J. Kearns (ed.), *New Vistas in Translator and Interpreter Training*. Special issue of *Translation Ireland*, 17, (1), 205–218.

Kelly, D. (2005), *A Handbook for Translator Trainers: A Guide to Reflective Practice*. Manchester: St Jerome.

Kelly, D. and C. Way (2007), 'Editorial', in *The Interpreter and Translator Trainer 1(1)*, pp. 1– 13.

Klopper, D. (ed.) (2002), *Language and Empowerment*. Special issue of *English Academy Review* 19.

Kluckhohn, F. R. and F. L. Strodtbeck (1961), *Variations in Value Orientations*. Evanston: IL: Row & Peterson.

Kruger, A. (ed.) (2000), *Translation Studies in South Africa*. Special issue of *Language Matters*, 31.

— (2004), *Corpus-based Translation Studies: Research and Applications*. Special issue of *Language Matters*, 35, (1).

Kussmaul, P. (1995), *Training the Translator*. Amsterdam/Philadelphia: Benjamins.

Lefevere, A. (1992), *Translation, Rewriting and the Manipulation of Literary Fame*. London and New York: Routledge.

Makubalo, G. (2007), ' "I don't know . . . it contradicts": identity construction and the use of English by high school learners in a desegregated school space', in *The English Academy Review*, 24, (2), 25–41.

McKinney, C. (2007), '"If I speak English, does that make me less black anyway?": "race" and English in South African desegregated schools', in *Language, Identity and English Education in South Africa*. Special issue of *The English Academy Review*, 24, (2), 6–24.

McKinney, C. and Soudien C. (2007), 'Editorial', in *Language, Identity and English Education in South Africa*. Special issue of *The English Academy Review*, 24, (2), 1–5.

Mossop, B. (2001), *Revising and Editing for Translators*. London: St Jerome Publishing.

Nongogo, N. (2007), '"Mina 'ngumZulu phaqa": language and identity among multilingual grade 9 learners', in *English Academy Review*, 24, (2), 42–54.

Nord, C. (1991), *Text Analysis in Translation: Theory, Methodology and Didactic Application of a Model for Translation-Oriented Text Analysis*. Amsterdam: Rodopi.

— (1997), *Translating as Purposeful Activity*. Amsterdam: Rodopi.

Peirce, C. S. (1966), *Collected Papers of Charles Sanders Peirce*, by C. Hartshorne, P. Weiss and A.W. Burks eds). Cambridge, MA: Harvard University Press.

Pokorn, N. (2005), *Challenging the Traditional Axioms: Translation into a Non-Mother Tongue*. Amsterdam: Benjamins.

Pope, R. (2000/1995), *Textual Intervention: Critical and Creative Strategies for Literary Studies*. London and New York: Routledge.

— (2002/1998), *The English Studies Book*. London and New York: Routledge.

— (2005), *Creativity: Theory, History, Practice*. London and New York: Routledge.

Rudwick, S. (2004), '"Zulu, we need it for our culture": Umlazi adolescents in the post-apartheid state', in *Southern African Linguistics and Applied Languages Studies*, 22, (3-4), 159–172.

Samovar, L.A. and Porter, R.E. (2001), *Communication between Cultures*. Belmont, CA: Wadsworth.

Schäffner, C. (2002), 'Discourse analysis for translation and translator training: status, needs, methods', in C. Schäffner (ed.), *The Role of Discourse Analysis for Translation and in Translation Training*. Clevedon/ Buffolo/ Toronto/ Sydney: Multilingual Matters, pp. 1–8.

Scollon, R. and Scollon, S. W. (2003/1995), *Intercultural Communication: A Discourse Approach*. Oxford: Blackwell.

Soudien, C. (2004), 'Constituting the class: an analysis of the process of "integration" in South African schools', in L. Chisholm (ed.). *Changing Class: Education and Social Change in Post-apartheid South Africa*. Cape Town: HSRC Press, pp. 89–113.

Steiner, G. (1975), *After Babel: Aspects of Language and Translation*. New York and London: Oxford University Press.

Towards Comprehending Spoken-language Educational Interpreting as Rendered at a South African University

10

Marlene Verhoef and Johan Blaauw

Introduction

In their study of the management of power relations within a typical community interpreting environment, R. Merlini and R. Favaron (2003: 226–227) reach the conclusion that, if community interpreters overtly view their task as involving an effort at reconciliation in order to create a common as well as an enabling communicative environment, they will fulfil a visible and transparent mediating role. Furthermore, when the notion of being both visible and transparent is unpacked, it is evident that the mediating role of interpreters working in situations where the interlocutors differ in terms of status (and where uneven power relationships therefore exist between interlocutors), power relations are co-constructed (and reconstructed) by the way the interpreter(s) position themselves in the communicative triad. Further, it appears from research done at the North-West University (NWU) in South Africa on interpreting services provided within the educational programmes of the University that the interpreters also view their task in terms of a social responsibility towards the end-users (De Kock and Blaauw, 2008; Olivier, Verhoef, 2008; Verhoef and Bothma, 2008).

What then characterizes spoken-language educational interpreting? Although the simultaneous mode of interpreting is used in classrooms, it has become apparent from the above-mentioned research that the educational interpreter's socio-communicative function cannot be ignored. Thus, this chapter not only seeks to determine the typological boundaries of this genre of interpreting as it has developed over the past four years at the NWU and other educational delivery sites where the University provides interpreting services, but also takes a closer look at the way in which perceptions of different role-players in the educational interpreting event provide empirical evidence of the expectations and views of the role of the educational interpreter.

Exploring the characteristics of spoken-language educational interpreting

Context

Educational interpreting developed naturally from community interpreting. In view of F. Pöchhacker's (2004/2007: 161) remark that professional interpreting is always situated in a particular social context that has a determining impact on the interpreting activity, it is evident that the educational setting is indeed a typical community-based setting, so that educational interpreting can be seen as a sub-type of community interpreting. However, after four years of service delivery it has become clear that educational interpreting cannot merely be defined in this way. For example, different teaching styles used within the educational environment have a direct bearing on the interpreting type – if lecturers use a formal lecturing style, the interpreting type tends towards the conference type, while if the teaching style shifts to more facilitative teaching, a related shift in interpreting towards the liaison-type of interpreting can be identified.

While community interpreting mostly utilizes the consecutive mode (both short and long consecutive, except in the case of sign-language interpreting, which is normally simultaneous), educational interpreting, as rendered at the NWU and elsewhere, takes place in the simultaneous mode. The next section aims to investigate the particular characteristics of spoken-language educational interpreting against the background of a theoretical exploration of the canonical modes and types of interpreting.

Fitting spoken-language educational interpreting into the modes and types paradigm

Introduction

Otto Kade (in Pöchhacker, 2004/2007: 10) states that interpreting is a separate form of 'Translation' which is determined by both immediacy of delivery and time-pressure, thus making it a typically ephemeral activity. The literature makes it clear that, regardless of the transitory nature of the activity, it is imperative that the interpreting product should demonstrate pertinent levels of sameness in relation to the source text – in terms of both intended meaning and pragmatic effect. In his overview of the historical development of the phenomenon of interpreting, Pöchhacker (2004/2007: 15) states that the development of interpreting should be viewed on a continuum, from isolated inter-social contacts at one end to institutionalized intra-social interpreting at the other. This language mediation ranges from typical expedition-type contacts (explorations, warfare, etc.), through transactional mediation (trade, diplomacy, etc.), to administrative-type mediation (e.g. law and justice, religious services, etc.). Obviously, such spheres of interaction not only influence the format of interpreting but also determine the choice of language modality (i.e. spoken or sign language).

Working modes of interpreting

More recent literature generally distinguishes two working modes: consecutive and simultaneous (cf. Riccardi, et al., 1998: 3; Jones, 1998: 7; Hsieh, 2003: 284; Pöchhacker, 2004/2007: 18). While it is acknowledged that the *consecutive* working mode refers to rendering the target text after the source text, and *simultaneous* interpreting refers to rendering the target text as the source text is being presented, it is clear that each of these modes includes a variety of delivery possibilities. S. Kalina (2005: 770) and E. Hsieh (2003: 284) report that consecutive interpreting is the oldest and most established mode of interpreting – it has even been referred to by AIIC (1982) as the *noblest* form of interpreting. Because this mode is characterized by delayed delivery, the use of notes and the skills of note-taking can play a role in the rendering of the target text. Depending on both the length of utterances/texts in the source-text which have to be interpreted and the levels of bi-directionality, there is a distinction in the literature (e.g. Pöchhacker, 2007: 19) between the classic/long consecutive (with notes and reduced bi-directional turn-taking) and short consecutive (without notes and with more bi-directional turn-taking). It is also acknowledged that short consecutive interpreting is the most frequently used mode for liaison-type community interpreting, where the interactants are involved in typical bilateral discussions with appropriate turn-taking (Pöchhacker, 2001: 415).

As regards the professional performance of consecutive interpreters, AIIC (1982) proposes that interpreters working in the consecutive mode should hone their public-speaking skills, make eye-contact with the end-users, and use their body language to 'project poise and confidence'. The simultaneous mode, characterized by 'speaking while listening' (Setton, 2001:1), implies simultaneity of a multitude of psycholinguistic tasks to be dealt with by the interpreter. Simultaneous interpreting is a demanding and complex task that concurrently involves various tasks such as listening, comprehension, information retention, retrieval, production and monitoring (Mizuno, 2005: 741).

The origins of simultaneous interpreting can be traced back to 1927, when it was used for the first time at the International Labour Conference in Geneva (Furmanek and Achenbach, 2004). However, simultaneous interpreting as it is known today dates back relatively recently to the Nuremberg Trials, when it was felt that consecutive or whispered interpreting would not provide defendants with a fair trial in their preferred languages (Gaiba, 1998: 30, Ramler, 2007: 9). W. Skinner and T. F. Carson (1990: 22) suggest that both the differences and the similarities between interpreting at Nuremberg and the current situation in the profession remain striking. While a relationship of rapport and familiarity was evident between the interlocutors and the interpreters, as indeed happens today, there was initial scepticism with regard to the trustworthiness of the interpreting product at Nuremberg (Gaiba, 1998: 37, Ramler, 2007: 10). The same doubt was identified in the minds of lecturers as to the accuracy of simultaneous interpreting at the NWU and subsequently had to be overcome (Blaauw, 2006: 14).

Interpreting types

While interpreting modes refer to the *form* of interpreting delivery, there is consensus that interpreting types describe the *function* of the act of interpreting by primarily denoting the communicative event that is mediated by means of the particular mode of interpreting. Merlini and Favaron (2003: 207) admit that an intricate terminological debate exists as regards the typological description of the various functions of interpreting and the places where interpreting takes place, and they are only prepared to distinguish between conference and *ad hoc* interpreting, where the latter serves as the superordinate term encompassing public service, community and liaison interpreting.

From Merlini and Favaron (2003: 207) and from other scholars working in the field of interpreting, it appears that a typological description of the functions of interpreting is vague and even troublesome (cf. Mikkelson, 1999). In fact, Pöchhacker (2001: 411) proposes that conference and community interpreting should be viewed on a continuum ranging from interpreting in an international sphere of interaction to interpreting within a social community. Therefore, for the purposes of this chapter, we will follow Pöchhacker's proposal that the 'social context of interaction' or 'setting' should be seen as a functional notion for denoting types of interpreting. Starting out from macro-directionality, in which the levels of interaction between interlocutors is a variable, we need to explore Merlini and Favaron's (2003: 206) distinction between conference and *ad hoc* interpreting in order to identify an appropriate niche for spoken-language educational interpreting as implemented at the NWU.

Conference interpreting predominantly takes place unidirectionally and in a particular format of interaction, and may happen in either the consecutive or the simultaneous working mode (Pöchhacker, 2007: 16). However, it seems clear that the simultaneous mode is gaining ground and is replacing the consecutive mode (Kalina, 2005: 771). According to Giovanna Pistillo (2005) conference interpreting is characterized by formal and structured speeches (sometimes provided to interpreters in printed format) as source texts, resulting in communication relying only to a limited degree on non-verbal elements. This viewpoint is in contrast to that of H. Bühler (1985: 50–51), who contends that, apart from auditory signals, conference interpreting is also reliant on visual signals, with regard to both the message and the context of social interaction.

In terms of the demand on conference interpreters to deal with particular topics, Beaugrande (1992 as quoted by Shlesinger, 1998: 6) points out that the categorization of conferences into *monster* and *thematic* types also has a bearing on the way in which conference interpreters do their work. While the former refers to parallel sessions on a variety of topics – which means that interpreters do not necessarily share situational and contextual knowledge with the participants – the latter has thematic coherence in as far as a paradigmatic delineation of themes, issues and topics exists. As regards the type of discourse dealt with by conference interpreters, Linell (1988 as quoted by Straniero, 2003: 167) states that conference interpreting could be regarded as 'intra-inter-professional discourse' in that interpreters work with a discourse that is being produced by professionals in particular fields. These observations all apply in varying degrees to spoken-language educational interpreting although non-verbal elements are perhaps of more significance than in conference interpreting where the speaker may be at some distance from parts of the audience.

In contrast to conference interpreting, community or social interpreting refers to the type of interpreting that takes place in the 'public service sphere to facilitate communication between officials and lay people' (Wadensjö, 2001: 33; see also Backes, 2007) According to O. Furmanek and H. Achenbach (2004) the term *community interpreting* was coined during the 1970s in Australia, from where it spread to other countries and regions, such as the USA and Europe. It is apparent from the literature that community or social interpreting (also known as *ad hoc interpreting, liaison interpreting,* or *public service interpreting*) refers to 'all types of interpreting which are not classified as conference interpreting' (Merlini and Favaron, 2003: 206; see also Hsieh, 2003: 285). H. Mikkelson (2004) suggests that community interpreting should be seen as an overall concept which includes informal interpreting rendered by amateurs in neighbourhoods and community agencies as well as 'a more formal occupation involving practitioners with training in medical, legal or social service interpreting', an approach shared by C. Wadensjö (2001: 33) and Hsieh (2003: 284). At the first international conference on community interpreting held in Canada in 1995, a definition of community interpreting was adopted that specifically refers to interpreting as a means of creating full access to public services, such as health, legal, education, government and social services (Wadensjö, 2001: 33; Mikkelson, 2004). Thus it is evident that interpreting types such as medical interpreting, mental health interpreting, educational interpreting and legal interpreting, can be regarded as typical functional fields of community interpreting (cf. Rudvin, 2006: 59). It generally takes the form of face-to-face bi-directional language mediation via the same person, which usually takes place in the short consecutive working mode (cf. Merlini and Favaron, 2003: 206; Gentile et al., 1996:17), although the simultaneous working mode is also gaining ground as delivery mode for this type of interpreting (Mikkelson, 1999).

The role of the interpreter in the community interpreting context is one of 'an interactive participant in cross-cultural communication rather than as a relayer of linguistic messages from one language to another' (Swabey, 2007). This view is echoed by M. Inghilleri (2003: 263), who asserts that the facilitation of bi-directional communication characterizes community interpreting insofar as 'a greater degree of "interpretation" of utterances based on contextual and cultural knowledge is granted to or expected of interpreters'. In fact, M. Rudvin (2006: 58) proposes that the community interpreter is obliged to 'negotiate and mediate between the interlocutors' culture, in the sense that s/he needs to fully understand both parties and communicate the respective communicative intentions'.

Given the generally unequal power relationship between interactants in a community interpreting context, interpreters are often inclined to act on behalf of the weaker party (Russo, 2005: 8–9; Kalina, 2005: 771). Mikkelson (2004) also observes that the community interpreter acts as advocate or cultural broker who goes beyond 'the traditional neutral role of an interpreter' by demonstrating a more distinct and noticeable presence in the communication process than does the conference interpreter (cf. Hsieh, 2003: 296). Such an advocacy or support role by the interpreter on behalf of the 'weaker party' is particularly evident in medical interpreting (Swabey, 2007).

In their analysis of this kind of advocacy role, Merlini and Favaron (2003: 210–212) argue that this role might have more to do with conciliation/reconciliation in the sense that the interpreter brings people together by creating an enabling and common communicative environment than with overt advocacy. By assigning to interpreters a social as well as an interpersonal conciliation-reconciliation role that is dependent upon the communicative setting in which the service is rendered, greater insight can be gained into this contentious issue. The implication of Merlini and Favaron's (ibid.) conciliation/reconciliation dichotomy is that the mediating role of interpreters working in situations with differentiated statuses and unequal power distributions between interactants will depend on the way in which these interpreters succeed in doing conciliation and reconciliation of the communicative intent.

Helge Niska (2002: 137–138) similarly accepts that the community interpreter fulfils diverse roles ranging from a neutral position, in which he refers to the interpreter as a linguistic conduit, to an involved role, where the

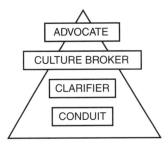

Figure 1. Diverse roles of community interpreters (Niska, 2002: 138).

interpreter acts as advocate. Instead, and following Diversity Rx (1998 as quoted by Niska, 2002: 138), he proposes that the role of community interpreters should be regarded as one of increasing levels of involvement, depending on the particular circumstances. This role is represented graphically as a triangle in Figure 1.

It could therefore be accepted that community interpreters only convey functional meaning during the bulk of their work (acting as 'conduits'), but it is also the case that at times the communication situation (less frequently and not during the bulk of their work) necessitates their further involvement so as to 'make the message accessible to the recipient', which means that they then act as *clarifiers*. Niska further explains that the interpreter occasionally has to become a culture broker if, for example, an explanation of a cultural issue is necessary to prevent misunderstanding from derailing a situation. Controversially, community interpreters sometimes also involve themselves on another level *outside* interpreting situations and act on behalf of service users when they feel a need to protect clients from bureaucracy or other forms of prejudice. All of these features and characteristics of both conference and community interpreting may have an effect on the nature of spoken-language educational interpreting, to which we turn below.

Towards a typological understanding of spoken-language educational interpreting

Spoken-language educational interpreting as rendered at the NWU could be said to be new, not only in terms of educational interpreting as such, but also in its use as a means to implement the multilingual language policy of the university (cf. Blaauw, 2006: 9; Verhoef, 2006: 89). Soon after the commencement of the educational interpreting services, a decision was taken that, for best-practice purposes, the service would be rendered in accordance with the professional scope and requirements of the interpreting profession as a whole.

Because the simultaneous working mode was used, it became evident that interpreters would have to be specifically trained and assessed primarily as simultaneous interpreters working in a particular niche area, namely the educational environment.

However, typological vagueness in relation to the activity subsists. Therefore, in the next section, the notion of 'spoken-language educational interpreting' is explored and unpacked on an interpreting-typological level in order to understand what precisely this activity entails.

Characteristics of spoken-language educational interpreting as rendered at the NWU

Introduction

It is apparent from the literature that the notion 'educational interpreting' has previously been used predominantly to refer to sign-language interpreting (VDDHH 1994: 2; Pöchhacker, 2004/2007: 163; Bolster, 2005: xiv; DEAFSA, 2006: 30). However, Mikkelson's (1999) explanation of educational interpreting would suggest that it is possible to extend this notion to spoken-language interpreting. According to her, this type of interpreting is used both in classrooms for students who do not understand the language of instruction, and in other education-related circumstances, such as school board meetings and disciplinary hearings, and adds that both workings modes (simultaneous and consecutive) can be used for delivery. The term 'academic interpreting' was initially used in the first scholarly articles on this relatively unique type of tertiary-level interpreting in the South African context (Blaauw, 2006: 7), but the decision was later taken to use the more familiar generic term 'educational interpreting', partly because this is the terminology used in the South African Qualifications Authority's registered unit standards for interpreting qualifications (SAQA, 2008).

Towards establishing a profile of spoken-language educational interpreters

When it comes to the profile of the spoken-language educational interpreter it is clear that the demands associated with simultaneous interpreting, regardless of the function of the interpreting event, are equally applicable to educational interpreters. The latter are also expected to demonstrate appropriate skills for successfully managing divided attention, continuous response, concentration, time pressure and a lack of access to the entire source text. Reference to Daniel Gile's well-known effort model (Gile, 1995: 159–190) shows that educational interpreters share the same variables as other simultaneous interpreters in terms of efforts (listening and analysis, short-term memory, production, co-ordination), demands on processing capacity (saturation and individual deficit) and memory (processing capacity, primary and secondary/short-term, long-term, immediate). The same understanding of the notion of working memory also applies. If we consider the various levels of processing and coping strategies, such as chunking, waiting, stalling and anticipating, it is evident that there are no differences in the demonstrable skills required of educational interpreters compared with those required of conference interpreters working in the simultaneous mode.

In fact, a close look at C. J. Kellet-Bidoli's (2002: 174–175) extensive list of the factors and aspects shared across working modes or types of interpreting, confirms that the personal qualities expected of interpreters in general coincide with those expected of educational interpreters. In stating that all modes of interpreting are influenced by the same environmental, experience-related, interpersonal, linguistic and situational factors, as well as expanding on the similarities among linguistic, paralinguistic, prosodic and other features that have a bearing on all modes of interpreting, it could be assumed that all interpreters need to possess the same primary requisite qualities. In fact, the literature also states that all interpreters should possess the following qualities, among others: good language skills, analytical skills, listening and recall skills, speaking skills and interpersonal skills, as well as both cultural and subject knowledge (cf. Mikkelson, 1999; Pöchhacker, 2004/2007: 113ff; Kalina 2005: 776; Clifford, 2005: 28–29). Finally, the literature provides no conclusive evidence that the models of the knowledge, skills and profiles of interpreters differ when it comes to their applicability to different interpreting functions. The requisite skills and attitudes could therefore be said to be generic.

In fact, A. L. Nilsson (1997: 550) states that 'all interpreters do the same job; we interpret between two languages'. The implication of this statement as well as of the above findings for the spoken-language educational interpreting service rendered at the NWU is that these interpreters are also expected to demonstrate the generic traits applicable to all professional interpreters, regardless of the working mode or the type of interpreting activity.

Demarcating the role and function of spoken-language educational interpreters

In contrast to the conclusion about the generic background and shared characteristics of interpreters, Angelelli (2004: 1) poses the following focused question: '(W)hy do we assume that all interpreters, regardless of their own individual differences or the social interactions within which they work, play their roles in the same way?' This question points to the relevance of defining the context of spoken-language educational interpreting at the NWU.

From research data collected at the NWU over the past four years (as part of an ongoing postgraduate study) a profile of the spoken-language educational interpreter is slowly emerging. This is discussed further below. In short, it is apparent that these interpreters fulfil a typically and primarily community interpreting role, albeit using the simultaneous interpreting mode, with varying levels of involvement according to the scale used in Niska's model (2002: 137–8), referred to above.

However, because end-users are not separated from non-users in the classroom situation – they all sit together in one class and receive education together – an equalization of the power relationship has been noted. 'Non-users' are in indirect contact with, and are therefore aware of the educational interpreting taking place. Their perceptions were surveyed based on the logic that they would give a more informed opinion of the value of educational interpreting than would students in classes where no interpreting was rendered, some of whom are probably not even aware of, the interpreting service. From longitudinal data gathered by means of questionnaires administered among both end-users and non-users of the educational interpreting services in the relevant classes, it became apparent that both parties perceive the service as opening up educational opportunities for students regardless of their language preferences.

The illustrative comments (English translations of original Afrikaans by the authors) shown in Table 1 are from the dataset of perceptions among both non-users and users of educational interpreting services. The data was collected during March 2006.

Overtly linked to the management of power relations, an aspect that is typical of community interpreting due to its core function of facilitating access to public services is the issue of the role and function of the interpreter as mediator of the communicative event. Based on the assumptions of Diversity Rx (1998), which propose diverse roles for interpreters depending on the needs

Table 1. Perceptions on educational interpreting services

Non-users	'Alle taalgroepe kan geakkommodeer word met tolkdienste'. *All language groups can be accommodated by means of interpreting services.*	(Respondent 587) [First-year female student enrolled for Pharmacy Studies]
	'Tolkdienste gee almal die geleentheid om die klas by te woon en te verstaan.' *Interpreting services afford all an opportunity to attend class and to understand.*	(Respondent 600) [First-year female student enrolled for Pharmacy Studies]
	'Almal kan nou by Potch swot'. *Everyone now can study at Potchefstroom.*	(Respondent 606) [Second-year female student, enrolled for Commerce Studies]
Users	*The class will be stalled without interpreters due to English students asking lecturers to repeat what they already said.*	(Respondent 38) [Second-year female student enrolled for BCom]
	Not everyone can speak the same language so interpreter helps a lot. And I understand him and can relate to teacher.	(Respondent 40) [Second-year male student enrolled for BCom]
	Because all of us get a chance of understanding at the same time …	(Respondent 58) [Second-year male student enrolled for BCom]

of the interactants, it appears as if spoken-language educational interpreters also adapt their roles and functions according to the interpreting circumstances and the needs of the interactants. A clear variable in this regard is the teaching style of lecturers. If lecturers show a preference for a more formal lecturing style, interpreters adapt to this and perform predominantly according to conventions typical of conference interpreting. However, if lecturers follow a style more typical of mediating the classroom discourse, interpreters tend to resort to community-type interpreting conventions (Verhoef and Bothma, 2008).

A research study conducted by Verhoef and Bothma (2008) clearly indicates that the primary challenge within the spoken-language educational setup relates to the interpreting of so-called surrounding communicative functions, which are vital for maintaining the referential and phatic functions of language. These findings correlate with the pyramid-shaped graphical representation of Diversity Rx as shown in Figure 1. In describing the position of the educational interpreter on the pyramid, it is apparent from the longitudinal dataset gathered at the University that the position of educational interpreter varies from that of a conduit to a clarifier, and even at times to that of a culture broker. It is evident from several focus-group discussions held with interpreters that they attach these labels to themselves, saying without exception that they view their task from a social responsibility point of view. The findings of H. Olivier (2008) concur with this viewpoint. In addition, the manner in which end-users approach interpreters outside the interpreting situation and consult them on issues related to the classroom discourse could also be indicative of the fact that these interpreters have a predominantly clarifying role. From the dataset it is interesting that end-users view interpreters differently depending on their academic background and age: clarifying questions posed to younger interpreters usually deal with administrative enquiries, while the type of questions posed to one of the retired professors rendering interpreting services usually dealt with academic questions related to content (also see Mathey and Verhoef, 2006).

Furthermore, it is also clear from research by Verhoef and Bothma (2008) that educational interpreters play a clear culture-broker role insofar as they have to achieve a pragmatic effect that accounts for both the context and the way in which utterances are conveyed and understood, taking the social, cultural and historical setting into consideration. From the dataset gathered by the Language Directorate it is clear that particular challenges are posed by the interpreting of culturally related expressions. It is important to mention that interpreters also view their mediating roles as a hybrid between clarifier and culture broker. Of particular interest is the fact that their motivation for being involved in the educational interpreting service tends towards that of being advocates. During a focus-group discussion with interpreters on the way in which they view their work, it became clear that they feel socially responsible for ensuring that end-users receive the correct information. It is noteworthy that these interpreters, although they value a good working relationship with the lecturers, do not express any sense of having a responsibility towards these lecturers (Mathey and Verhoef, 2006).

From the preceding it is apparent that enough empirical evidence exists from the data gathered at the NWU to justify the fact that educational interpreters view themselves predominantly as mediators of the communicative event in order to enable end-users to enjoy access.

Reverting to Merlini and Favaron's (2003: 205, 210, 212ff) view of the role of the community interpreter as one of conciliation and re-conciliation between the participants in the communicative event, it seems that this mediating role of educational interpreters resides in the fact that, by virtue of the advantage resulting from their linguistic, cultural and contextual knowledge, they are best equipped to manage the communicative function of providing an interpreting service. This means that educational interpreters continuously reposition themselves on the pyramid either as a conduit or an advocate. The reconciliating position of the educational interpreter on the pyramid is determined by the particular communicative setting, including the lecturing style of the lecturer, the subject content, the size of the class group and the working relationship between interactants and the interpreter.

According to Merlini and Favaron (2003: 212) the reconciliation role refers to the establishment and maintenance of overall efficiency in the tripartite communication involving an interpreter. This points to the fact that the mediating role of the interpreter as a secondary communication participant should be aimed at decreasing the communicative distance between the interactants. While the conciliation role refers to the interpreting process, it is evident that the reconciliation role refers to the production of an appropriate target text, taking into consideration the different contexts. In this regard, the data gathered as part of the quality management process of the educational interpreting service reveals that educational interpreters working at the NWU frequently, like all interpreters, revert to a number of interpreting strategies to cope with the associated challenges. For example, for items which are culture-specific interpreters often make use of brief paraphrasing to explain the background of a particular expression. The interpreting of culture-specific jokes, however, does continue to pose particular challenges for interpreters, regardless of experience in this field of interpreting.

On an ethical level, interpreters face further challenges when lecturers unintentionally use pejorative language, for example when a large unruly class is called to silence by a lecturer who shouts, 'Shut up!', or when a culturally insensitive comment is made, such as referring to 'African time'. One possible solution put forward (albeit not accepted interpreting practice and not encouraged by the interpreter trainers) was to deal with this challenge by not interpreting the source-text speaker in the conventional first-person form, but rather to use the more remote third person, that is, in the form of reported speech introduced by 'The lecturer says . . . , in order for the interpreters to distance themselves from what is said.

Conclusion

From the preceding explanation it is evident that the notion 'educational interpreting', historically referring predominantly to sign-language interpreting, can easily be expanded to include spoken-language interpreting in education situations. It is evident that the tripartite communication setup within this distinctly community-type setting requires exploration, and consequently a clearer definition, of the roles of these interpreters.

Summary

This research was initiated by the question posed by Merlini and Favaron (2003: 226–227) regarding the task and role of community interpreters working in the service industry where interpreting is used to enhance access to public services. It was stated that if community interpreters (including educational interpreters) overtly view their task as an attempt at conciliation and reconciliation in order to create an enabling and common communicative environment, this would result in inclusive mediation.

From the argument in this chapter, based on research done at the North-West University where spoken-language educational interpreting is used as a separate language medium, it is clear that, although simultaneous interpreting is used as the working mode, the characteristics of the educational type of interpreting are determined by the role and functions of educational interpreters, and not by the characteristics of the processes and products of interpreting. In other words, it is evident that the definition of educational interpreting as a distinct type of interpreting does not rely on a description of either the processes or the products of interpreting, but on the ways in which the interpreters who render this service view themselves in terms of the communicative role they have to fulfil.

In terms of the typological boundaries of this type of interpreting as it has developed over the past four years at the NWU, it could be stated that spoken-language educational interpreting shares the generic characteristics and qualifications applicable to all forms and functions of interpreting. It also requires similar qualities in terms of the profile(s) of the ideal interpreter(s). However, it is evident from the empirical data that the distinction arises at the level of the role and function of interpreters in this particular setting. While they work within the broad community interpreting paradigm, it is clear that these interpreters continuously vary their position on the continuum of the roles of the community interpreter according to the individual context. Depending on the situation, they position themselves predominantly somewhere between clarifiers and culture brokers (in terms of the triangle presented in Figure 1).

Although evidence also exists that, if needed, they can act as advocates for the end-users of the service, it is nevertheless clear from the data that these interpreters place a high premium on a good working relationship with lecturers. In this regard it might be appropriate to view spoken-language educational interpreting as it has developed at the NWU as a role-determined type of community interpreting where interpreters, for the sake of the optimal mediation of the triadic communicative events in the interpreted lectures, are continuously involved in the processes of conciliation and reconciliation.

References

AIIC (1982), Practical Guide for Professional Conference Interpreters. Geneva: AICC. Available at: www.aiic.net/ViewPage.cfm/article21.htm (accessed 23 May 2008).

Angelelli, C. V. (2004), *Revisiting the interpreter's role.* Amsterdam/ Philadelphia: John Benjamins.

Backes, B. (2007), 'Social Interpreting. A Crucial Instrument for Service Providers in a Multicultural Society: Rights, Obligations, Impact', Paper read at the *1st International Forum of Translation Interpreting and Social Activism.* University of Granada, 28–30 April.

Kellet-Bidoli, C. J. (2002), 'Spoken-language and signed-language interpreting. Are they really different?', in G. Garzone, G. and M. Viezzi (eds), *Interpreting in the 21st century: challenges and opportunities.* Amsterdam/Philadelphia: John Benjamins, pp. 171–179.

Blaauw, J. W. H. (2006), Interpreting with limited training: experiences in the interpreting of academic lectures at the North-West University, *Translation Ireland,* 17, (1), 7–21.

Bolster, L. (2005), *Time-compressed Professionalization: the Experience of Public School Sign Language Interpreters in Mountain-Plains States.* (Unpublished Ph.D. Dissertation), Virginia: Virginia Polytechnic and State University. Available at: http://en.scientificcommons.org/1529969 (accessed: 30 January 2008).

Bühler, H. (1985), 'Conference interpreting: a multichannel communication phenomenon', *Meta,* 30, (1), 49–54. Available at: www.erudit.org/revue/ meta/1985/v30/n1/002176ar.pdf (accessed 10 February 2008).

Clifford, A. (2005), 'From model to competency: the role of interpreting theory in learning, teaching, and testing', Conference abstracts of the 50th Anniversary Conference entitled *Professional Education of 21st Century Translators and Interpreters,* Monterey Institute of International Studies. Available at: gsti.miis.edu/conference/cab.htm (accessed 8 February 2008).

De Kock, E. and Blaauw, J. (2008), 'Are longer interpreting turns than the norm possible?' in M. Verhoef and T. du Plessis (eds), *Multilingualism and Educational Interpreting: Innovation and Delivery.* Pretoria: Van Schaik.

Deaf Federation of South Africa, (2006), *Deaf Education Position Paper.* Discussion document. Available at: www.deafsa.co.za (accessed 10 February 2008).

DEAFSA see Deaf Federation of South Africa.

Diversity Rx. (1998), 'Choosing a role', adapted from 'Bridging the Gap', Interpreter Training Program. Courtesy of Cindy Roat, Cross-Cultural Health Care Program. Available at: diversityrx.org/HTML/MOIPR3.htm (accessed 10 February 2008).

Gaiba, F. (1998), *The Origins of Simultaneous Interpretation: The Nuremberg Trial.* Ottawa: University of Ottawa Press.

Gentile, A., Ozolins, U., and Vasilakakos, M. (1996), *Liaison Interpreting: A handbook.* Melbourne: Melbourne University Press.

Gile, D. (1995), *Basic Concepts and Models for Interpreter and Translator Training.* Amsterdam: John Benjamins.

—(2005), 'Directionality in conference interpreting: a cognitive view' in R. Godijns, and M. Hindedael (eds), *Directionality in Interpreting. The 'Retour' or the Native?* Ghent: Communication and Cognition, pp. 9–26. Available at: www.cirinandgile.com/05Directionality.rtf (accessed 8 February 2008).

Hsieh, E. (2003), 'The Importance of Liaison Interpreting in the Theoretical Development of Translation Studies'. Available at: faculty-staff.ou.edu/H/I-Ling.Hsieh-1/download/Hsieh2003-2.pdf (accessed 2 February 2008).

Inghilleri, M. (2003), 'Habitus, field and discourse: interpreting as a socially situated activity', *Target,* 15, (2), 243–268.

Jones, R. 1998. *Conference Interpreting Explained.* Manchester: St. Jerome.

Kalina, S. (2005), 'Quality assurance for interpreting processes', *Meta,* 50, (2), 768–784. Available at: www.erudit.org/revue/meta/2005/v50/n2/011017ar.html (accessed 23 May 2008).

Mathey, G. and Verhoef, M. (2006), 'The critical role of trust in classroom interpreting – setting the norms and assessing the performance of interpreters in the North-West University (NWU) classroom interpreting project', Paper read at 2nd IATIS Conference, *Intervention in Translation, Interpreting and Intercultural Encounters,* Cape Town, 12–14 July 2006.

Merlini, R. and Favaron. R. (2003), 'Community interpreting: reconciliation through power management', *The Interpreters' Newsletter,* 12, 205–229.

Mikkelson, H. (1999), *Interpreting is Interpreting – or is it?* Available at: www.acebo.com/papers/interp1.htm (accessed 9 February 2008).

—(2004), *The Professionalization of Community Interpreting.* Available at: www.acebo.com/papers/protslzn.htm (accessed 9 February 2008).

Mizuno, A. (2005), 'Process model for simultaneous interpreting and working memory', *Meta,* 50, (2), 739–752. Available at: www.erudit.org/revue/meta/2005/v50/n2/index.html (accessed 5 February 2008).

Nilsson, A. L. (1997), 'Sign language interpreting in Sweden', *Meta,* 42, (3), 550–554.

Niska, H. (2002), 'Community interpreter training – past, present, future', in G. Garzone, and M. Viezzi (eds), *Interpreting in the 21st Century: Challenges and Opportunities.* Selected papers from the 1st Forli Conference on Interpreting Studies, 9–11 November 2000. Amsterdam/Philadelphia: John Benjamins, pp. 133–144.

Furmanek, O., and Achenbach, H. (2004), Interpreting *for the Community: A Brief History of Interpreting.* Available at: http://lrc.wfu.edu/community_ interpreting/pages/history.htm (accessed 2 February 2008).

Olivier, H. (2008), 'Process, product and performance: exploring the differences between conference interpreters and educational interpreters', in M. Verhoef, and T. du Plessis (eds), *Multilingualism and Educational Interpreting: Innovation and Delivery*. Pretoria: Van Schaik.

Pistillo, G. (2005), 'Building Interpreters' Intercultural Competence' in *Quality in Translation: Academic and Professional Perspectives*, Proceedings of the IV Conference on Training and Career Development in Translation and Interpreting, Universidad Europea de Madrid, 25–27 February 2004.

Pöchhacker, F. (2001), 'Quality assessment in conference and community interpreting', *Meta*, XLVI, (2), 410–425. Available at: www.erudit.org/revue/meta/2001/v46/n2/003847ar.pdf (accessed 23 May 2008).

—(2004/2007), *Introducing Interpreting Studies*. London and New York: Routledge.

Ramler, S. (2007), *The Origin and Challenges of Simultaneous Interpretation: the Nuremberg Trials*. Available at: www.someya-net.com/10-JAIS/Kaishi2007/00_FINAL/03-18%20Ramler_YS.pdf (accessed 5 February 2008).

Riccardi, A., Marinuzzi, G. and Zecchin, S. (1998), 'Interpretation and stress', *The Interpreters' Newsletter*, 8, 93–106.

Rudvin, M. (2006), 'Issues of culture and language in the training of language mediators for public services in Bologna: matching market needs and training', in D. Londei, D.R. Miller, and P. Puccini (eds) *Insegnare le lingue/culture oggi: il contributo dell'interdisciplinaritá*. Bologna: CeSLiC.

Russo, M. (2005), *Language and Culture ... A journey into Interpreters' Human, Cultural, and Linguistic Awareness*. Address delivered at the Tarleton State University, 10 February 2005. Available at: www.tarleton.edu /~honors/Russo_lecture_fin_pdf_s05.pdf (accessed 23 May 2008).

South African Qualifications Authority (2008), Registered unit standard: 'Categorise new and existing information into working memory'. Available at: http://regqs.saqa.org.za/viewUnitStandard. php?id=116797 (accessed 21 April 2008).

Shlesinger, M. (1998), 'Corpus-based interpreting studies as an offshoot of corpus-based translation studies'. *Meta*, 43, (4), 1–8. Available at: www.erudit.org/revue/meta/1998/v43/n4/004136ar.pdf (accessed 5 February 2008).

Setton, R. (2001), 'Deconstructing SI: a contribution to the debate on component processes', *The Interpreters' Newsletter*, 11, 1–26.

Skinner, W. and Carson, T. F. (1990), 'Working conditions at the Nuremberg Trials', in D. Bowen, and M. Bowen, M. (eds) *Interpreting – Yesterday, Today and Tomorrow*. American Translators Association Scholarly Monograph Series, Volume IV, pp. 14–22.

Stranieiro, S. F. (2003), 'Norms and *quality* in media interpreting: the case of Formula One press-conferences', *The Interpreters' Newsletter*, 12, 135–174

Swabey, L. (2007), *Healthcare Interpreting: Research and Resources*. Available at: www.asl.neu.edu/nciec/ resource/docs/MedicalInterpretingSwabey.pdf (accessed 4 February 2008).

VDDHH see Virginia Department for the Deaf and Hard of Hearing.

Verhoef, M, (2006), 'Tolking as afleweringsmodus in universiteitsklasse. 'n Bespreking en analise van die Dagbreektrusttolkprojek aan die Potchefstroomkampus van die Noordwes-Universiteit', *Tydskrif vir Geesteswetenskappe, Moedertaalonderrigsupplement*. Junie, 89–99.

Verhoef, M. and Bothma, R. (2008), 'Assessing the role of the interpreter in facilitating classroom communication' in M. Verhoef, and T. du Plessis (eds), *Multilingualism and Educational Interpreting: Innovation and Delivery*. Pretoria: Van Schaik.

Verhoef, M. and du Plessis, T. (eds). 2008, *Multilingualism and Educational Interpreting: Innovation and Delivery*. Pretoria: Van Schaik.

Verhoef, M. (2008), 'Accounting for paralanguage and non-verbal communication in the educational interpreting service rendered at the NWU', in M. Verhoef, and T. du Plessis (eds), *Multilingualism and Educational Interpreting: Innovation and Delivery*. Pretoria: Van Schaik.

Virginia Department for the Deaf and Hard of Hearing (1994), 'Educational Interpreting and the Virginia Quality Assurance Screening (VQAS)'. Available at: www.eric.ed.gov/ERICDocs/data/ ericdocs2sql/ content_storage_01/0000019b/80/14/ca/f4.pdf (accessed 10 February 2008).

Wadensjö, C. (1998/2001), 'Community interpreting', in M. Baker (ed.), *Routledge Encyclopedia of Translation Studies*. London and New York: Routledge, pp. 33 –37.

Simultaneous Interpreting: Implementing Multilingual Teaching in a South African Tertiary Classroom

Anne-Marie Beukes and Marné Pienaar

11

Chapter Outline

Background

In South Africa the language policies of tertiary-education institutions have been a point of serious concern and debate since the dawn of democracy in 1994. This has been the result of changes in South Africa's language policy and hence a rapid change in demographics at higher education institutions. Historically English and Afrikaans have dominated the higher education landscape and African languages have seldom been used as medium of teaching and learning. However, since 1994 the need to transform this landscape has had a significant impact on the language dispensation in higher education. In this regard two important policy documents emanating from the national Department of Education have had a decisive impact.

Higher education in South Africa was radically restructured during the period 2002 to 2004 following a rationalization programme announced by Government in the National Plan for Higher Education in 2001. The restructuring process reduced 36 universities and technikons (tertiary institutions with a technical focus) to 22 universities through mergers and incorporations of existing higher education institutions. The rationalization process not only changed the configuration of South Africa's higher education institutions, but also impacted on issues related to languages of learning and teaching (LOLT) at these institutions, issues that have a long history of conflict and controversy. S. Murray (2002: 435) contextualizes language in education matters in apartheid South Africa as follows:

> It is a truism to say that policies of language and education are inherently political, but nowhere more so than in South Africa where language has been closely bound up in the system of ethnic and racial division. . . . A racially and ethnically segregated education system was central to the maintenance of these boundaries.

While recognizing the critical role of language and access to language 'to ensure the right of individuals to realize their full potential to participate in and contribute to the social, cultural, intellectual, economic and political life of South African society' (DoE, 2002: 4), the National Plan for Higher Education in South Africa (DoE, 2001) is clear that ethnolinguistic forces such as the need to be an 'English university' or an 'Afrikaans university' would no longer determine the nature of the language dispensation. The Language Policy for Higher Education (2002) acknowledges the status quo in higher education where English and Afrikaans are dominant languages of learning and teaching, but rejects the need for designated Afrikaans universities since this notion 'runs counter to the end goal of a transformed higher education system' (DoE, 2002: 12). The 'simultaneous development of a multilingual environment in which all our languages are developed as academic/scientific languages' (DoE, 2002: 5) is the challenge that higher education must respond to. In the interest of effecting a transformed higher education system as envisaged by the National Plan for Higher Education, universities should 'unabashedly and unashamedly' become 'South African' (DoE, 2002: 12).

Historically Afrikaans-medium universities[1] in particular have been affected by these policy and demographic pressures to re-evaluate their monolingual teaching practices and to provide for teaching in English (Du Plessis, 2006; Giliomee and Schlemmer, 2006). Most historically Afrikaans-medium universities have in fact undergone 'a sociolinguistic metamorphosis' (Du Plessis, 2006: 87) and now offer tuition both in English and (increasingly less) in Afrikaans. Student demographics and language preferences at the University of Pretoria (UP) bear witness to the changing face of higher education. In 1990 only 20 per cent of UP's students were English-speaking. Although classes were offered in Afrikaans at the time, English students were afforded the opportunity to write all tests and exams in English. In 2006 some 59 per cent of UP's undergraduate student population indicated that their preferred LOLT was English, while almost 68 per cent of postgraduate students chose English as a LOLT. In addition, more than 2,200 international students from 60 different countries were registered at UP in 2005 (Grové, 2006).

At the University of Johannesburg (UJ), the introduction of English as a LOLT in 1998 has steadily led to an imbalance in the number of students in Afrikaans and English classes respectively, with a ratio of approximately 1: 4 in favour of English. However, students attending English classes are not necessarily first-language speakers of English. During 2003 a study was conducted in which a series of seven lectures in Development Studies, where the lecturer was of Ugandan origin, was interpreted into Afrikaans for the benefit of those students who preferred to attend Afrikaans-speaking classes. The study was conducted against the background of the university's former language policy (which prescribed parallel-medium teaching), the inability of certain academic staff to teach in Afrikaans and the feeling of some staff members that the homogenous nature of the Afrikaans classes was not conducive to class discussion.[2]

From the 2003 study it became evident that the use of simultaneous interpreting as an alternative to parallel-medium teaching was not without its shortcomings, and it was concluded that 'although there is technically speaking no reason why simultaneous interpreting cannot be used as an alternative to duplicating classes, . . . the hegemony of English could stand in the way of a fully fledged interpreting service' (Pienaar, 2006: 38).

The study recommended that:

> it might be a solution not to limit interpreting to Afrikaans classes only, but to do away with parallel medium instruction and rather introduce double medium instruction where lecturers use their language of preference coupled with interpretation into the other language(s) (emphasis added). This will allow students the benefit of the knowledge base of the lecturer; the lecturer will have the benefit of

speaking his/her language of preference; students should benefit from using their language of preference and furthermore multiculturalism will be enhanced as making use of the interpreting equipment will not be restricted to one group only.

(Pienaar, 2006: 38)

Interpreting and language policy implementation in higher education

Simultaneous interpreting is a useful language policy management mechanism in the sense that it facilitates access to information in a multilingual context. Recent years have witnessed the introduction of whispered interpreting in the South African higher education context to address the challenges posed by the changing landscape of universities (Verhoef, 2002; Van Rooy, 2005; Pienaar, 2006; Verhoef, 2006; Blaauw, 2007; Le Roux, 2007; Verhoef, 2007; Verhoef and Blaauw, 2007). While a range of indigenous languages are used on a daily basis in a variety of domains in South Africa, English is now the de facto academic lingua franca of higher education. The reality of transformation in higher education has resulted in an increased demand for the use of English as language of learning and teaching at historically Afrikaans universities.

An example of innovation devised to meet the challenges presented by the Language Policy for Higher Education (2002) is provided in the interpreting service offered by the North-West University (NWU), where a fully fledged interpreting service has been operational since 2004 on its Potchefstroom campus. Following an experiment to establish whether students who spoke an African language as first language would benefit from English tuition – be it by means of simultaneous interpreting or by the direct use of English as medium of instruction – and also to ascertain if Afrikaans-speaking students would be disadvantaged by the use of English as medium of instruction, B. Van Rooy (2005: 86) reported as follows:

As far as the straight-forward comparisons between Afrikaans and English as media of instruction are concerned, it is clear that Afrikaans learners perform much better in Afrikaans classes than in English classes, while Black learners perform much better in English classes than in Afrikaans classes.

Following the results, it was recommended that simultaneous interpreting from Afrikaans into English be implemented at the Potchefstroom campus; that Afrikaans be used as medium of instruction for Afrikaans-speaking students and that further research be undertaken into the feasibility of rendering a simultaneous interpreting service from English into Afrikaans.

(See Blaauw (2007: 19) for a detailed exposition of the establishment and current status of the fully fledged simultaneous interpreting service offered at the NWU.)

Another case in point regarding the increased demand for the use of English as language of learning and teaching at historically Afrikaans universities, and the focus of this study, is the University of Johannesburg situated in the Gauteng province, one of South Africa's linguistically most diverse provinces. However, it should be borne in mind that the student body at the Potchefstroom campus differs significantly from that of the former RAU (now UJ). The majority of students at Potchefstroom are Afrikaans-speaking. By 2004 students who preferred English as medium of tuition (first and second language speakers) outnumbered Afrikaans-speaking students by approximately 4: 1 at the former RAU.

This chapter reports on a research project by the Department of Linguistics and Literary Theory at the University of Johannesburg, which sought to investigate the success of simultaneous interpreting in a classroom context characterized by a high degree of linguistic diversity. From a language management perspective, gauging language attitudes and perceptions in such a classroom situation may point to possible challenges that could impact on the implementation of a policy of multilingualism in the higher education context. An important objective of this project was therefore to explore some of the factors that influence the use of simultaneous interpreting in a classroom context, such as the values that students attach to, or associate with, their mother tongues, primary languages[3] or other languages.

A changing context: the University of Johannesburg

The University of Johannesburg was established on 1 January 2005, after incorporating the East Rand Vista campus and the Soweto Vista campus with Rand Afrikaans University (RAU) in January 2004, and merging in January 2005 with the Technikon Witwatersrand (TWR). The merger took place in accordance with the Minister of Education's proposals – issued in December 2002 and approved by Cabinet – for the transformation and restructuring of the institutional landscape of the higher education system. Retaining the campuses of the merging institutions resulted in UJ having five campuses: the Auckland Park Kingsway Campus (the main campus), the Doornfontein Campus, the Auckland Park Bunting Road Campus, the Soweto Campus and the

East Rand Campus. UJ is one of the largest residential universities in South Africa with more than 40,000 full-time students.

When RAU was officially opened in 1967 it did not have an official language policy, but in accordance with the university's aim to be Afrikaans in spirit and character, Afrikaans became the language of learning and teaching at this institution for the next 20 years. This situation changed gradually from the late 1980s when non-Afrikaans-speaking students began enrolling. Measures to accommodate students who preferred English as their LOLT were introduced: study guides were made available in English and students also wrote examinations in English.

However, over the last few years of RAU's existence its language dispensation changed fundamentally as a result of the influx of students who preferred English as their LOLT. The process of introducing parallel-medium instruction at RAU began in 1997, when it was decided that departments would offer courses on a parallel-medium basis. In practice this resulted in separate classes, study guides and tutoring for English- and Afrikaans-speaking students. In addition, RAU provided resources to support its multilingual policy such as translation and whispered interpreting facilities[4] and services (see Table 1 for an exposition of whispered interpreting services provided at RAU/UJ).

Table 1. Whispered simultaneous interpreting services provided at RAU in 2004 and UJ in 2005

Type of meeting/event	Number of meetings/ events interpreted	
	2004	2005
Council meetings	4	1
Institutional Forum meetings	8	1
Senate meetings	5	4
Faculty board meetings	16	16
Management Committee meetings	1	1
N.P. van Wyk Louw Memorial Lecture	1	
Lectures in Dept. of Anthropology & Development Studies	9	
Student Service Centre		3
Disciplinary hearings		1
UJ welcome function		1
FSAC meeting		1
TOTAL	**44**	**29**

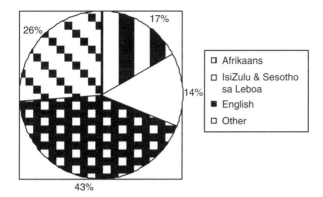

Figure 1. Language distribution at UJ according to students' home language – 2005
(Source: UJ Institutional Development).

Contrary to the situation when its predecessor, RAU, was established in 1967, the UJ's student profile is now characterized by a high degree of diversity (see Figure 1 for a breakdown of students' language distribution per home language).[5] It is important, however, to note that this data, captured from registration forms, does not necessarily reflect the current sociolinguistic reality of UJ's students since the forms only capture bilingual proficiency in the Afrikaans-English configuration, but not in the English-African language configuration.

In line with trends at other South African universities the majority of students prefer English as a LOLT. At the Auckland Park Kingsway campus only 16.5 per cent of students preferred Afrikaans as a LOLT in 2005 (see Table 2).

The UJ is committed to transforming itself into an African university that reflects and accommodates the cultural and linguistic diversity of its clients. Figure 1 indicates a campus that has transformed from being previously monolingual into one that is linguistically diverse. A draft language policy developed in June 2006 in support of UJ's vision (UJ 2006a: 1) recognizes:

1. different languages as an asset to, and a reflection of, the rich diversity of the South African nation;
2. the important role of language in promoting respect for people's human dignity, and realizing the objective of the transformation process to build a free and just democracy; and
3. the barriers formed by language practices in the past, also in education, and the need to cultivate instead a spirit of mutual tolerance, respect and inclusiveness in all matters relating to language.

Table 2. Language distribution according to preferred medium of instruction at UJ in 2005 (Source: UJ Institutional Development)

	Campus	PREFERRED LANGUAGE		
		Afrikaans number of students	English number of students	Total number of students
Postgraduate	Auckland Park Bunting	1	572	573
	Auckland Park Kingsway	1098	5544	6642
	Doornfontein	9	1234	1243
	East Rand		38	38
	Eloff St		24	24
	Soweto		49	49
	TOTAL	**1108**	**7461**	**8569**
Undergraduate	Auckland Park Bunting	1	7491	7492
	Auckland Park Kingsway	3500	16243	19743
	Doornfontein	2	6699	6701
	East Rand		678	678
	Eloff St		275	275
	Soweto		1671	1671
	TOTAL	**3503**	**33057**	**36560**
GRAND TOTAL		**4611**	**40518**	**45129**

UJ's draft language policy with its emphasis on promoting linguistic diversity as enshrined in the constitutional language clause must also be viewed in the context of government's Language Policy for Higher Education regarding the important role of higher education in promoting multilingualism (DoE, 2002: 14–15):

> The Ministry encourages all institutions to consider ways of promoting multilingualism. . . . Clearly, change in the diversity of student and staff profiles, . . . and the creation of a receptive institutional culture which embraces linguistic diversity are . . . crucial ways for promoting a climate where all people feel affirmed and empowered to realize their full potential.

UJ's draft language policy therefore designates the preferred languages of the Gauteng province, that is, 'Sesotho sa Leboa, isiZulu, English and Afrikaans, as its primary languages for academic, administrative, communication and marketing purposes' (UJ, 2006a: 2). The university is committed 'to preserve and develop on all its campuses the designated languages in particular' and to 'recognize the importance of the use of the first language'

(UJ, 2006a: 2). The university is also committed to providing progressively for teaching, learning and assessment in these four languages 'taking the existing position as the point of departure' (UJ, 2006a: 2).

As far as the existing position at UJ is concerned, the status quo which preceded the merger is maintained. English is therefore currently the only language of learning, teaching and administration on all campuses, with the exception of the Auckland Park Kingsway campus. At this campus English and Afrikaans (the latter to an increasingly lesser extent) are used as languages of learning and teaching and for administrative purposes. The bilingual policy on the UJ Auckland Park Kingsway campus is perfectly in line with the Language Policy for Higher Education. This policy makes it clear that 'the Ministry acknowledges that Afrikaans as a language of scholarship and science is a natural resource' (DoE, 2002: 11). Hence the Ministry argues that universities may, 'through a range of strategies, including the adoption of parallel and dual language medium options' (DoE, 2002: 12), retain Afrikaans as a LOLT. At undergraduate level both languages are used as LOLT and at postgraduate level the medium of tuition is determined on an *ad hoc* basis (Table 2).

Extending the interpreting service: Plan A

In accordance with the changing face of student demographics, and following the results of the 2003 interpreting study, the Department of Linguistics and Literary Theory at UJ embarked on a project at the beginning of 2006 in which the two second year groups (English and Afrikaans respectively) in the Literary Theory module of Linguistics and Literary Theory 2 (LIW2) would not be split according to language preference, but rather incorporated into one. The idea was that the medium of teaching would be English or Afrikaans, with interpreting provided also into isiZulu. IsiZulu was chosen since the draft language policy of the University of Johannesburg identified isiZulu and Sesotho sa Leboa as the two indigenous languages (apart from Afrikaans) that need to be promoted within the university context. The intention was to start with isiZulu and to later extend the interpreting service to Sesotho sa Leboa. In practice this would have meant that when a class was offered in Afrikaans, it would be interpreted into English and isiZulu and when offered in English, it would be interpreted into Afrikaans and isiZulu. The hypothesis was that the incorporation of the two existing language groups,

Table 3. Language profile of Linguistics and Literary Theory 2 (LIW2) students at UJ in 2006

	Language	Mother tongue		Primary language	
		N	%	N	%
1	English	8	34.78	16	64
2	Afrikaans	6	26.09	5	20
3	isiZulu	1	4.35	1	4
4	Setswana	1	4.35		
5	Sesotho sa leboa	1	4.35	1	4
6	isiXhosa	2	8.7		
7	Xitsonga	1	4.35		
8	SiSwati	1	4.35		
9	Sesotho	1	4.35		
10	German	1	4.35	1	4
11	Greek			1	4
	TOTAL	**23**	**100.02**	**25**	**100**

coupled with interpreting into a third language, would counteract some of the problems encountered in the previous study where the hegemony of English seemed to have been a barrier in the use of simultaneous interpreting as an alternative to parallel medium teaching.

However, when the department met with the group at the beginning of 2006, it was clear that the experiment could not be done as only one student spoke isiZulu as a first language. As far as other mother tongue and primary languages were concerned, the statistics as shown in Table 3 emerged.

Due to the extreme diversity, with 11 languages in a group of 23 students, and also given the fact that only one student each indicated isiZulu and Sesotho sa Leboa as primary languages, it was decided not to use this particular group as it did not make sense to provide a service that would potentially benefit only one additional student.

Extending the interpreting service: Plan B

Following the experience referred to in Plan A above, it was then decided to focus on the students in Linguistics and Literary Theory 1 (LIW1). In order to determine the linguistic diversity of the class, a short questionnaire, which was made available in English and Afrikaans, was distributed to all students during the first meeting (see Appendix A). Apart from sociolinguistically relevant biographical information, the questionnaire also attempted to ascertain which languages were most commonly used as primary and additional languages. Furthermore, certain questions were indirectly aimed at establishing students' attitudes and opinions towards specific languages, their thoughts and beliefs on diversity and their language preferences, as well as their assessment of the value of particular languages as languages of learning and teaching.

The design of the questionnaire was based on the assumption that attitudes towards diversity and the use of languages in education may affect the success of introducing whispered simultaneous interpreting as a mechanism to promote the university's multilingual language policy. The questionnaire was administered in class and was completed by 103 students. Completed questionnaires were analysed by the Department of Statistical Services of the UJ. The results shown in Table 4 and Figures 2 and 3 are based on their analysis.

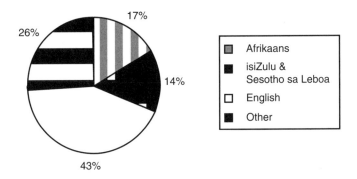

Figure 2. Distribution of students' mother tongue in Linguistics and Literary Theory 1 course at UJ in 2006.

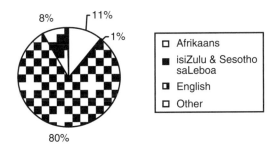

Figure 3. Distribution of students' preferred primary languages in Linguistics and Literary Theory 1 course at UJ in 2006.

Table 4. Language profile of Linguistics and Literary Theory 1 (LIW1) students as per mother tongue, primary language and other languages at UJ in 2006

	Language	Mother tongue[6] N	%	Primary language[7] N	%	Other home language(s)[8] N	%	Other SA language(s) N	%
1	English	44	42.72	80	80	7	10.45	10	12,66
2	Afrikaans	17	16.5	11	11	22	32.84	31	39,24
3	Eng & Afr			1	1	1	1.49		
4	IsiXhosa	9	8.74	2	2	2	2.99	3	3,8
5	IsiZulu	7	6.8	1	1	5	7.46	22	27,85
6	Sesotho sa leboa	7	6.8			4	5.97	2	2,53
7	Setswana	6	5.83			2	2.99	5	6,33
8	Sesotho	4	3.88	3	3	5	7.46	4	5,06
9	SiSwati	3	2.91			1	1.49		
10	Xitsonga	1	0.97			1	1.49	1	1,27
11	Tshivenda	1	0.97			1	1.49		
12	IsiNdebele					2	2.99		
13	German	2	1.94						
14	Arabic								
15	Greek	1	0.97	1	1				
16	Gujarati	1	0.97	1	1	3	4.48		
17	Urdu					3	4.48		
18	Hindi					1	1.49		
19	French					1	1.49		
20	Dutch					1	1.49		
21	Polish					1	1.49		
22	Danish					1	1.49		
23	Portuguese					1	1.49	1	1,27
24	Italian					1	1.49		
25	Malawian language					1	1.49		
	TOTAL	103	100	100	100	67	99.99	79	100,01

The high degree of linguistic diversity as far as the mother tongue was concerned was evident once again.

Language attitudes in a higher education context with whispered simultaneous interpreting

The research project is based on the assumption that gauging language attitudes and perceptions may give an indication of the challenges that could influence the implementation of a policy of multilingualism in the higher education context. The project was aimed at bringing to light the impact of students' attitudes towards particular languages (their mother tongues, primary languages and other languages) and the value they attach to or associate with languages in the higher education context against the backdrop of the role of English as the preferred LOLT. Another primary aim was to ascertain the possible repercussions of these attitudes for simultaneous interpreting in the classroom. The study was informed by the following psychosociological factors that may impact on using simultaneous inter-preting as a language management tool in a linguistically diverse educational environment:

> Any policy for language, especially in the system of education, has to take account of the attitude of those likely to be affected. In the long run, no policy will succeed which does not do one of three things: *conform to the expressed attitudes* of those involved; *persuade* those who express negative attitudes about the rightness of the policy; or seek to *remove the causes of the disagreement*. In any case knowledge about attitudes is fundamental to the formulation of a policy as well as to success in its implementation. (Lewis in Baker, 2006: 211 emphasis added)

The high degree of diversity of the LIW1 class is evident from Table 4, which indicates that 103 students speak 13 different mother tongues (10 of which are official languages of South Africa) and seven primary languages (five are offi-cial languages). Students' language preferences are also presented in Figure 3. There is a shift towards English as primary language: whereas some 40 per cent of students claim that they grew up using English as their mother tongue, 80 per cent choose to use English on a daily basis (i.e. as their primary language).

Students' language preferences as captured in Figure 3 must be read in con-junction with their responses to Question 28, that is, 'In which language would you prefer to study for tests or exams?' Some 50 per cent of the students indi-cated that they would prefer their mother tongue compared to 41 per cent who opted for their primary language. The apparent contradiction of using English as a primary communication vehicle points to an integrative attitude towards English as opposed to an instrumental attitude resulting in their preferring to use the mother tongue for assessment purposes (cf. Baker, 2006). The high social value of English is a determining factor: students clearly viewed English as the prestigious language to be used for public 'status-raising situations' in 'the larger, dominant community' (cf. Myers-Scotton, 2006: 110) where the judgments of the peer group during interaction are considered to be of paramount importance.

According to M. Pienaar (2006) the single most important consideration for using whispered simultaneous interpreting in a context marked by the dominance of English-speaking students as an alternative to duplicating classes is the impact of the hegemony of English. Afrikaans-speaking students who initially had expressed a need for tuition in Afrikaans in the course of a few weeks increasingly became reluctant to use the interpreting services. This was attributed to the fact the students were all second-language speakers of English and did not wish to draw attention to the fact that they found it difficult to follow the classes in English. The results of the questionnaire administered to the LIW1 and LIW2 classes echo Pienaar's findings that Afrikaans students prefer tuition through the medium of their mother tongue: two-thirds of the Afrikaans-speaking students in the LIW1 class indicated their preference for being taught through the medium of their mother tongue (Table 5). The study aimed to determine what these students' response to simultaneous interpreting in the classroom would be, a factor that we argue is of pivotal importance should the university wish to honour its commitment 'to preserve and develop on all its campuses the designated languages in particular' and to 'recognize the importance of the use of the first language' (UJ, 2006a: 2).

Yet, the fact that one third of the LIW1 class had the option to attend classes taught through the medium of Afrikaans, but opted for English medium classes instead, could be indicative of a possible language shift alluded to above, also among Afrikaans-speaking students. However, the reasons for this tendency still need to be investigated further.

Table 5. Choice of language of tuition by Afrikaans-speaking students in LIW1 and LIW2 classes (N = 22) at UJ – 2006

Course	Afrikaans		Afrikaans & English		English	
	N	%	N	%	N	%
LIW1	11	50	0		5	22.73
LIW2	4	18.18	1	4.54	1	4.54
TOTAL	**15**	**68.18**	**1**	**4.54**	**6**	**27.27**

Extending the interpreting service: Plan C

Against the background of a linguistically highly heterogeneous student population, it was decided to offer a 14-week module in Cross-Cultural Communication B in all four languages prescribed by UJ's language policy via simultaneous interpreting. The module boasted a sufficient number of first-language speakers of these languages to warrant offering a simultaneous interpreting service.

The Cross-Cultural Communication module is a semester course offered over a period of 14 weeks. The group of 95 students was divided into two classes of 48 and 47 students each with an even distribution of primary-language speakers of the four designated languages of UJ (English, Afrikaans, Sesotho sa Leboa and isiZulu) in both groups (see Table 6). During the first seven weeks, Group A received their main lectures, one tutorial per week and their learning guides in English only, whereas Group B had their learning guides made available to them via the University's online learning tool, *Edulink*, in English, Afrikaans, Sesotho sa Leboa and isiZulu. This included a glossary of difficult terms with lexical equivalents and definitions in the four languages.

Table 6. Language profile of Cross-Cultural Communication B students at UJ in 2006

		Frequency	Percent	Valid percent	Cumulative percent
Valid	1 English	32	33.3	33.7	33.7
	2 Afrikaans	7	7.3	7.4	41.1
	3 isiZulu	17	17.7	17.9	58.9
	4 isiXhosa	8	8.3	8.4	67.4
	5 siSwati	2	2.1	2.1	69.5
	7 Sesotho	8	8.3	8.4	77.9
	8 Sepedi	4	4.2	4.2	82.1
	9 Tswana	11	11.5	11.6	93.7
	10 Tshivenda	2	2.1	2.1	95.8
	11 Xitsonga	1	1.0	1.1	96.8
	12 French	1	1.0	1.1	97.9
	13 Kiswahili	1	1.0	1.1	98.9
	14 Chichewa	1	1.0	1.1	100.0
	Total	**95**	**99.0**	**100.0**	
Missing	System	1	1.0		
Total		**96**	**100.0**		

Although lectures and tutorials were presented in English, a simultaneous interpreting service, using mobile interpreting equipment (the Sennheiser system) and whispered interpreting using the simultaneous mode was available in all classes and tutorials. During this period, the students in Group B were encouraged to use their primary languages. This was possible by virtue of the fact that the isiZulu and Sesotho sa Leboa interpreters were able to interpret from other Nguni and Sotho languages into English and effectively meant that only six students (those who spoke Tshivenda (2), Xitsonga (1), Kiswahili (1), Chichewa (1) and French (1)) in the combined Group A and B did not have the option of using their primary language to address the lecturer or tutor. After seven weeks all language facilitation interventions were withdrawn from Group B, and Group A was given access to the translated learning guides, glossaries and an interpreting service in classes and tutorials.

The rationale behind the research design was twofold: firstly it was to establish whether language facilitation intervention would impact on students' results and secondly to enable the researchers to determine the students' views on the practical use of language facilitation comparatively, that is, both groups would have been exposed to the same course material, the same lecturer and the same tutors in English only, as well as in a context where language facilitation was provided.

During the course of the 14 weeks, the students, the lecturer, the tutors and the interpreters were interviewed to obtain their views on *inter alia*, the quality of the interpreting, whether or not the interpreting was experienced as a barrier, problems encountered, and so on. At the end of the 14-week period, students were required to complete a questionnaire. The questionnaire dealt with different aspects related to the project, that is, language preference and proficiency, the availability of learning material in languages other than English, computer proficiency and *Edulink*, as well as interpreting (cf. Pienaar, 2007 for a detailed discussion of the questionnaire and results).

Conclusion

Since the key to successful language management is judicious decision-making, the choice of enhancing learning and teaching practice in a highly diverse higher education context by using whispered simultaneous interpreting should be informed by situated language demographics and a sound understanding of the dynamics of current language attitudes and beliefs (ideologies). The extreme linguistic diversity that characterizes the student profile of the University of Johannesburg has serious implications for the use of simultaneous interpreting as a sustainable alternative to parallel medium teaching and even more so for the extension of the medium of tuition to include the two other languages indicated in the University's draft language policy, namely isiZulu and Sesotho sa Leboa. Furthermore, a tendency is also towards a language shift where non-native speakers of English are shifting towards English, either by not attending Afrikaans-medium classes, when they are Afrikaans-speaking, or, in the case of African language-speaking students, by indicating English as their preferred language of tuition.

However, if one returns to the words of Lewis quoted above in which it is stated that a language policy, if it is to succeed, either has to conform to the attitudes of those involved, or, alternatively, has to persuade those who express negative attitudes about the acceptability of the policy, or has to seek to remove the causes of the disagreement, we are of the opinion that simultaneous interpreting does indeed have a role to play in the tertiary classroom. This is particularly relevant in the case of UJ where university policy allows for the use of two languages as LOLT, especially as far as changing negative attitudes is concerned.

The project also aimed to establish in what way the implementation of multilingualism would impact on language attitudes and beliefs. However, the mere fact that it took six months to find a group that was suitable for the experiment does point to the impact of diversity on the suitability of offering a simultaneous interpreting service.

From a language management point of view, all policy interventions should, after all, be researched and evaluated to establish their impact and sustainability. The language attitudes and beliefs (ideologies) and the hegemony of English in the context of the linguistic diversity of the student profile at a South African metropolitan university (in this case the University of Johannesburg) hamper the applicability of such a service if only a very small percentage of students benefit. But then again, it probably depends on the motives and objectives of rendering such a service. Questions such as the following need answers: Is it done to extend the benefits of mother tongue education and in so doing 'persuading those students with negative attitudes about the rightness of the policy and approach' (Lewis, 2006: 211)? Is it done to protect and develop minority languages? In the case of parallel-medium teaching, is it done to protect a particular minority language? Or is it done to accommodate a language policy, which, on the face of it, does not reflect the realities, preferences and attitudes of the community it is meant to serve?

Consequently, this study has to conclude that, notwithstanding the possible benefits of simultaneous interpreting as an alternative to parallel and multi-medium teaching, these benefits do not mean that it is necessarily feasible or appropriate in all contexts.

Notes

1. These universities, which in the past offered tuition primarily through the medium of Afrikaans, are the North-West University (NWU) – previously the University of Potchefstroom (PU), the University of Johannesburg (UJ) – previously the Rand Afrikaans University (RAU), the University of the Free State (UF) – previously the University of the Orange Free State (UOFS), the University of Pretoria (UP) and the University of Stellenbosch (US).
2. See Pienaar (2006) for an exposition of this interpreting project.
3. 'Mother tongue' refers to the language with which the respondent grew up, while 'primary language' refers to the language the respondent uses most on a daily basis (cf. Question 8 and 9 in Questionnaire, Appendix A).
4. The whispered simultaneous interpreting services entail the use of portable interpreting equipment, that is, the Sennheiser system with rechargeable headset-receivers and a microphone. The advantage of this equipment is that the interpreter sits among the users, hence no separate booths are required.
5. For the purposes of this study 'home language' refers to the language regularly spoken at home by the student and his or her parents (cf. Question 10 in Questionnaire, Appendix A).
6. The language the respondent grew up with.
7. Not the language the respondent grew up with, but the language the respondent uses most on a daily basis.
8. Other South African languages spoken by respondents.

References

Baker, C. (2006), 'Psycho-sociological analysis in language policy', in T. Ricento (ed.), *An Introduction to Language Policy. Theory and Method*. Maldon: Blackwell Publishing, pp. 210–228.

Blaauw, J. (2007), 'Interpreting with limited training: experiences in the interpreting of academic lectures at the North-West University, South Africa', in J. Kearns (ed.), *Translation Ireland. A special issue. New Vistas in Interpreting Training*, 17, (1), 6–21.

Department of Education (DoE) (2001), *National Plan for Higher Education in South Africa*. Pretoria: Ministry of Education.

—(2002), *Language Policy for Higher Education*. Pretoria: Ministry of Education.

Du Plessis, T. (2006), 'From monolingual to bilingual higher education: the repositioning of historically Afrikaans-medium universities in South Africa', *Language Policy*, 5, 87–113.

Giliomee, H. and Schlemmer, L. (2006), 'n Vaste plek vir Afrikaans: Taaluitdagings op kampus. Stellenbosch: Sun Press.

Grové, N. (2006), ''n Volhoubare plek vir Afrikaans in hoër onderwys en regeringsteun daarvoor II'. Available at: www.litnet.co.za (accessed 10 February 2007).

Le Roux, M. (2007), Die rol van die opvoedkundige tolk in 'n tersiêre klaskamer. Unpublished MA dissertation. Johannesburg: University of Johannesburg.

Murray, S. (2002), 'Language issues in South African education: an overview', in R. Mesthrie (ed.), Language in South Africa. Cambridge: Cambridge University Press, pp. 434–448.

Myers-Scotton, C. (2006), Multiple Voices. An Introduction to Bilingualism. Malden: Blackwell Publishing.

Pienaar, M. (2006), 'Simultaneous interpreting as an aid in parallel medium tertiary Education', Stellenbosch Papers in Linguistics (SPIL), 33, 27–42.

—(2007), 'Four languages, one classroom: "Reasonably practicable"'?, Southern African Linguistics and Applied Language Studies, 25, (3), 401–418.

University of Johannesburg (UJ). (2006a), Language policy. Subcommittee draft, 7 June 2006. University of Johannesburg.

—(2006b), Information supplied by Institutional Development Section. University of Johannesburg.

Van Rooy, B. (2005), 'The feasibility of simultaneous interpreting in university Classrooms', Southern African Linguistics and Applied Language Studies, 23, (1), 81–90.

Verhoef, M. (2002), 'Successful classroom interpreting services of the North-West University'. Available at: www.puk.ac.za/opencms/export/PUK/htlm/nuus/nuus253 (accessed 15 May 2006).

—(2006), 'Reeks: Die Afrikaanse universiteit van die toekoms: Waar kennis en taal mekaar insluit: die NWU-model'. Available at: www.brainyqoute.com/quotes/authors/a/albert_einstein.html (accessed 2 November 2006).

—(2007), 'What about quality management for educational interpreting services at the NWU?' Paper presented at Combined Annual LSSA/SAALA SAALT Conference at the North-West University, July 2007.

Verhoef, M. and Blaauw, J. (2007), 'Simultaneous interpreting in the university classroom', Translatio, 1&2, 14–16.

Appendix A: Questionnaire

Biographical information

1. Age
2. Male or Female
3. Name of city/town or suburb in which *you* currently live
4. Name of city/town or suburb in which *your parents* currently live
5. What are your parents' occupations?

    a. Father:
    b. Mother:

6. What career do you plan to follow after completion of your studies?
7. Field of study

    a. Are you enrolled for a language course at the UJ?
    b. If so, name the course (i.e. French 1A and 1B):

8. Mother tongue (the language with which you grew up)
9. Primary language (in other words, not the language with which you grew up, but the language you mostly use on a daily basis)
10. Other home language (that are regularly spoken at home – i.e. mother and father speak different languages)
11. Which other South African languages do you speak?
12. Languages taken at matric level and symbol obtained for each.
13. Language or languages of tuition at pre-primary level.
14. Language or languages of tuition at primary school level
15. Language or languages of tuition at high school level
16. Name the school you matriculated at
17. In which province is the school?
18. Which language did you choose as the language of tuition at the UJ?
19. Why?
20. In which language would you like to receive tuition at the UJ ?
21. Why? (mark with an X)

    a. It is my primary language and therefore the language in which I learn and perform best and it will therefore open doors in the future.
    b. It is my home language and therefore the language in which I learn and perform best and it will therefore open doors in the future

    c. It is the language used in the business world and it will therefore open doors in the future

    d. Other reason

22. My best friends speak –

    a. the same mother tongue as I: Yes/ No

    b. languages other than I : Yes / No (name the language or languages)

23. I am comfortable in the company of speakers of other languages: Yes / No
24. Do you think that your mother tongue is important to achieve success in your future career? Yes / No
25. If not, why not?
26. Which one of the languages that you speak do you find most beautiful?

    a. Why do you find this language so beautiful?

27. Which one of the languages that you speak do you find the ugliest?

    a. Why do you find this language so ugly?

28. In which language would you prefer to study for tests or exams? (mark with an X)

    a. My mother tongue

    b. My primary language

    c. My second language (that is not my mother tongue and also not my primary language).

    d. It doesn't matter

29. Why?

Index